LAST CHANCE TO SEE

IN THE FOOTSTEPS OF DOUGLAS ADAMS

For Douglas Adams.

Co-conspirator and much-missed friend.
With great admiration for all you did for conservation.

LAST CHANCE TO SEE

IN THE FOOTSTEPS OF DOUGLAS ADAMS

WRITTEN & PHOTOGRAPHED BY
MARK CARWARDINE

FOREWORD BY
STEPHEN FRY

Collins

HarperCollins Publishers
77–85 Fulham Palace Road
London W6 8JB

www.harpercollins.co.uk

Collins is a registered trademark of HarperCollins
Publishers Ltd.

First published in 2009

© Mark Carwardine and West Park Pictures Ltd 2009
Photography © Mark Carwardine except: front cover,
p10, p42 (Will Edwards), p194, p221 (Don Merton), p250
(Jake Drake-Brockman), p214 (Ben Southwell)
Maps by graphixasset.com
Foreword © Stephen Fry

13 12 11 10 09
10 9 8 7 6 5 4 3 2 1

A catalogue record for this book is available from the
British Library.

ISBN 978 0 00 729072 7

Collins uses papers that are natural, renewable and
recyclable products made from wood grown in sustain-
able forests. The manufacturing processes conform to
the environmental regulations of the country of origin.

Associate Publisher: Myles Archibald
Cover design: James Annal
Proofreader: Janet McCann
Designer: Marc Marazzi

Colour reproduction by Butler Tanner & Dennis
Printed and bound in Great Britain by Butler
Tanner & Dennis

CONTENTS

Foreword by Stephen Fry   6

In the Beginning   12

1   Travelling Case for a Seal   16

2   Danger: Rebels Coming   68

3   Bits of Other Animals   116

4   Dear Old Ralph   164

5   Poisoned Dagger   222

6   Singing the Blues   256

One More Thing...   312

It's a Wrap! Last Chance
to See Travel Statistics   315

Last Chance to Help...   316

Acknowledgements   317

Index   318

FOREWORD

I first met Douglas Adams some time in 1983. I can't imagine what we actually did for the first seven months of our friendship – twiddle our thumbs and yawn, I suppose – but at last in January 1984 the first Apple Mac was launched and from then on we visited each other every day to swap and play. Our interests for the next year or so centred entirely around inanimate electronic equipment and its habit of not working – if we gave the natural world a second thought it was when we looked out of the window and wondered if a thunderstorm was brewing. Lightning strikes could cause a power outage or even a spike or surge in the line that might damage our precious toys. So much for nature.

Time passed. One day, much to my surprise, Douglas went off to Madagascar on a peculiar journalistic mission that had to do with a rare species of lemur. On his return I began to notice an alteration in my reliably geeky-nerd companion. He read Richard Dawkins's *The Selfish Gene* and *The Blind Watchmaker* and gave me copies telling me that my life would be changed. Which it was. What Nils Bohr said of quantum mechanics is true of evolution, 'if you're not shocked then you haven't understood it properly.'

I had been sharing a place in Dalston at this time with a group of friends from university, but we were now at the stage where it was possible to consider splitting up and buying our own flats and houses. I wanted to find a place in Islington, but also felt that I needed time to look around and wait for the perfect property. Perhaps I should rent first? I off-loaded my tedious residential worries on Douglas one afternoon as we sat in his study staring at a Mac and wondering, for the thousandth time, if we could stop it going 'boing' and closing down whenever we tried to do something unusual with it.

'Why don't you stay here for a year?' he suggested. 'You can house-sit for me. I've decided to go round the world for twelve months seeking out rare animals.'

'You've de-whatted to go round the what, whatting out *whats*?'

Douglas explained that his journey to Madagascar had lit a fire within him that would not go out. In the company of a zoologist called Mark Carwardine he had

Opposite
Stephen and Mark
on their first trip,
to the Amazon.

found and photographed the elusive lemur known as the 'aye-aye', an experience, together with reading Dawkins, that had made him realise that the technology that now most excited him was the one that had evolved over millions of years and resulted in him and me and ultimately the device that wouldn't stop going 'boing'. He really wanted to understand this business of life and extinction. He and Mark had hit it off straightaway and the plan was now to find seven more species like the aye-aye that were in imminent danger of disappearing for ever.

The result was Mark and Douglas's *Last Chance to See*, a book and a BBC radio series. While the intrepid pair were travelling the globe, I duly stayed at Douglas's house fielding the occasional call and request. This was the time before faxes were in general use, let alone emails or texts, so communication and flight reservations and other travel details had to be expedited by landline and telex. It was not unusual to be awoken at three in the morning by a Douglas too excited by what was happening around him to have worked out time differences. 'Can you telex Garuda Air and tell them we want to change our flight?' he would yell down the phone. I would copy down the names of islands, ports and towns I had never heard of and make calls to countries I couldn't point to on the map.

The book was a remarkable success. I do not believe it has ever been out of print, a testament to the importance of the subject and to Douglas and Mark's natural story-telling abilities, charm, wit and unforced writing styles. Alarm about the environment, issues of conservation, pollution, habitat degradation and species

endangerment existed before *Last Chance to See*, but they were far less the common currency of concern than they are now. Mark and Douglas's book focused general worry into a particular understanding of the clock that was ticking on the future of wildlife in so many corners of the planet. Every campaign needs heroes, faces that represent the issue at stake. Icons, we would say now. It was typical of Douglas, and as I later found out of Mark too, that their icons should be such strange and (at first glance) unprepossessing animals as the Amazonian manatee, the aye-aye and the kakapo. There is something in the solemn oddity, the idiosyncratic earnestness of these species that tears at the heart with greater urgency and pathos than the more photogenic and glamorous pumas, dolphins and pandas. Nature admits of no hierarchy of beauty or usefulness or importance. We like to think, entirely wrongly, that we, mankind, are nature's last word, at the summit of evolution, or that animals 'at the top of the food chain' are somehow more important than animals at the bottom. *Last Chance to See* showed us all that a bumbling earth-bound parrot is as good a symbol of the beauty and fragility of the natural world as a soaring condor and that a plug-ugly nocturnal lemur with a twiglet for a middle finger can represent the glory of creation quite as aptly as a meerkat or an orang-utan.

I was proud to know Douglas, pleased to have been even tangentially connected with his and Mark's great and pioneering project, but I cannot honestly say that over the following fifteen or so years I gave *Last Chance to See* much more thought. I re-read it once, I think, and began to develop my own small wildlife interests – involving myself in two films and a book about the spectacled bear in Peru and narrating a handful of the BBC's Natural World documentaries.

On 11 May 2001 I was shocked and heartbroken to hear of the sudden and wholly unexpected death of Douglas Noel Adams – the DNA at the core of so much that I loved and valued in the world. He was just 49 years old. The years since have passed and every day I have missed Douglas as a friend, teacher and companion. How can I know what to think of iPhones and iMacs, compact cameras, GPS devices and Blu-ray players without Douglas here to offer his unique sideways view?

Then one day in 2007, out of the blue, I had a phone call. Might I consider travelling, with Mark, back to those animals that had formed the principal cast list of *Last Chance to See*, this time filming the experience for television? I sounded myself out, I sounded Mark out and then I sounded the BBC out. We all seemed to be in agreement that the time was right. Out of the eight species Mark and Douglas had originally chosen it seemed that two were already functionally extinct (the northern white rhino and the Yangtze river dolphin) – in other words, a quarter of their almost random snapshot of vulnerable species had been wiped from the map of creation. Mark told me at our first meeting that he believes whichever eight critically endangered species they had chosen back then the chances are that a quarter would now be extinct.

It fell out that this documentary filming project would have to go hand in hand with another that I was doing for the BBC in which I visited every state of the USA, so for a time I was worried that I would not be able to take on the commitment. Willingness and cooperation on all sides ensured that it could be done, however, and in January 2008 I flew from Miami, Florida to Manaus, Amazonia to join Mark and start work on the first film, which was to feature the Amazonian manatee.

Mark has written these adventures up with that mixture of zoological mastery and human insight that characterises him and raises him so far above the level of most professional naturalists and conservationists. He has been very modest about himself, however. Let me just say that without his energy, enthusiasm, local knowledge and refusal to accept second best, neither *Last Chance to See* the television series nor this new book could ever have been completed. There is no length to which Mark will not go in order to observe an animal, photograph it and, if needs be, save it from peril. He has put his own life in the severest possible danger time and time again in his work for anti-poacher patrols in Africa and Asia, all at the service of protecting rhinos, elephants and tigers from those who would slaughter them wholesale for gain. The more endangered the species become, the higher the price their horns, tusks and penises command for the 'traditional medicine' market in the Far East and the more willing poachers are to kill anyone who comes between them and their route to riches. Mark talks rarely and self-deprecatingly of his courage in putting himself in the line of fire, but it is a more extreme proof of what anyone would observe if they saw Mark in the wild under any circumstances: commitment, passion and extraordinary zest. No matter how many times he has seen an animal before, Mark will want to see it again. He will climb mountains, ford streams and penetrate steamy malaria-infested swamps just for one glimpse. Not only that, but he will encourage, belabour and enthuse any large, sweaty unwilling companions who happen to be lumbering at his side wishing there were better phone signals and air-conditioning available.

I embarked on this whole project honestly believing I had bitten off more than I could chew. I am no physical hero: I am clumsy, overweight, unfit and uncoordinated. The first episode of filming began with me falling off a floating dock and smashing my right humerus. Yet somehow, a year and a quarter later, I had lost much weight and was happily hurling myself into physically demanding conditions that I would have wept and gibbered at before. The life-changing benefits of the filming experience I owe to the animals and to Mark. That he and I never quarrelled is testament to his extraordinary good temper and sweetness of nature. He tolerated the presence of an amateur, idler and dilettante and proved a perfect teacher and matchless travel companion.

Most importantly of course, through Mark I also met and befriended the extraordinary, enchanting and rare creatures that you are about to meet now. I hope the experience inspires you to consider what you might do to help, in however small a way, the work of conservation that goes on around the world to save these and other species from no longer existing.

If this book and our adventures have any purpose it is to help with the conservation conversation. Are the animals worth saving because they hold an important place in the great interconnected web of existence? Are they worth saving because they might one day yield important clues and compounds to help us with medicine or some other useful technology? Or are they worth saving because they are the beautiful achievement of millions of years of natural selection? Extinction is a natural part of creation, this is unquestionably true: yet no matter what one's views on climate change or global warming, it is impossible, impossible, to deny that man-made alterations to habitat are threatening thousands of plant and animal species across the planet at an unprecedented rate and scale. So the question is perhaps not 'why should we save them?' but 'what right do we have to destroy them?'

Let us never stop talking about the creatures we share the planet with. The first step is to know them a little better.

Stephen Fry

IN THE BEGINNING

No one believed me when I said I was going to the Amazon with Stephen Fry. It must have seemed about as likely as taking Johnny Rotten to the opera, or joining the Dalai Lama for a week of downhill skiing in Holland.

When I mentioned that we were going to a particularly remote corner of the world's greatest rainforest to look for a large, black, sleepy animal easily mistaken for an unusually listless mudbank, they merely stared at me as if I'd taken leave of my senses.

But, sure enough, the Amazon was the first (and, as it happened, nearly the last) stop on a whirlwind year-long world tour.

Two days after Christmas 2007 we set off on a 145,000-kilometre (90,000-mile) journey to eight different countries on five continents in search of the weird and the wild. Our aim was to come face to face with some of the rarest and most peculiar animals on the planet: from nocturnal ET-like lemurs in Madagascar and tourist-eating dragons in Indonesia to flightless and charmingly gormless parrots in New Zealand and square-lipped rhinos in war-torn Congo.

Along the way, we hoped to meet some of the remarkable people whose fearless and gritty determination, sometimes in the face of tremendous personal danger, is all that has kept most (though, sadly, not all) of these animals from going extinct.

Stephen and I had known one another a little since the late 1980s (enough to say 'hello' and 'how are you?' and, more recently, 'can't you get reception on your iPhone either?'). But we'd barely sat in the same car together, far less shared cabins, huts, tents, far-flung adventures or tropical diseases. Suddenly, for better or for worse, we were being thrown together on a lengthy, often uncomfortable, occasionally quite gruelling and, once or twice, quite traumatic journey that would challenge our evolving friendship, test our patience, put our best-laid plans through the wringer and even cross-examine our medical skills.

'I must confess I'm quite nervous about this whole enterprise,' admitted Stephen. 'I like my creature comforts rather more than I like my creatures.'

Opposite
Mark and Douglas in Robinson Crusoe's cave in the Juan Fernandez Islands, off the coast of Chile.

But there was method in our madness. We'd decided to retrace the steps I had taken exactly twenty years earlier with a mutual friend – the late Douglas Adams, who very sadly died in May 2001.

In 1985, the *Observer Colour Magazine* agreed to send Douglas, a comedy writer better known for *The Hitch Hiker's Guide to the Galaxy*, to an otherworldly island in the middle of the Indian Ocean to look for an endangered nocturnal lemur called an aye-aye (exactly the kind of weird and wonderful creature that a writer of humorous science fiction might concoct on a really creative day).

It was a ground-breaking idea. Bear in mind that this was in the good old days, when endangered species and orphaned children could leave their dens or houses in complete safety, without having to pose next to D-list celebrities with falling ratings and crocodile tears. The aye-aye had never met a celebrity before, let alone one of Douglas's stature (in both senses of the word).

Douglas's mission was to report on conservation efforts in Madagascar, in his own inimitable style, by taking a unique and imaginative look at some of the wild animals and even wilder people that professional zoologists tend to take for granted. As he explained at the time: 'My role, and one for which I was entirely qualified, was to be an extremely ignorant non-zoologist to whom everything that happened would come as a complete surprise.' My own role, basically, was

to arrange plenty of wildlife encounters, help him identify what he was looking at and make sure he came back alive.

We met for the very first time at the airport in Madagascar's capital, Antananarivo, and spent three hilarious and thought-provoking weeks bumbling through Malagasy jungles and red tape. Against all the odds we came face to face with an aye-aye, undeniably the strangest animal either of us had ever seen, for a fleeting few seconds near the end of the trip.

The best way to tell if you get on with someone is to be thrown together for a couple of hard weeks' travelling and spend night after night sleeping on a wet concrete floor in the middle of a jungle. We found that we got on extremely well. In fact, we enjoyed the experience so much that we hatched a rather ambitious plan to do it all over again, half a dozen times. We put a big map of the world on a wall, Douglas stuck a pin in everywhere he fancied going, I stuck a pin in where some of the most endangered animals were, and we made a journey out of every place that had two pins.

Three years later we set off.

Actually, to be fair, it wasn't quite that simple. Arranging all those long-haul trips to remote corners of the globe in the days before adventure travel became as normal as a £4 gallon of petrol, and long before anyone had even heard of

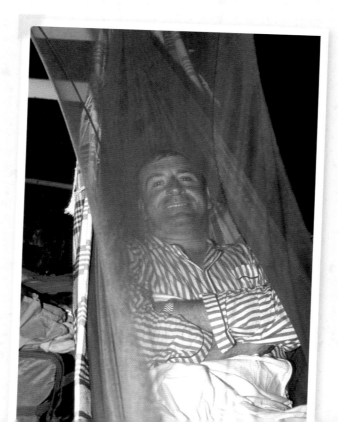

email, deserves more than a merry 'so we set off'. Let me rephrase it. Instead of 'three years later' please read 'after hundreds of unbearably slow clank-clank-clanking telexes, dozens of typewriter-and-Tippex-written letters (most of which never arrived), goodness knows how many barely audible, pre-booked, long-distance phone calls, and thousands of grey hairs later'... we set off in search of more endangered species.

Eventually, everything was in place: the schedules were set, naturalists the world over were ready and waiting, our passports were stamped with a mind-boggling array of visas, and multitudinous flights, boats and hotels were booked.

Then Douglas called to announce that he hadn't quite finished his latest novel, and would I mind doing it all over again?

I did do it all over again and, eventually, we had lots of life-changing, awe-inspiring and hair-raising experiences, presented a radio series, wrote a book about our adventures (called *Last Chance to See*) and became firm friends in the process.

Now history has repeated itself. It's the same pins in the map, but this time it is Stephen who has been sleeping in the middle of jungles and sharing life-changing, awe-inspiring and hair-raising experiences to find out how all those wild animals – and their protectors – have got along in the years in between.

This is our story.

1

TRAVELLING CASE FOR A SEAL

Stephen reminds me a little of Douglas: unnaturally bright, exceedingly well read, enthralled by obscure facts and figures, never without a pocketful of weird and wonderful gadgets or an Apple Mac, and very tall.

He strode into the Arrivals Hall, head and shoulders above his fellow passengers, wearing a slightly crumpled light-blue shirt, a blue-and-white striped blazer favoured by wealthy yacht owners, beige chinos, a deep golden suntan after spending Christmas in the Caribbean, and a broad smile.

I had the fleeting impression of Crocodile Dundee arriving for the first time in Manhattan, except in reverse, if you see what I mean.

Admittedly, I was a little apprehensive. Stephen is no Crocodile Dundee. Travelling with him was going to be like travelling with Wikipedia permanently online. He knows pretty much everything about everything. I've never heard him struggling to recall a person, a place, a fact or a figure (I probably have, of course, perhaps once or twice, but I'll be damned if I can remember when).

Sure enough, next to him I felt unnaturally short, pitifully pale and extraordinarily dim. It wasn't his fault. Stephen is far too unassuming and generous to make anyone feel in any way deficient on purpose. But he's the kind of person who makes you continually question your own intellect. Why on earth didn't I know the name of the Key Grip in the 1987 film *The Princess Bride*, how many syllables there are in a dodecasyllable, which was the last place in Britain to be

Opposite
Stephen has a few minutes to spare, so he decides to learn Portuguese.

converted to Christianity, when Daniel O'Connell became Lord Mayor of Dublin, what a quatrefoil is, or so many other things from countless topics of conversation that cropped up during our travels together?

Sometimes it felt as if we were on two different channels – he on BBC News and me on the Home Shopping Channel. At one point I actually wrote a rather desperate-sounding note in my diary: 'Must read more'.

But I sought refuge in the knowledge that my work as a zoologist takes me to the world's wildernesses for so many months every year that my mind has been broadened and my bowels loosened more often than I care to remember. A lifetime of being on the move, unrecognisable food, strange beds (or no beds at all), communicating by sign language, and hair-raising or life-changing experiences made a month-long expedition to the Amazon seem quite normal.

In fact, to be honest, I feel more like a fish out of water when I'm at home, wearing slippers, watching telly.

Stephen, on the other hand, is more at home at home – at least, appearing on telly rather than watching it. His natural habitat is a television or radio studio. He's by no means a stranger to travel or even wildlife (he's the only person I know who has been on an expedition to search for Paddington Bear in Peru) but, let's face it, you're unlikely to bump into him in an outdoor shop with armfuls of mosquito repellent and Imodium.

It didn't even cross my mind at the time, but he was a little apprehensive too.

'I felt quite nervous of you,' he admitted later. 'I was expecting to feel very foolish if ever I said "what's that?" and you'd give me one of those long, burning looks as if you couldn't believe there's a sentient being on the planet who is unaware of what a capybara is, or whatever it might have been.'

Opposite
A welcoming face in the Amazon.

Below
Stephen ready for anything in his expeditionary gear.

We did have at least one thing in common. Our Amazon adventure had been occupying our thoughts a great deal over the previous year or so, and we were both thrilled and eager to get started. Although it was already well past midnight we had a great deal to talk about, and we talked about it until we could barely keep our eyes open.

Not once, strangely, did we talk about potential dangers. The jungle is full of bottom-emptying and life-threatening hazards. Yellow fever, hepatitis, meningitis, tetanus, rabies, giardiasis, cholera, typhoid, Chagas' disease, bilharzia, dengue fever, several strains of malaria and leishmaniasis immediately come to mind. The Amazon is the perfect place to go if you'd like to increase the odds of dying from something you've never even heard of.

In fact, if the Amazon were in Britain, the Health and Safety Executive wouldn't allow it at all.

Most exciting, among all the potential hazards, you could be killed by an animal

that hasn't yet been named by science: perhaps a rare species of poison-dart frog, a chigger that no one has had the time (or bothered) to investigate, a well-camouflaged spider, or a particularly secretive venomous snake.

By the way, if you want to be cleverer than almost everyone else on the planet (even so-called 'experts' who write about these things) here's an interesting fact. Dangerous snakes are not poisonous. They are venomous, and there's a big difference. For something to be poisonous it has to be ingested (or, in some cases, touched). An animal that is venomous, on the other hand, actually injects its poison with a bite or sting. Try to bring it up in casual conversation – everyone will be amazed.

While we're on the subject of potential misadventures, perhaps worst of all (certainly commonest of all) is traveller's diarrhoea, especially if you're on the move every day, staying hundreds of kilometres from the nearest loo, and filming. The trots, the runs, dysentery, gastroenteritis or Montezuma's revenge are all part and parcel of travelling (Stephen's philosophy, quite rightly, is that travel boils down to laundry and bowels). You simply have to choose whether to go for amoebic dysentery or bacterial dysentery, and the ghastly concoction of microbes lurking in virtually everything you eat or drink will take care of the rest.

In reality, of course, these things sound much worse from afar. There's probably more chance of getting deep-vein thrombosis on the cramped long-haul

Opposite
Aerial view of part of
the largest nonstop
expanse of pure,
unremitting nature
on earth.

flights from London to São Paulo and on to Manaus than of being struck down by a deadly disease or bitten by an animal that's venomous not poisonous.

What we hadn't anticipated was something the Health and Safety Executive would probably have warned us about, had we bothered to ask, and that's the risk of slipping on a wet wooden boardwalk in the dark at 5am. But now we're getting ahead of ourselves.

Whether or not jungles keep you awake at night, overwhelmed with awe and wonder, you'd have to be a lump of rock not to be impressed by the Amazon Basin. If you're like most people, and it occupies a murky, something-to-do-with-jungles place in the back of your mind, you deserve a good slap for failing to grasp the sheer scale and splendour of the largest nonstop expanse of pure, unremitting nature on earth.

Imagine a place nearly the size of Australia, spread across no fewer than eight different countries and one overseas territory (Peru, Bolivia, Ecuador, Colombia, Venezuela, Brazil, Guyana, Suriname and French Guiana). Then cover it with all the jungles, or tropical rainforests, from Africa and Southeast Asia (indeed, half of all the jungles left on earth). Add the world's mightiest river (watercourse connoisseurs will get cross if I say 'longest', because the Amazon is 'only' 6,448 kilometres (4,030 miles) long – 222 kilometres (139 miles) shorter than the record-breaking Nile); and crisscross the entire region with a mind-boggling spider's web of 1,100 major tributaries (many of which are among the world's largest rivers in their own right). And then, like the icing on a cake, fill it up with nearly one-fifth of all the free-flowing fresh water in the world.

I would say it defies description, but then I'd have to delete the last paragraph.

Larger than the whole of western Europe, and draining half the total landmass of South America, it bombards you with sensory overload at every turn. Compared with lesser parts of the world, even its palms look palmier and its rain feels considerably wetter.

But there's more. This vast territory of trees and water is home to something like one in ten of all known species of plant and animal. Counting them can be tricky and time-consuming, even for people who like to do such things, so we can only guess at total numbers. But here's a recent list: 427 mammal species, 1,294 birds, 378 reptiles, 3,000 fish and 40,000 plants. I don't know anyone who's even tried to count the insect species, so let's just say that there are more than you can shake a stick at. Millions of them.

Now, the bad news is that all these figures are wrong. New species are being

If the Amazon were in Britain, the Health and Safety Executive wouldn't allow it at all.

found in the Amazon almost daily, so by the time you read this they'll be completely out of date. But the good news is that, if you can tell a waxy-tailed planthopper from a South American palm weevil, or a kissing bug from a peanut-headed bug, you could take a couple of weeks off work, set up camp in a quiet corner of the rainforest, and discover a whole assortment of species entirely new to science.

You could name them, too, though you'd have to be drunk. Judging by the names dreamed up by many experts, one can only assume there is a serious drinking problem among the world's zoologists: I have little doubt that whoever came up with no-eyed big-eyed wolf spider, dik-dik, bongo, blob fish, burnt-neck eremomela or Bounty Islands shag had more than one celebratory drink to toast their great discoveries.

A friend of mine once named a new species of sea slug after his wife; she didn't like it.

Alternatively, you could take a proper sabbatical and go in search of something really newsworthy. Vast areas of the Amazon remain as unexplored as in the days of the early adventurers, so you could set off to find the warring women who apparently fight like the Amazons of Greek mythology or the tribe reputed to have their feet facing the wrong way to deceive trackers.

The last thing you'd expect to stumble upon in the Amazon is a large city. But, sure enough, plonked in the middle of this natural unexplored treasure trove is just that: a city of 1.7 million people in northern Brazil, called Manaus.

Manaus is where our adventure really began.

Our challenge was to find one of the least-known and most outlandish animals on the planet. We were going in search of an Amazonian manatee, the first endangered species on our list.

There are several species of manatee around the world (informatively named the West Indian, West African and Amazonian manatees, plus the closely related but less informatively named dugong), all belonging to a group of aquatic mammals officially called the sirenians. They're better known as sea cows.

We were looking for the smallest and hardest to find. Found only in the Amazon Basin, from the river mouth to the upper reaches of calm water tributaries in Brazil, Colombia, Ecuador, Guyana and Peru, the Amazonian manatee is shy and retiring and likes to keep itself to itself.

With a wonderfully carefree rotund body, predominantly black skin the texture of vinyl, a bright pink belly and diamond-shaped tail, a cleft lip, a unique

Below
A great potoo – who comes up with these names?

Our challenge was to find one of the least-known and most outlandish animals on the planet.

sixth sense, a reputation for farting more than any other animal on the planet, and an affinity for remote corners of tropical rainforest rarely penetrated by humans, the Amazonian manatee is not your average endangered species.

It was first described as a cross between a seal and a hippo, though it's not related to either. Douglas Adams more aptly portrayed it as 'not so much like a seal as like a travelling case for carrying a seal in'. There is nothing else quite like this perfect piece of evolutionary engineering in the world.

In the old days, when men were men and manatees were much more common, sailors used to confuse them with mermaids. Or so they say (the word 'sirenian' comes from the seductive 'siren' of Greek mythology – part-woman, part-fish). I like manatees, a lot, but I'm not sure I'd be so keen on a 400-kilo marine temptress with a bristly face.

Clearly, it's not just zoologists who've been drinking too much.

Manatee-ologists say that the Amazonian manatee is active both during the day and at night. But 'active' is probably too strong a word. It is spectacular mainly for its single-minded determination to do everything as slowly and calmly as possible.

Most of the time it eats, then farts, then sleeps. Sometimes it just farts and sleeps. It doesn't leap out of the water to perform breathtaking acrobatics like a dolphin, jump daringly from tree to tree like a monkey, or hang upside down like a sloth. Its main activity is doing nothing much at all.

Oh, and it is vegetarian (not that there's anything wrong with being vegetarian – I'm just saying so by way of introduction).

The Brazilians call it the *peixe-boi*, or ox-fish, which pretty much sums it up.

On the plus side, it is a mammal and that means it has to breathe air. This is where things start to get pretty exciting. When it rises to the surface of the river to take a breath, it pokes its bristly snout nearly a centimetre into the tropical world outside for as long as a second at a time. Few people have seen this happen in the wild (a manatee can stay submerged for twenty minutes, which means there are often tediously long gaps between bouts of such awe-inspiring activity) but, needless to say, most of them have never forgotten it.

Despite weeks of trying, Douglas and I had failed to see one all those years ago. Actually, that's not strictly true. Our jungle guide saw a manatee disappear beneath the surface of a remote tributary of the Rio Negro, I saw the ripples after it had disappeared, and Douglas nearly saw the ripples. We consoled ourselves with the thought that we'd more or less breathed the same air as a manatee.

Stephen and I were determined to do even better.

But first a bit of luxury. The roughing it, the creepy-crawlies, the piranhas-for-breakfast survival cuisine, the jungle-borne diseases and the frightening lack of electrical sockets to plug in Stephen's Apple Mac could all come later. Stephen, like Douglas Adams before him, was more used to comfortable hotel rooms larger than my flat. Like reintroducing an orphaned manatee to the wild, he had to be habituated first. Some things definitely call for a warm-up.

So we courageously booked ourselves into the surprisingly comfortable Tropical Hotel, on the outskirts of Manaus, and bivouacked for the night in our air-conditioned hotel rooms.

'We' were seven of us altogether. We'd brought a BBC film crew with us (although they'd probably say it was the other way round – they brought us) to make a TV series about our adventures: Stephen and I, a four-person team from the UK and translator Marina Barahona De Brito. We were planning to meet up with Ivano Cordeiro, our Fixer, in a few days' time. We didn't have a baggage handler or a chef or a masseuse, but with the BBC determined to cut costs we thought we'd try and muddle through.

Manaus is the biggest city in the world's biggest forest. While much of the Amazon Basin remains unexplored, this particular part of it has been very heavily explored indeed – not least by coach-loads of tourists. It's the launch pad for a motley collection of half-day, full-day, several-day and one-week jungle adventures.

Surrounded by rainforest and water, some 1,450 kilometres (906 miles) from the open ocean, the city sprawls along the Rio Negro near its confluence with the Rio Solimões.

These two great rivers have different densities, temperatures and speeds, so they run side by side for several kilometres without mixing. You can actually see a distinct line between them – the dark, Guinness-coloured water of the Negro on one side and the light-brown *café-au-lait*-coloured Solimões on the other. After years of creative thinking, brainstorming and lively debate by an army of geographers, strategic planners, publicity agents and marketing consultants, the powers that be decided to call it the 'Meeting of the Waters'.

Above
The salmon-coloured opera house, or Amazon Theatre, is so out of place in Manaus it might as well be on the moon.

Below left
Sprawling into the
surrounding jungle –
the city of Manaus.

Below
The imaginatively
named 'Meeting of the
Waters'.

Eventually, the two rivers grudgingly begin to mix, creating all sorts of intriguing whorls and eddies more like an Impressionist painting. And when they've finished, they form the mighty Amazon.

The city itself is best known for its sumptuously grand, salmon-coloured opera house. The Teatro Amazonas, or Amazon Theatre, was completed in 1896 at a time when Manaus was a rubber boomtown and temporarily had an overblown status in the world economy. With its exuberant red velvet seats, crystal chandeliers, Brazilian wood (polished and carved in Europe), Italian marble and 36,000 individually decorated ceramic tiles, it is so out of place amid the hot and humid streets of utilitarian, grime-coloured buildings it might as well be on the moon.

But the best thing about Manaus is the fish market (I realise that only a zoologist – or a fisherman – would have the audacity to say anything so ridiculous). I would never normally admit this to anyone, but I really do like fish markets, despite having to get out of bed at an ungodly hour to see them at their best.

Anyway, there's no denying that the warehouse-sized fish market in Manaus is in a league of its own: a five-star deluxe version unparalleled by fish markets in lesser parts of the world. It's not all sweetness and light (it also bears testimony to the industrial-sized fishing fleets now monopolising the market and openly flouting laws and regulations designed to protect Amazonian fish stocks), but it's worth losing a few hours' kip for.

But here's the thing: it is far and away the best place to see some of the most peculiar and unbelievable fish you could ever imagine in your wildest dreams. A temple to biodiversity, it's the next best thing to a lifetime of diving in the Amazon (except, of course, all the stars of the show are dead) and gives a wonderful insight into an ecosystem that harbours half of all the freshwater fish species in the world.

Manaus fish market, or Mercado Municipal Adolpho Lisboa to give it its proper name, is a bustling place. Every morning, as many as 100 fishing boats dump their colourful catches into large wooden boxes on the shore of the Rio Negro and then porters run, literally, with these heavyweight aquatic menageries balanced precariously on their heads. They race along the wobbly wooden jetty floating on metal drums, up the concrete steps, over the road and into the white-tiled market. There to meet them in the gloomy light, illuminated only by 15-watt bulbs hanging from a web of bare wires, is an army of fishmongers dressed in bloody aprons and equipped with long, curved knives.

The stalls were soon piled high with a truly eye-catching collection of weird and wonderful fish of all shapes and sizes. Many looked as if they had just been lowered down from a spaceship recently returned from a galaxy far away.

We found 1.5-metre (5-foot) long red and grey pirarucu – unfriendly-looking, grumpy-old-man-faced fish with creepy little eyes, mouths like World War II landing craft and long, barbed tongues. Among the largest freshwater fish in the world, pirarucu are reputed to leap out of the water and grab small birds from overhanging branches.

Next to them were grouper-like, olive-green tambaqui. Roughly half the length of the pirarucu, these fruit and nut eaters loiter beneath trees in the flooded forest and wait for breakfast, lunch and dinner to fall right into their mouths. They are armed with powerful, crushing teeth like the molars of a sheep to grind down the tougher parts of their food.

Elsewhere in the market there were fish that looked like large silver coins, others resembling the porcelain models used to adorn fancy ornamental ponds, snaky fish with zebra stripes, salamander-like fish with fleshy fins, enormous catfish with whiskers that would make your average moggy purr with pride, and perfectly round spotty stingrays like multicoloured Frisbees.

We even found some long-bodied, big-eyed aruanas, or water monkeys, which specialise in surface-to-air attacks on insects that sit around all day, rather un-wisely, on branches above the water.

We saw more species of fish in a couple of hours in the fish market than I've seen during a lifetime of wildlife watching in Britain: there is no more graphic insight into the hidden underwater world of the Amazon.

Piranhas were everywhere and, as we watched, several different species were unloaded by the crate-full. My favourite were the red-bellies, which live up to their name with glowing red undersides and caudal fins – they must look like neon signs underwater. If you are partial to a surfeit of tiny throat-stabbing bones in your fish, piranhas make good eating. The locals like them because, de-spite a complete lack of scientific evidence, they are used as a cure for everything from baldness to a lack of virility (perhaps the two are connected, after all?).

I feel sorry for them (piranhas, not bald people). Their reputation as vicious pack-hunting monsters devouring villains in jungle B-movies is, well, utter non-sense. It's President Theodore Roosevelt's fault. He came back from a hunting trip in South America, nearly a century ago, telling tall stories of 'the most fero-cious fish in the world'. Experts quickly latched on to his wild imagination and warned that piranhas made 'swimming or wading an extremely risky pastime over about half the entire South American continent'. Now that the tabloid press has latched on to the idea, there is no separating fact from fiction.

Opposite
Visiting Manaus fish market is the next best thing to a lifetime of diving in the Amazon (except, of course, all the stars of the show are dead).

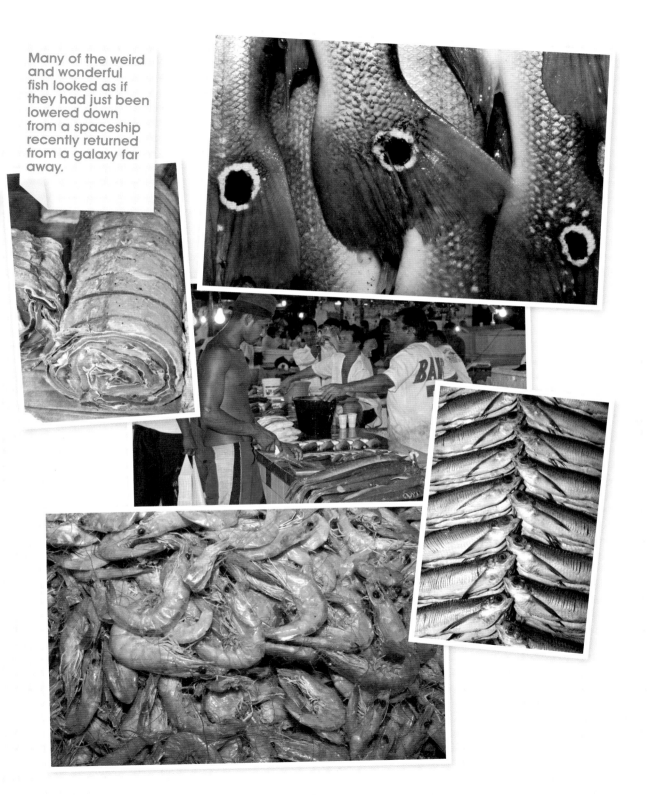

Many of the weird and wonderful fish looked as if they had just been lowered down from a spaceship recently returned from a galaxy far away.

The people most at risk are fishermen, as so many local men have discovered for themselves. Their missing fingers are the somewhat predictable result of attempting to remove fishing hooks from inside piranhas' mouths.

Under the circumstances you'd probably give an almighty bite, too.

The next day we were up at the crack of noon to catch a fast boat to a jungle lodge, just an hour away.

We would have left sooner, but Stephen was busy thrashing about in his hotel room. I went to see if he was okay and found him looking hot and flustered and trying to force a pile of neatly folded clothes into a bright-yellow stuff sack. I watched patiently, for as long as I could stop laughing.

'You know you don't *fold* the clothes,' I said, 'you *stuff* them into a stuff sack. That way they take up less space.'

Stephen gave me a sideways glance, and for a fleeting moment looked a bit cross. It wasn't like him at all. He muttered something about a smart arse.

'Anyway, you don't need to look neat and tidy,' I ventured, 'because we're on an expedition.'

He glanced at my crumpled shirt, slightly torn trousers and muddy boots. Then he grabbed his pile of clothes, ruffled them up like a tramp rifling through a rubbish bin, and stuffed the tangled mess into the sack.

'Oh,' said a slightly embarrassed Stephen, once voted the most intelligent man on television, 'is that why it's called a stuff sack?'

Our jungle lodge was a hotchpotch of ramshackle wooden towers and nearly 300 stilted rooms, interlinked by a precarious and rickety eight-kilometre (five-mile) wooden boardwalk. It was like an Amazonian theme park right in the middle of the Amazon. It took the jungle out of the jungle. It made everything seem artificial. Even its own wobbly boardwalk felt like the collapsible bridge at Universal Studios.

According to the official bumph, it was Jacques Cousteau's idea. I think he may have been suffering from the bends at the time. Anyone who thinks anything so big and brash and out of place is a good thing must have missed some of the lessons.

I guess it was designed for the kind of people who think a naturalist is someone who runs naked through the woods. But for me it doesn't really count as 'exploring the Amazon'.

Maybe I'm alone in my aversion. Western lawyers would love the place. Gradually being reclaimed by the surrounding jungle, it had undoubtedly seen better days as its labyrinthine network of walkways and buildings was filled with cracked and creaking floorboards, gaping holes, splintered handrails and a variety of other litigation-inspiring hazards.

And judging by the picture-studded notice board in reception, the lodge was frequently visited by the high and mighty – everyone from Helmut Kohl and the Swedish royals to Jimmy Carter and Bill Gates – and to make such luminaries feel right at home the lodge had not just one, but no fewer than three helipads.

It did have one redeeming feature: its idyllic location, bang in the middle of the flooded forest. This is what the Amazon is all about. The water depth varies greatly throughout the year – reaching a peak in April or May and falling to its lowest level some time in October – thanks to the cycles of snowfall and thaw in the Andes. At the lodge, for instance, the water level can rise and fall by as much as 15 metres (50 feet) in a single year. The impact on the forest and its wildlife is phenomenal.

Nonetheless, intrepid adventurers like us feel out of sorts surrounded by loud and insensitive tourists wearing loud and insensitive shirts and oversized baseball caps. Whatever wildlife happens to be nearby, these are the kind of people who will be facing the other way and talking about the traffic in London, the weather in Munich or the best place to buy chocolate-chip ice cream in Seattle. I was once on a whale-watching boat in the Pacific, and we were trying to listen to the haunting sounds of a singing humpback whale, but we could barely hear above the incessant babble of indistinguishable people in loud shirts noisily swapping baseball caps to see who had the biggest head.

They may want the sensation of adventure, without the unpleasantness and inconvenience of adventure itself, but we didn't. We were on a proper expedition and, as a matter of principle, in a determined effort to appear as professional as possible, resisted the temptation to have our hair done in the beauty salon or watch *The Simpsons* on satellite television or hide in our air-conditioned rooms to avoid the gruelling heat and humidity of the real jungle outside.

Admittedly, we failed to resist the temptation to lie in hammocks by the pool, sipping caipirinhas. But no one is perfect. And, to be fair, we occasionally looked up to watch the local squirrel monkeys and white-fronted capuchins and to make the most of high-speed wi-fi on our laptops.

Besides, we were recovering from New Year's Eve. We hadn't drunk too much, unfortunately, but we were struggling to cope with a combination of jet lag and hazy memories of a dark beach on the shores of the Rio Negro surrounded by jungle, with a huge bonfire, a firework display to rival the opening ceremony of the Beijing Olympics, a motley collection of biting insects, pink champagne in dainty little glasses, and a blur of singing and dancing.

After a lot of debate and soul-searching, we managed to convince ourselves that our serious lying-down time was a productive and essential part of the jungle habituation process.

Eventually, a couple of days and a couple of dozen caipirinhas later, Stephen was almost ready to be released into the wild. We decided to start by getting wet.

The worst thing about swimming in the Amazon isn't what you might expect. It's certainly not crocodile-like caiman, which are large enough to eat the smaller members of a film crew, but rarely do. And it's not bull sharks, which rather alarmingly leave the open ocean and make their way as much as 3,700 kilometres (2,310 miles) upriver, past Manaus and far beyond.

Stingrays, admittedly, can be slightly worrying. They lie flat on the river bed, waiting for you to step on them, and then give you an almighty sting that is so excruciatingly painful you have to run, not walk, to the nearest doctor. But if you shuffle your feet in the muddy or sandy shallows, rather than marching like a trooper, they are more likely to get out of your way than get out their secret weapon.

It's certainly not piranhas, and it's not even two-metre (six-foot) long electric eels or anacondas the length of minibuses.

Opposite
Stephen undergoing an essential part of the jungle habituation process.

No, the worst thing about swimming in the Amazon is the tiny candiru fish (pronounced can-dee-roo). Otherwise known as the toothpick fish, vampire fish or (more disturbingly) the willy fish, this is a parasitic freshwater catfish just a few centimetres long.

Eel-shaped and translucent (so it's virtually impossible to see underwater) the candiru has a voracious appetite for blood. On a normal day it seeks out unsuspecting larger fish by following the flow of water from their gills. It dives underneath the gill flaps, opens its umbrella-like spines to lock itself in position and draw blood, and then drinks and drinks and drinks. It may consume so much blood that its body visibly expands, like that of a leech. Eventually, the little sponger unhooks its spines and sinks to the bottom of the river to digest its meal.

If you happen to be swimming in the Amazon, and peeing, the candiru fish will happily follow the flow of your urine back to its source. Before you can whip up your trunks it will swim straight into your penis and inconveniently lodge itself right inside your urethra. The pain, apparently, is spectacular.

If you are unfortunate enough to be *candirued*, the best option is to get to a hospital before infection causes shock and death, or your bladder bursts. Failing that (a likely scenario if you happen to be in a remote corner of the Amazon), the next option is to chop off your penis.

Alternatively, there is a traditional cure that requires the use of two local plants: the juice of the jagua tree or the pulp of the buitach apple. These are supposed to be brewed into a hot tea that apparently dissolves the skeleton of the fish within a couple of hours (a synthetic version of the brew has been used in the past to dissolve kidney stones). Be wary of some survival books that rather unconvincingly suggest you insert the buitach apple into the affected area.

The main problem with such traditional cures is that, if you're anything like me, you won't have a clue a) where to find a jagua tree or a buitach apple, or b) how to know if you actually do. But if you think you're capable of calmly flicking through a field guide, inevitably written in Portuguese, with a candiru fish and its open umbrella firmly lodged inside your penis, and then organising a nice little campfire to brew a piping-hot cup of tea with your correctly identified traditional plants, then you might just be okay.

The only good news is that, despite rumours to the contrary, it's perfectly safe to stand on the riverbank and pee into the Amazon below. A candiru fish cannot, no matter how hard it tries, leap in mid-air and work its way upstream like a salmon.

I digress. We weren't about to swim in the Amazon just to see if we could avoid penis penetration by a fish with a spiny umbrella. We wanted to swim with a blushing dolphin.

Opposite
Men overboard –
Stephen and Mark
about to snorkel with
pink river dolphins.

The pink river dolphin, or boto, is the kind of animal young children paint at school. A particularly naïve teacher might relegate the exuberant splashes of dazzling pink, the chubby cheeks, the gratuitously long beak crammed with crushing teeth and the gargantuan designer flippers to a wild and fertile young imagination. But pink river dolphins are real – a celebrated Amazonian speciality.

Their pink colour is caused by blood flowing immediately beneath the skin. It becomes even pinker when they are excited or aroused, and as they get older.

We found 'our' dolphins surprisingly easily (actually, they found us), tucked away in a quiet backwater far from the hubbub of the lodge. They were used to being fed by local villagers and, as soon as they spotted the boat, started leaping about excitedly. And blushing bright pink. They raced one way, then did a handbrake turn and raced back the other way.

Unlike most other dolphins, which have fused neck vertebrae (enabling them to swim fast and turn without breaking their necks), Amazon river dolphins have flexible necks that can bend remarkably well, as an adaptation for swimming in the flooded forest and weaving between all those submerged roots and trunks.

Stephen is rarely short of something to say, but for a few moments, admiring the dolphins around the boat, he was speechless. Then his remarkable powers of observation returned.

'They're unmistakably dolphinous,' he remarked. 'If there is such a word.' Indeed.

We squeezed into our smelly, damp wet suits, rinsed out our snorkels, spat in our masks, climbed down the steps of a floating platform anchored in the middle of the river and stepped into the lukewarm waters of the Rio Negro.

The visibility below the surface was dreadful – less than half a metre (20 inches) – and when I stretched my arm out in front of me I could barely see my fingertips. It was virtually impossible to tell what, if anything, was down there. I glanced across at Stephen, goggle-eyed and smiling as much as he could with a snorkel rammed into his mouth, as he stared into the gloom. The dark, tannin-rich water made this alien underwater world surprisingly red in colour and, for a moment, he looked like an astronaut recently landed on Mars.

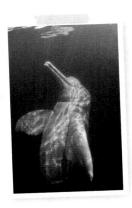

I followed his stare – and there, right in front of us, was a dolphin. Roughly the same size as Stephen and as pink as an embarrassed teenager's blush, it was hanging vertically in the water and staring straight back.

Within minutes, we were being pushed and shoved and bumped by five or six different dolphins. They would suddenly appear between our legs, under our arms, over our shoulders or right in front of us peering inquisitively into our masks. They pushed and shoved one another, too, in their boisterous efforts to get a closer look at these strange beings from the land of loud shirts and baseball caps.

Photography was almost impossible – the dolphins were either too close, touching me or prodding the lens with their beaks, or they were whizzing around too far away and barely visible in the murk.

But watching them at such close range gave us a unique fish-eye view. Their eyes were tiny (though they can see reasonably well both under water and above the surface), and, like many dolphins, their long mouths were angled upwards in the shape of a permanent smile. This is an expression that cannot be changed – they continue to 'smile' when they are unhappy, in intense pain, and even when they are dead.

The proper way to tell a river dolphin's mood, by the way, is to look at its bulging forehead (known in the scientific world as the melon). This changes shape like the forehead of an Ood from the Ood-Sphere, in *Dr Who*, and can appear swollen and globular or shrunken and lumpy. Frustratingly, no one has yet deciphered the code (perhaps not surprising, given that male zoologists can barely fathom the changing moods of female zoologists, and vice versa, let alone those of pink river dolphins).

They also have the most peculiar chubby cheeks, making them look like guilty children with their mouths full. In fact, they are so chubby they hamper the dolphins' downward vision and, bizarrely, may explain why botos frequently swim upside down – it's probably a simple adaptation to help them see better.

It's easy to understand why such unlikely-looking animals are steeped in myth and legend. According to one particularly imaginative myth, perpetrated by early missionaries, the dolphins come out at night and turn into handsome young men, complete with black top hats and Edwardian waistcoats; they then ravish young village girls and impregnate them before returning to the river at first light. It was an inspired way of explaining the sudden appearance of pink babies in the local Indian population.

Best of all, legend has it that pink river dolphins are charged with protecting the very animals we had come to the Amazon to see. Apparently, if you really want to see a manatee you must first make peace with the dolphins.

So far so good.

Getting around in the Amazon can be time-consuming. It's not a happy place for efficient people with a sense of urgency and a superlative quartz watch that is guaranteed to lose no more than 0.5 seconds a day (but then if you're living so close to the edge that your life is thrown into disarray by normal mechanical timepieces that lose more than 0.5 seconds a day, a bit of time in the Amazon would probably do you some good). There are virtually no deadlines or roads in the region and most of the boats seem to take the best part of a manatee's 60-year lifetime to reach the end of the jetty.

It was all well and good for the early explorers, who had months or even years to get from A to B, and no pressing engagements back home. But we were on a tight BBC schedule. Stephen had to get back to the UK in time for multitudinous TV recordings and I had to be on several different continents for multitudinous other reasons. Sadly, we didn't have months to spare.

So we did what most people do under the circumstances. We hitched a ride on a missionary floatplane.

Missionary pilot Captain Wilson Kannerberg did the usual pre-flight checks, bowed his head in prayer, leaned back on a seat cover made of wooden beads normally used by Greek taxi drivers, and reached for the throttle.

Stephen was watching from the back and had that look on his face men get when their girlfriends start winding up tough guys in public. Not scared exactly, but wishing he were somewhere else. Wisely, he chose to ignore the religious mutterings from the cockpit and buried himself in a Portuguese–English dictionary, purchased at the airport. He had nearly two hours to learn Portuguese from scratch. Given that he already spoke French, German, Dutch and Spanish, and had a strong grounding in Latin and Greek, I was mildly shocked that he didn't speak Portuguese already. But he was remedying the situation fast and I felt sure he'd be fluent by the time we arrived. I speak English and American.

On a wing and a prayer, we flew 350 kilometres (220 miles) south of Manaus and began searching for a converted wooden ferryboat called the *Cassiquiari*. After a few theatrical swoops and turns over the jungle canopy, we found it tucked away in Arauazinho Creek, a tributary of the Rio Aripuanã, and thanked the Lord when Captain Wilson successfully landed with a splash and aplomb right alongside our home for the next few days.

'Have I told you about my flatulence?' asked Stephen, as we gathered our belongings and clambered down onto the plane's gargantuan float. He'd heard a malicious rumour that we would have to share a cabin. 'Or that I'm a pyromaniac? And did I mention my stabbing obsession?'

We were greeted by the boat's skipper, Miguel Rocha, along with the guarantee of two entirely separate cabins. Such was Stephen's cheering response,

Opposite
Missionary pilot Captain Wilson landing on a tributary of a tributary of a tributary of the Amazon with a splash and aplomb.

Miguel might have announced the end of income tax for one and all.

There was, however, no power in Stephen's private cabin. And that meant no power for his Apple Mac.

'Right, that's it,' he said. 'We're going back.'

'Never mind,' I replied consolingly, trying not to laugh. 'It'll be alright.'

He looked a little wide-eyed and panicky as he tried to force his laptop plug into a cracked and rusty once-was-a-plug-socket hole in the cabin wall. 'There's no never mind about it. I cannot go four days without power.'

I left the cabin, in mock despair.

'You may well despair, but not as much as I do.'

Miguel was a gentle, calm man in his late-60s. Born in the forest, but brought up in the city, he was one of nineteen brothers and sisters. His grandfather crossed the Atlantic from Portugal in the 1880s and his grandmother was a native Indian. This made him a caboclo, one of the so-called 'forgotten people' of the Amazon – mixed-race descendants of European settlers and Amerindians. The caboclos get none of the rights of the indigenous forest-dwellers and are ignored by government and aid agencies, and Miguel was leading their fight for recognition.

He'd been exploring the Amazon Basin professionally since 1981 and knew a thing or two about life in the jungle.

Opposite
Two men in a boat –
searching for one
of the rarest and
most elusive animals
on earth.

We had a long, relaxing lunch on the rear deck, poring over an Amazon-sized map of the forest and planning our mini-expedition. By the time we'd finished we had convinced ourselves that our chances of finding a manatee were actually quite good.

Then it rained.

We happened to be in the Amazon during the rainy season. It would have been a bit rich to complain – after all, rain is the whole point of a tropical rainforest. The clue is in the title.

But there's rain and there's RAIN! I have rain at home, in Bristol. Rather a lot, as it happens. To be fair, it doesn't rain all the time (the week before I left it had rained only twice – once for three days and once for four days), but I've always been convinced that I live in the rainiest corner of Britain, if not the entire known universe.

Until, that is, I checked the figures. Bristol doesn't even register on the scale. My garden receives less than a quarter as much rain in a typical year as the Amazon (not the whole of the Amazon – just an area the same size as my garden).

But the biggest difference is that the Amazon has more professional rain. My garden gets a seemingly endless grey drizzle that starts around the beginning of January and continues through to the latter part of December. Meanwhile, the Amazon gets a heartfelt torrential downpour once or twice a day, complete with unforgettable displays of lightning and ear-splitting thunder, and that's that. The daily ritual opening of the heavens would make Steven Spielberg's special effects department glow with pride, but here's the point: there's plenty of time in between for everyone to go outside and do things without an umbrella.

Rain stopped play while we were filming at least once every day, typically between midday and 2pm, making an excellent excuse to break for lunch. Sometimes it rained at other times, too, making an excellent excuse to break for caipirinhas or a snooze. The prognosis was unlikely to improve for several months, until the end of the rainy season, but we were always optimistic and never quite got the hang of this new daily routine.

It was like spending a couple of hours every day in a power-jet shower.

We watched the rain lashing against the side of the *Cassiquiari*, pouring off the blue tarpaulin roof, running across the deck in torrents and visibly swelling the creek. Then it was time for a nap. There were hammocks hanging from the rafters and I picked a bright red one, crawled inside and fell into a deep sleep.

There's a technique to sleeping in hammocks: you don't lie in them straight, as in holiday brochures or dreamy advertisements for tropical drinks. You lie in them diagonally. That way it's possible to lie completely flat and, over the years, you don't end up with a permanently bowed back and forever curled up like a frightened armadillo.

I woke with a start to find the entire crew standing around me, filming.

'Welcome to my world,' muttered Stephen in his very rich, very warm, very English, best TV voice.

Stephen, meanwhile, had been counting mobile phones. He owns 121 altogether, at the last count, but was disappointed to discover that he had only six of them with him in the Amazon. Not a single one had reception. I made a mental note to buy him a satellite phone for his next birthday.

Opposite
Travelling deeper and deeper into the flooded forest.

The rain stopped as suddenly as it had started, and we were able to embark on our mission (I suppose we could have started earlier but we didn't want to get wet).

Before searching for manatees we had to find Ivano, our fixer for the rest of the trip. Sure enough, as promised, he was ready and waiting for us in a delightful little settlement carved into a particularly wild and remote corner of jungle. Called Arauazinho, after the creek, and with just five families forming a population of fewer than thirty people, this teeny homestead of stilted wooden houses was too small to be called a village.

I liked Ivano immensely. Short enough to stand at the table during mealtimes, as bald as a baby manatee and never without a mischievous grin, he had the habit of addressing everyone he met as if he wanted to marry their daughter. He made the perfect fixer – a man who, if he wanted to, could persuade Prince Charles to eat genetically modified crops.

My only slight complaint is that Ivano introduced us to a long-haired Dutchman. This Dutchman talked so slowly, and in such a dreary monotone, that whenever he opened his mouth all you could hear was the sound of doors closing.

Ivano made the perfect fixer – a man who, if he wanted to, could persuade Prince Charles to eat genetically modified crops.

He was utterly obsessed with what he claimed to be a new, smaller species of manatee, which he'd already named the dwarf manatee. It's found only in Arauazinho Creek, apparently, and he wouldn't talk about anything else.

We'd offer him a beer and he'd say something like 'Why don't they call the beer "Dwarf Manatee Beer" instead of "Brahma Beer"?' We'd invite him to join us for dinner on the boat and, quick as a flash, he'd say 'We could watch my video of dwarf manatees while we're eating.'

The Dutchman had been studying wildlife in the Amazon for decades, partly because he liked animals and partly because he was on the run. When we briefly managed to change the subject from dwarf manatees, with the help of a large jug of caipirinha, he told us hair-raising stories of warrants for his arrest issued by both the Brazilian and Dutch governments. He never satisfactorily explained exactly what he was supposed to have done, but it sounded serious.

We'll call him Hairy van Pit-bull, just in case (speaking in monotone isn't bad

enough to justify a long spell in a Brazilian jail – and he claimed to be innocent of all the other, unspecified charges).

In theory, I suppose, he could be right and there may indeed be such a thing as a dwarf manatee. After all, there are pygmy blue whales, lesser white-toothed shrews and dwarf caiman. But Hairy was one of those people who could have sworn blind that our names were Mark and Stephen and we wouldn't have believed him. To make matters worse, his best evidence seemed to consist of a blurry home video of a vaguely diminutive manatee (most likely a youngster) lasting no more than a few fleeting seconds. It was pretty iffy, to say the least.

He was clearly a bright man. He was fluent in even more languages than Stephen (Dutch, English, Portuguese, French, German, Spanish and taki-taki – the mother tongue of the Creoles, once spoken by African slaves working on plantations in Suriname) and was the author of scientific papers on everything from wild pigs to a lost cousin of the Brazil-nut tree. But something was clearly amiss.

I wondered if it might be possible to be an unbearable bore in one language, but an exceptionally witty and enlightening raconteur in another. Perhaps, if we had made the effort to learn taki-taki, we'd have seen him in an entirely different light?

Naturally, both Stephen and I did the diplomatic soft-shoe shuffle and oozed as much politeness as we could muster. Despite our frustration, we couldn't help feeling sorry for him. His whole world revolved around persuading the rest of the world that dwarf manatees are real. We even agreed to a 20-kilometre (12-mile) wild-goose chase, up the infamous clearwater creek, to search for his little hobbyhorses.

It would only take 15 minutes to reach them, he assured us. Half a day later we decided to go back and return to the mother ship, leaving Hairy to sulk and us to revel in the brief period of heavenly peace.

We said our goodbyes, politely but not too enthusiastically, and climbed back on board the *Cassiquiari* with renewed *joie de vivre*.

I asked Ivano about his own encounters with more customary, proper-sized manatees. He laughed.

'I love manatees,' he said. 'They taste better than beef.'

He admitted that he hadn't actually seen a manatee in the wild, and launched into a happy few minutes reminiscing about eating manatee meat as a child. He

could barely stop licking his lips as he described its tender, melt-in-the-mouth texture and the unique, slightly almond-flavoured taste.

I'd heard about almond-tasting sea cows before. The Amazonian manatee has a long-lost relative, called Steller's sea cow, which once lived in the Bering Sea between Kamchatka and the western tip of the Aleutian Islands. Three times the size of its Amazonian cousin, this monster among manatees was discovered by the crew of the Russian brig *St Peter*, who were shipwrecked on Bering Island in November 1741. In fact, the weak and scurvy-ridden castaways survived only by eating their friendly neighbourhood sirenians.

Fortunately, one of the crew happened to be a naturalist, Georg Wilhelm Steller, who spent much of his enforced time on the remote uninhabited island recording information about the animals he and his crew were scoffing. I feel for Steller. It's hard enough studying wildlife at the best of times, without the added pressure of friends and colleagues eating your subjects as fast as you can write. He did it, though, and made the only detailed written record of the habits and appearance of the sea cow that was later to bear his name.

With full stomachs, the shipwrecked survivors cobbled together an escape boat and, some ten months and many almond-tasting, human-trusting sea cows later, made it back to the Russian mainland. But they blabbed about their miraculous discovery and prompted a rush of hunting expeditions. The sea cows didn't stand a chance. They provided three square meals a day, and endless snacks in between, while the hunters killed fur seals, otters and other fur-bearing animals for big profit.

The outcome was predictable. Just 27 years after its discovery, Steller's sea cow officially became extinct. The last one was killed in 1768.

Graca, our boat's cook, overheard Ivano waxing lyrical about almond-tasting manatees and called out from the galley. I hadn't seen her so enthusiastic and animated. She described some manatee recipes from her own childhood and told us about manatee-hunting expeditions with her father, armed with nothing more than a home-made harpoon and a rope. They would sit for hours in their little wooden boat, in complete silence, until a manatee surfaced near enough for her father to strike. Then they waited patiently for the injured animal to tow them around and tire itself out.

I asked Ivano and Graca if they still eat manatee meat today. Never, they told me. It's illegal.

I pushed them a little more.

'Well, you can still buy manatee meat on the black market in Manaus. Sometimes you can get it, but it's not easy.'

'Do you miss it?' I asked.

Opposite
Hot? Every morning
arrived complete with
a full body sweat.

'A lot,' laughed Ivano.

I left it at that.

The next day we returned to Arauazinho and met one of the villagers, Francisco, as well as his wife Ennis, their seven smiley children and just a few of their innumerable chickens and goats. Francisco had kindly agreed to help us find manatees. He'd seen them just the day before, feeding on water lilies in a hidden lake behind the creek.

Manatees are not just vegetarians – they are greedy vegetarians. They eat a heck of a lot. In fact, they can eat up to ten per cent of their body weight in a single day. That's the equivalent of me eating ninety three-course meals a day. They are fussy eaters, too, scoffing just a few, carefully selected species of aquatic plants and nothing else.

Understandably, the few carefully selected species of aquatic plants don't like it at all. So they've developed a special anti-manatee device. What they've done is to stuff themselves with silica, which is hard and abrasive and wears out the manatees' teeth very quickly (ironically, silica is used in toothpaste for precisely the same reason – but to remove plaque rather than the actual teeth).

The manatees wouldn't allow themselves to be outwitted by a few plants and responded – not by carefully selecting other species of plants – but by growing replaceable teeth. They have a canny conveyor-belt system in which all their teeth move forward about a millimetre a month; as the front ones wear out, and fall out, they are replaced by the next in line.

I had woken up feeling quite ill with heatstroke on the morning Francisco offered to help, and was trying to alternate between filming, lying down, and feeling sorry for myself. But Francisco's sighting, almost within a stone's throw of where we were standing, had triggered a surge of adrenalin and I couldn't bear the thought of missing our best chance yet of seeing a manatee.

We manhandled Francisco's canoe out of the creek, up a steep bank, through the tangled forest and across to the hidden lake. It was hard to do it quietly. Actually, it was downright impossible. Francisco never uttered a word and effortlessly sauntered through the jungle in complete silence, like a ghost in slippers. The rest of us bumbled about like drunks in a coffee shop, stumbling over hidden roots, yelping in pain every time we gashed our legs, cursing whenever we were seized by horrible grasping plants, stepping on each and every snapable twig, swatting irritable mosquitoes, and in the end giggling uncontrollably at the absurdity of it all.

By the time we reached the lake I suspect every local manatee had either moved somewhere else, or died of old age.

Unwaveringly optimistic, though, we launched the canoe and paddled quietly

(relatively quietly) across to the far side. We cruised along the shoreline, weaved in and out of the half-submerged trees, zigzagged backwards and forwards in the open expanse in the middle, and every so often waited in silent (relatively silent) anticipation.

But all our efforts were in vain. We didn't see a manatee disappear beneath the surface of the lake. We didn't see the ripples made by a disappearing manatee. We didn't even nearly see the ripples.

For the next two days we searched rivers and lakes and ploughed tributaries and tributaries of tributaries.

Then we gave up.

It was such a disappointment. I really thought we might be lucky and so wanted to see an Amazonian manatee – even fleetingly – in the wild. But if there were manatees in the Aripuanã, they'd chosen to stay concealed in the river's murky waters.

We'd been outmanoeuvred by one of the slowest creatures on earth.

Francisco didn't know of any other likely places to look. We tried to console ourselves in the knowledge that if he didn't know anywhere else to look, that was definitive. Definitely not knowing was at least better than vaguely not knowing.

Next morning we called Captain Wilson on the satellite phone, reported calm conditions, and settled down to wait for the flight back to Manaus.

The thought of going home (or, at least, returning to the familiarity and relative comfort of the Tropical Hotel, in Manaus) made Stephen bound around the deck with renewed energy and enthusiasm. I've no doubt he had enjoyed our little escapade enormously, but I think four consecutive wi-fi-free nights in the jungle was just about enough.

I have a maddeningly low boredom threshold and simply cannot leave the house without something to keep me occupied, just in case my train is delayed, I get caught in a traffic jam or the person I'm meeting happens to be late. My worst nightmare would be to get kidnapped and be forced to cope with days, weeks or (heaven forbid) months of captivity without a notepad and pen, a book, a magazine, a solar-powered laptop … anything to while away the time.

How anyone can embark on a 12-hour long-haul flight without a bulging bag of stuff to keep them busy for at least 14 hours (allowing for delays) I'll never know. The mere thought of doing nothing but stare out of the window makes me feel downright fidgety.

Except in the Amazon, of course, where there are plenty of reasons to stare out of the window.

The scale of the jungle beggars belief. Describing it as big is like describing Bill Gates as fairly well off. 'Big' doesn't even register on the scale. New York is big. Wembley Stadium is big. The Amazon is absolutely bloody ginormous. As we climbed above Arauazinho not-quite-a-village, and banked towards Manaus, the forest stretched out below us, unbroken except for the occasional mighty river or creek, as far as I could see in every direction.

It made me want to say something. My brain couldn't possibly grapple with this staggeringly, achingly beautiful expanse of verdant green. It was exploding with superlatives that wanted to get out.

I caught Stephen's eye. He'd stopped learning Portuguese for a moment and, like me, was staring in disbelief out of the window.

'Oh my God!' I said.

'I know,' he nodded, knowingly.

We both felt better.

Some of the trees were considerably taller than others. This may seem like an obvious thing to say, but jungles have a small number of very tall trees whose role in life is to tower majestically above the main canopy. They form what is

known in the trade as the 'emergent layer' and they might as well be in the Sea of Tranquillity, they are so difficult to reach and so death-defyingly hard to study. As high as 70 metres (235 feet) above the ground, these emergents give a whole new meaning to the term 'out on a limb'.

Immediately below them is the thick leafy realm of the forest canopy. This is the heart of the rainforest – home to the vast majority of the Amazon's large trees and, indeed, most of its animal and plant species. It forms a more or less continuous cover of foliage some 40 metres (130 feet) above the ground, and blocks out pretty much all the sunlight. To be precise, it blocks out 98 per cent of the sunlight (living in the gloom underneath must be like living under a particularly expansive, dark-green golfing umbrella).

The science of navigating and studying the jungle canopy is called 'dendronautics'. If you fancy a career change, with more day-to-day risks than coal mining, deep-sea diving or flying with the Red Arrows, this is the job for you. It's perfect for dinner-party conversation because, joy of joys, you would be allowed to call yourself a dendronaut.

As a dendronaut, you will be able to fire ropes into the jungle trees with a crossbow, erect elaborate cranes with rotating jibs, build precarious walkways, climb to dizzying heights using nothing but ropes and pulleys, and even fly

above the forest canopy in a wonderful assortment of motorised hot-air balloons, tethered helium balloons and airships straight out of a science-fiction movie. You'll also get to live in a real-life vertigo-inducing tree house.

Best of all, since dendronautics is still in its infancy and the jungle canopy is one of the last largely unexplored frontiers on earth, there's a very good chance that you will come across something entirely new to science. The forest above a forest is believed to harbour literally millions of species, from lianas and bromeliads to frogs and monkeys, which are just waiting to be discovered.

Stephen was still staring out of the window. Every so often he'd shout 'macaw' or 'eagle' or 'oooph!' (there was a lot of turbulence with black rain clouds gathering for the next torrential downpour) to anyone who would listen.

I think we saw more wildlife from the plane, flying over the jungle canopy, than in four days of exploring from the *Cassiquiari*.

The striking thing about wildlife-watching in the Amazon is that you don't get to do it very often. Far from being overwhelmed by the forest's world-renowned biodiversity – it was once described as 'the most alive place on earth' – much of the time we were decidedly underwhelmed by the apparent absence of anything remotely resembling an animal.

The reason is simple: ingenuity. Competition for food is so intense that rainforest animals live in constant fear for their lives. They have to be clever and resourceful to avoid being eaten (or, at least, to avoid being reduced to gibbering nervous wrecks and dying from stress-induced heart attacks). Experts at concealment and camouflage, they simply can't afford to be seen.

So it was our own fault, really, that we didn't see very much. Unlike the jungle's super-predators, with their finely tuned senses, our pretty useless urban eyes, ears and noses were virtually incapable of spotting anything – unless it actually landed on us and bit really hard.

What we did occasionally see were the animals that deliberately make themselves conspicuous, or simply don't care whether they are seen or not. These showy jungle inhabitants tend to be either fast-moving, like birds, or inedible and dangerous, like poison-arrow frogs.

Halfway into the journey, it dawned on me that we were probably flying over vast areas of forest that no one had ever walked through, let alone explored or studied.

When Europeans first arrived in the early 16th century, the Amazon had an indigenous population of about six million people living in some 2,000 nations and tribes. Nobody can agree on exactly how many have survived the onslaught of western civilisation, but fewer than 700,000 is the most widely accepted figure.

There are many reasons for the disappearance of so many 'noble savages' (as early Europeans called them), but disease is perhaps the most significant. The explorers and early settlers unknowingly brought smallpox, measles, tuberculosis, influenza and a host of other deadly illnesses with them. The Indians had no immunity and were utterly helpless. Tens of thousands perished. Ironically, many never even came into direct contact with the outside world – entire tribes were annihilated by germs that travelled faster than their European carriers.

Then, as if things weren't bad enough, Jesuit missionaries dedicated to spreading Catholicism terrified the hapless Indians by warning that this wave of sickness and death was God's punishment for their lack of faith.

The number of indigenous people living in the Amazon seems to have increased slightly in recent years, perhaps because they have acquired a certain level of resistance to at least some of those diseases. Against the odds, there are still more than 200 indigenous groups in the region, talking 170 different languages and dialects, and at least 50 of them rarely or never have contact with the rest of the world.

But the depressing reality nowadays is that there's more chance of stumbling upon mechanical diggers and bulldozers in the Amazon than of meeting indigenous people.

If you fancy a career change, with more day-to-day risks than coal mining, deep-sea diving or flying with the Red Arrows, try dendronautics – the science of navigating and studying the jungle canopy.

Since 1970, almost one-fifth of the entire Amazon rainforest has been destroyed. That's equivalent to an area the size of England, Scotland, Wales, Northern Ireland, the Republic of Ireland, Germany and Denmark combined.

You couldn't dream up a bigger list of more damaging activities if you tried: cattle ranching, land clearance for soya-bean plantations, small-scale subsistence agriculture, logging, and a mixed bag of commercial agriculture, mining, urbanisation and dam construction are responsible for most of the damage. Construction of the 5,000-kilometre (3,125-mile) Trans-Amazonian Highway (which bisects Amazonia and opens up vast areas of land to settlement and development) certainly hasn't helped. Even misguided government policies, and outrageously inappropriate World Bank projects, have contributed to the environmental havoc.

So why aren't we all shocked and appalled and waving our arms about in despair?

I think it's because we tire of hearing about rainforest destruction. I remember writing articles predicting doom and gloom in the Amazon twenty years ago and I quoted similarly horrendous figures – 'an area the size of Belgium lost every year' springs to mind. Two decades of the same old revelations make them less shocking than they used to be. Our senses are dulled as the relentless stories of devastation become little more than background noise.

What's really frightening is that nothing much seems to have changed since deforestation first hit the headlines. Actually, that's not true – it's getting worse.

Have all those years of campaigning, fund-raising, pleading, cajoling and cautioning by so many individuals and conservation groups made the slightest difference?

I suppose the positive response would be to say that it must, surely, have slowed things down. But clearly it hasn't slowed things down anywhere near enough.

We couldn't leave Brazil without seeing a manatee (or at least a manatee biologist), and the best place to do that happened to be a short taxi ride from the hotel. Right in the centre of Manaus.

I remembered meeting a charming and delightful manatee biologist (how can someone who devotes their entire working life to studying manatees be anything but charming and delightful?) at the National Institute for Amazon Research. In fact, Douglas Adams and I had spent a couple of days with her, along with several orphaned manatees in her care, when we were in Manaus in the late 1980s.

Opposite
Almost one-fifth of
the entire Amazon
rainforest has been
destroyed since 1970.

What's really frightening is that nothing much seems to have changed since deforestation first hit the headlines. Actually, that's not true – it's getting worse.

Vera da Silva was still at the Institute (known locally as the Instituto Nacional de Pesquisas da Amazonas – or INPA) and was as charming and delightful as I remembered her. She was one of a handful of people responsible for discovering most of what we know about Amazonian manatees (which, as it happens, isn't very much – but that's not their fault).

We agreed wholeheartedly that neither of us had changed one little bit in twenty years and walked towards a large concrete tank, complete with two enormous windows and four adult Amazonian manatees.

They were farting and sleeping. As we approached, one of them started walking along the bottom of the tank – literally walking, using its long, stubby front flippers to pull itself along in a bouncy, slow-motion way, like an astronaut walking on the moon. We couldn't believe our luck: an active manatee.

Stephen stood and watched it for a few moments.

'Oh my, I think I'm in love,' he said, utterly spellbound. 'They've got that slow grace that big animals, such as elephants, seem to have.'

We stood and watched the manatees farting and pretending to be weightless, plump and graceful at the same time, and marvelled at their sheer loveableness.

You're probably wondering why we were so taken with these preposterous animals, and I can understand your scepticism. The problem, I think, is that

Travelling Case for a Seal

Amazonian manatees don't photograph particularly well (that's not a criticism – I don't photograph well, either, as my passport photograph spectacularly testifies). Look at a picture of a manatee in a book and you get the impression of an animal that only its mother, or a zoologist, could possibly find attractive.

But we were completely captivated. They looked so gentle, so harmless, so innocent … so sweet. I can't believe I just said that. I never say an animal is 'sweet'. It's so unprofessional. In my defence, though, it was actually Stephen who said it first – more of a 'sooooo sweeeeeeet'. And, besides, he's absolutely right.

We'd been filming for over an hour, trying to think of other, more colourful and imaginative words to describe our new-found friends, and were failing miserably. I think it was the heat. We were trying to do it in the relentless glare of the tropical sun.

The day we visited the Institute was staggeringly hot and humid. Having said that, describing any particular day in Manaus as staggeringly hot and humid is a little like describing one particular sloth as exceptionally upside down. It's rarely anything else.

Give me sub-zero temperatures, biting winds and icicles hanging off the end of my nose any day. I find high humidity a source of unadulterated misery. For most of the trip, every morning arrived complete with a full body sweat that stayed with me for the rest of the day. After a while, I had the permanent look of a red-faced Japanese macaque in a hot spring and felt hugely embarrassed about it from the moment we set foot in Brazil to the moment we left.

A couple of times I noticed super-cool Vera giving me a strange look as streams of perspiration trickled down my neck, off my chin, across my forehead and into my eyes like a series of dripping taps. She must have thought I'd been sweating buckets nonstop in the twenty years since we'd first met.

But I had a crafty plan to cool off and have a really close encounter with a manatee at the same time. I was also very keen to take some underwater shots – few people have had the chance to photograph these secretive creatures. I asked Vera if I could get in the tank. She hesitated for a moment, glanced at the colossal pile of diving kit I happened to have with me, just in case, and said 'yes'.

I spent two glorious hours under water, with the four manatees and about four tonnes of manatee poo. I think they were excited. In fact, by the time I was ready to get out, there was so much excitement in the water I could barely see the manatees themselves.

They were a little nervous at first (who can blame them?) but got increasingly confident and inquisitive and, by the end of my dive, were out-and-out friendly. They peered into my mask, gently touched me with their tails and even nuzzled me with their rubbery snouts. Every time I tried to photograph one, another would inevitably be watching closely from the sidelines. If they had cameras, I swear they would have been taking pictures too.

Gently, I ran my hand over the largest manatee's back. He didn't seem to mind. It was surprisingly bristly. At first glance Amazonian manatees look bald, but their bodies are sparsely covered in short, wiry hairs (about one per square centimetre: eight per square inch) that are connected to a rich network of nerves. These are believed to give them a kind of sixth sense – by detecting slight pressure changes underwater – that may explain how the animals are able to navigate in their murky riverine home without bumping into things.

Nothing would have compared to encountering an Amazonian manatee in its natural habitat, of course, but a couple of hours in INPA's tank was the next best thing.

I doubt if I will ever get another chance. As manatee numbers diminish, it will get increasingly difficult to see them wild and free. Rainforest destruction, dam building and accidental drowning in commercial fishing nets have all been taking their toll. Hunting, too, has long been a major threat. More than 200,000 were killed during the period 1935–54, for their meat, oil and hides, and although hunting at commercial levels has largely stopped, many thousands have been killed in the years since.

I couldn't stop thinking, while making friends with 'my' four manatees, how their placid temperament (like that of the iconic dodo) made them all too easy to drive towards extinction.

It's impossible to say how many are left. Maybe 10,000; maybe more, maybe fewer. But let me put it this way. In the 1980s, there were reports of as many as 1,000 manatees huddled together in a single river or lake. Nowadays, a gathering of half a dozen is considered quite a lot.

I would have stayed in the tank for longer, but Vera was keen to show us her babies. Hidden away in a quiet corner of the Institute were three more tanks. These were much smaller than the main one – more like the kind of paddling pools children in Kensington or Chelsea might play in – and provided a temporary home for half a dozen orphaned manatees.

As well as studying manatees, the staff at INPA provide round-the-clock care and attention for injured adults and orphaned calves. More and more youngsters had been arriving at this makeshift rehabilitation centre in recent years, and no one knew why. Perhaps it indicated a growing population or a greater awareness among the local people? More likely, it was an alarming sign that more adults were being killed.

Vera pointed out some rope marks on the orphans' tails. Young calves are curious and naïve and relatively easy to catch. Hunters tie ropes around their

Above
Feeding a baby manatee with bottled milk – some people get all the best jobs.

Opposite
The Amazonian manatee was first described as a cross between a seal and a hippo, though it's not related to either. There is nothing else quite like this perfect piece of evolutionary engineering in the world.

tails, tether them to lakeside trees, and wait while the frightened animals call out in distress. As sure as manatees are endangered, their mothers come to their rescue – and almost certain death.

Vera asked if we'd like to feed one, with a bottle of exceptionally rich milk. Stephen was desperate to have a go, and she showed him how. He held the tiniest calf firmly under its chin, with its head just above the surface so it could breathe, and tenderly pushed a baby's bottle between its enormous, prehensile lips.

With a flipper resting on the great man's arm and a line of milk dribbling down one cheek, the minuscule manatee closed its eyes and sucked and slurped really loudly. If Stephen were a manatee his eyes would have been closed, too, and I'm sure he'd have been dribbling down one cheek. The two mammals – one already endangered and the other about to be (as you will soon discover) – were in seventh heaven.

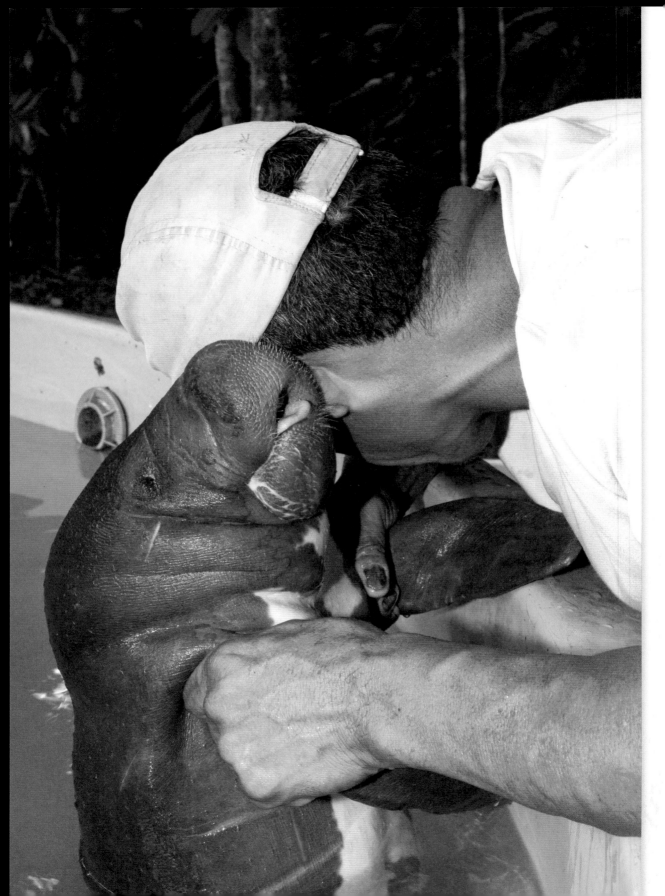

Opposite
A baby manatee
confides in the man
charged with nursing
it back to health.

After a rejuvenating couple of days marvelling at manatees and poring over emails, we were ready for our final expedition into the wi-fi-free jungle beyond Manaus. This was the part of the trip we'd been looking forward to the most: we were going to release an orphaned manatee back into the wild.

We took a scheduled flight 700 kilometres (440 miles) west, to a small town called Tefé, and set up base camp in the Anilce Hotel.

If you're ever given a year to live, move to Tefé. Founded as a base for missionaries in the 17th century, it's pleasant enough, with a Central American flavour to its buildings and streets, but there is absolutely nothing to do. Every day lasts an eternity. I asked a couple of people how they spent their spare time there: 'reading', said one; 'watching DVDs', said the other.

It reminded me of an Icelandic friend's response to a visitor who asked what there is to do in his remote village in the winter. 'Well, in the summer there is fishing and fornication,' he said, 'and in the winter there is no fishing.'

We were fortunate, though, because we had things to do and people to see. We waited for the customary storm of the day to drop its customary load and then set off to find the offices of the Mamirauá Project.

We'd flown halfway across the Amazon to meet an honorary member of the project, called Piti. Rescued from a fishing net with a nasty wound in his back (probably made by a harpoon), Piti was a baby manatee. He had been nursed back to health by the staff of the project and was about to embark on the first leg of a long journey to be released back into the wild.

We found the offices, eventually, floating on a wooden platform in the middle of the river, and introduced ourselves to two of the staff: Miriam Marmontel and Carolina Ramos.

If you're a single male zoologist, looking for a suitable study subject, I would recommend Amazonian manatees. You would be part of an elite group of specialists studying an enigmatic and endangered animal. Plus Amazonian manatee-ologists are all passionate and intellectual and, in my limited experience, would all turn heads on the streets of London, Paris or New York.

I couldn't think of anything intelligent to say.

'Please can we see your manatee?' sounded a little lame, or rude, or both.

Stephen took over.

'Please can we see your manatee?' he said.

We walked around the wooden platform, which was rolling slightly in the wake of a passing boat, picked our way past several garden sheds or offices (it was hard to tell which), and there in front of us was a bright blue fibreglass tank full of murky water. We leaned over the side, and saw Piti's little back breaking the surface.

Miriam and Carolina introduced us to Michelle, who had been Piti's nurse and confidante for the past few months.

The three girls asked who would like to help prepare Piti for his impending expedition. My hand shot into the air faster than a chameleon's tongue.

We carefully drained the water from his tank, until he was floundering around like an eel in an empty bath, and gently manhandled him onto the wooden floating jetty to be weighed and measured. He twisted and writhed. There was no hint of aggression, no lashing out, no biting. He simply wanted to demonstrate that he could out-wriggle us if he really wanted to. Michelle crouched down beside him and whispered something in his ear. He listened carefully and, miraculously, calmed down.

I was instructed to hang on to his tail, in case he didn't like being weighed and measured, and was thrilled to be able to help.

He farted.

This was not your average laugh-it-off friend-in-the-pub kind of fart. It was a lengthy, ear-splitting, far-reaching fart.

Stephen stepped back.

'At least he's not a meat-eater,' he remarked, trying to be helpful and positive.

Then he farted again. This time it was a shockingly wet fart which I felt hitting my shirt, dribbling down my shorts and then running down my leg. I glanced up, gasping for air. Stephen was standing on the far side of the tank.

Miriam pronounced Piti large enough to travel, so we lifted the anxious manatee out of his pongy postcard from the wild and started carrying him to another tank, ready and waiting on the deck of a boat called the *Com te Abreu*.

'Watch your feet!' Stephen called, helpfully, from behind a garden shed.

The plan was to take Piti 160 kilometres (100 miles) into the heart of one of the biggest jungle reserves in Brazil where, ultimately, he would be set free.

We hoisted the unwitting little manatee onto the deck of the *Com te Abreu* and into his temporary new home. With a wriggle and a splash, he disappeared beneath the surface.

We said our goodbyes to Miriam, Carolina, Michelle and Piti, and arranged to meet early the following morning.

But you know what they say about the best-laid plans? Without the benefit of hindsight, little did we realise that we were also about to embark on our biggest and toughest adventure yet.

It was still dark when we rolled up, lifeless and uncommunicative, at the appointed ungodly hour.

Opposite & below
Mark, Michelle and Piti, preparing for a journey into the heart of one of the biggest jungle reserves in Brazil. But you know what they say about the best-laid plans?

Suddenly, there was a thump and a blood-curdling scream.

It started to rain.

We commandeered two boats, just large enough to carry eight of us and 31 pieces of kit, and slowly motored out into the middle of the river. We found the *Com te Abreu*, which was moored alongside the floating wooden platform, and squeezed into a small gap in front of her bow.

Stephen got out first. I set foot on the wet platform a few seconds later, just as he disappeared behind the main boat.

Suddenly, there was a thump and a blood-curdling scream.

I turned the corner to see him lying by the side of the *Com te Abreu*, almost within touching distance of Piti in his tank, with a look of sheer horror and agony etched into his face.

Stephen never claimed to be the first to fall for an animal like Piti, though I dare say few have done it quite so dramatically. Everything seemed to be hurting – his arm, his shoulder, his back, his head, his ribs, his knee. He was feeling sick and yelping in pain with the slightest involuntary movement. But it was his right arm that seemed particularly bad, and we were worried because he was complaining of numb fingers and a 'weird' feeling in his elbow.

We were less than three weeks into a four-week trip. We weren't quite at the end of the universe, but for a while that morning it felt pretty close.

There's nothing worse than seeing a friend in pain, and feeling unable to do anything to make it better. We made him as comfortable as we could, under the circumstances, and waited for help.

The next few hours are a blur of satellite phone calls, BBC medical kits, boat journeys, jungle clinics, plaster of Paris, injections, pouring rain and howls of pain. And all the time we were being filmed. Cameraman Will, ever the professional, kept his finger on the button.

Eventually, after a lot of agonising debate and soul-searching, we split the crew in two. Will, Tim (Sound) and Sue (Assistant Producer) stayed with Piti,

Opposite
We should have taken
notice of the omens.

while the rest of us returned to Manaus.

Captain Wilson had responded to our SOS and, surprisingly quickly, half of us were in the air heading towards proper medical help. I looked across at Stephen, eyes shut, slumped in his seat, with his shirt tattered and torn and his arm in a temporary plaster. The adventure was over and we were alone with our thoughts.

All I could think about during the two-hour flight was that it could have been much worse. Stephen could so easily have knocked himself out and fallen into the fast-flowing river. I had visions of the rest of us diving in, holding our breath, feeling around in the darkness under the hull, in the vague hope of finding and rescuing him.

The next 24 hours were awful – another blur of clinics, X-rays, blood tests, heart checks and second opinions. At least we got a firm diagnosis. His right arm was broken, very badly, in three places. We decided to get him to Miami for a delicate and potentially dangerous operation to put it right.

But just when you think things can't get any worse, they do. I woke up with food poisoning and was vomiting every half an hour or so. A doctor was supposed to come to the hotel to clear Stephen for flying, but didn't. Then we discovered that he couldn't fly anyway, unless we could remove the fresh plaster cast from his arm (and all we could muster was a pair of curved nail scissors). In all the kerfuffle we lost the crucial hospital X-ray, and then mislaid the key to the storeroom where we kept all the kit. Tim and I were running around like headless chickens, while Stephen (who had slept in his torn and tattered clothes and looked as if he'd just stumbled out of the jungle after being raised by a troop of howler monkeys) was limping around with an unexpectedly stiff leg.

Stephen and Tim eventually made it to Miami – only after persuading the airline to hold the flight – while I hitched another ride on Captain Wilson's floatplane to catch up with the remnant crew, and Piti.

I had the GPS coordinates of the *Com te Abreu*, hastily written on the back of a laundry list following a crackly satellite phone call from Sue, and after the usual death-defying swoop over the rainforest the missionary plane touched down in the nick of time. Against all the odds, I'd caught up with them just as Piti was about to be released.

Miriam had sent out a message inviting the children of five local villages to come and meet their new, and still rather anxious, neighbour. As we closed in on Piti's final destination, news of his arrival had been spreading. By boat and canoe, in twos and threes, and then in a flood, they came. Most had never seen a manatee before.

The staff of the Mamiraua Project had built a temporary wooden enclosure next to a village overlooking the release site, where Piti could become acclima-

Stephen had slept in his torn and tattered clothes and looked as if he'd just stumbled out of the jungle after being raised by a troop of howler monkeys.

tised to his new home until it was time to be released fully into the wild.

We carefully lifted him out of his tank, carried him across another floating wooden platform and gently lowered him into his halfway house. He disappeared beneath the surface of the murky water, but not before releasing a tell-tale trail of bubbles that said simply 'I'm okay.'

We collapsed in laughter.

I watched his ripples for a while and then glanced at Miriam, Carolina and Michelle. They were hugging one another, with tears in their eyes. This was their big day, the result of months of planning and preparation, and they cared so much about Piti and his wild and endangered relatives.

They had a dream. They hoped that the enthusiasm of all those children, for one baby *peixe-boi*, would feed back through families and traditional hunting communities and make manatees something to cherish rather than hunt. If their dream came true, Piti's new-found freedom would be just the beginning and they would repeat the care and release of orphaned manatees across the Amazon Basin.

The next day I managed to speak to Stephen on the satellite phone. He was in surprisingly good spirits, under the circumstances, as he awaited his operation.

I was worried that he might be having second thoughts about our future travels together, but I think even he was surprised to discover just how much he was missing his home from home in the jungle.

'Wherever we meet next,' he said, though, 'it is firmly understood that Stephen never leads, he only follows, and everybody helps him onto boats. Because he's a clumsy arse. That's just got to be understood.'

And that was that. After all the mad panic of the past few days, both Stephen and Piti were in safe hands and there was nothing left to do. As we began the 12-hour boat journey back to Tefé, picking our way along the backwaters of the Amazon, I crawled into a hammock and slept.

Opposite
If Miriam's dream comes true, Piti's new-found freedom will be just the beginning, and more and more orphaned manatees can be released across the Amazon Basin.

2

DANGER: REBELS COMING

A four-hour operation and several recuperative months later, we were on the road again. This time Stephen had a steel plate and no fewer than ten aluminium screws in his arm, along with an impressive 25-cm (10-inch) scar – ample proof of his official new status as intrepid adventurer.

Our next stop was Africa.

Twenty years ago, Douglas Adams and I visited Garamba National Park, in the northeastern corner of Zaire.

I say 'Zaire' because that's what the country was called while we were there, but it changes its name more often than The Artist Formerly Known as Prince. It was originally called Congo Free State, then Belgian Congo, then Congo-Léopoldville, and finally Zaire. Actually, it's not even true to say 'finally Zaire' because since our visit it has changed its name yet again. Now it is called the Democratic Republic of Congo, or just DR Congo, or even DRC for short. It's not to be confused with one of its many neighbours, the Republic of Congo, otherwise known as Congo-Brazzaville or just the Congo, which is a former French colony rather than a Belgian one.

No one ever said African politics, or geography, was supposed to be easy.

When people talk about 'darkest Africa', this is usually where they have in mind. It is a land of jungles, mountains, enormous rivers, volcanoes, more exotic wildlife than you'd be wise to shake a stick at, hunter-gatherer pygmies who are

Opposite
The Country Formerly Known as Zaire isn't the safest place to live if you're an elephant.

Below
Stephen the adventurer returns – complete with steel plate and ten aluminium screws holding his broken arm together.

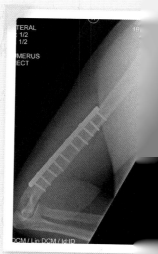

still largely untouched by western civilisation, and one of the worst transport systems anywhere in the world (ignoring our own transport system in Britain, of course).

Anyway, we went to The Country Formerly Known as Zaire to look for one of the rarest animals on the planet: the northern white rhino.

The northern white rhino has had a tough life. To be fair, it wasn't too bad for the first few million years. It's just the last hundred years that have been sheer hell.

It was common at the time of its discovery, in 1903, and lived in five different countries: Chad, the Central African Republic, Sudan, Uganda and the DRC. But it was highly sought-after by sports hunters and poachers (having two horns made it doubly attractive) and its numbers plummeted. By 1965, the population had dropped to 5,000; by 1980, there were just 800; and, by 1984, it had reached a frightening low of just fifteen animals left.

Those last survivors, hanging on by a thread, were under the protection of a skeleton staff, with little training, virtually no money, and no equipment. Basically, if a poacher wanted to kill a rhino, all he had to do was to turn up.

But that wasn't the only problem. Hunting and poaching aside, the DRC lies in the heart of war-torn Africa. It has been fighting a series of complex, many-sided wars for umpteen years. Millions of people have died and many more have been displaced from their homes. No wonder: it's an immense country (about eighty times the size of Belgium) with more than 200 ethnic groups. And, to make matters worse, many of these ethnic groups spill over the borders with all nine countries surrounding the DRC, adding a multifaceted international twist to the turmoil.

I don't pretend to understand the complexities of the situation in the region, but the DRC's problems seem to be even greater than the ethnic quarrelling that tends to make world news. The battleground is as much about the country's rich natural resources as it is about tribal warfare. As one Congolese official noted while we were there: 'It's interesting that the rebels aren't in any areas that don't have minerals.'

The DRC could be one of the wealthiest countries in Africa, but it is actually one of the poorest. It's rich in timber and in virtually every mineral known to man, from gold and diamonds to copper and tin. It is also a major source of coltan, or columbite-tantalite to give it its full name, the 'black gold' metallic ore that is a key ingredient in mobile phones, DVD players and laptops. And it is believed to hold huge reserves of oil and gas. But ever since King Leopold II of Belgium made the country his personal property in 1885 (in cahoots with the famous explorer Henry Morton Stanley) and exploited it mercilessly for its

Expatriates living in this humanitarian disaster zone have given the DRC their own name – they say the acronym stands for 'Danger: Rebels Coming'.

rubber and ivory, the allure of those resources has proved to be a curse, provoking and intensifying the never-ending conflict.

Expatriates living in this humanitarian disaster zone have given the DRC their own name – they say the acronym stands for 'Danger: Rebels Coming'. It's scarily apt, under the circumstances.

So this is the setting for the northern white rhino's last stand, in Garamba National Park.

Garamba is about 5,000 square kilometres (2,000 square miles) in size, although I realise that means absolutely nothing to most of us. How big is 5,000 square kilometres? Well, it's about the size of Luxembourg, Liechtenstein, Mauritius and the Isle of Man combined, if that helps. Or, as Douglas once said, it's 'roughly the size of part of Scotland'. In other words, it's very, very big.

There were 22 rhinos rattling around the park when Douglas and I were there in 1989 – and that was the entire world population in the wild.

We managed to stalk one on foot, creeping to within about 20 metres (66 feet) before it stopped grazing, lifted its head and made a dash for it, hurtling off across the plain like a nimble young tank. Then we hitched a ride in the park's anti-poaching patrol Cessna 185. As we flew across the savannah (which looked like stretched ostrich skin from the air) we saw a second rhino. Suddenly, as

we passed a screen of trees, we saw another two: a mother and calf, eyeing us suspiciously from behind a bush. In fact, during that three-hour flight we saw a total of eight different rhinos. It was quite a sobering thought – we had just encountered more than a third of the entire world population.

But we left feeling surprisingly positive. Garamba was better protected than it had been in a long time. During our visit, there were 246 trained staff, with six vehicles, permanent guard posts throughout the park, mobile patrols all in contact with one another by field radio, and a couple of light aircraft.

Against all the odds, for the next twenty years the dedicated team ran an extremely successful project and countered much of the trouble. At one point, the northern white rhino population actually doubled in size. But protecting wildlife on a battlefield was unimaginably tough. Rangers were even forced to patrol with hand grenades and rocket launchers (captured from the poachers) as well as their own AK47s.

With the benefit of hindsight, I think Douglas and I were being naïve in our optimism. Given Garamba's unhappy and chequered history, slap-bang in the middle of a lawless and relentless war zone with frequent armed conflict, we should have suspected trouble ahead.

Indeed, there was trouble ahead. Lots of it.

By the time Stephen and I were travelling in Africa, the park was surrounded by armed refugees, guerrillas from Uganda's Lords Resistance Army, Congolese rebels from the National Congress for the Defence of the People, military camps belonging to the Sudan People's Liberation Army, a motley collection of mercenaries, undisciplined and chronically underfunded Congolese army troops, and horse-riding Muharaleen elephant poachers. And that's not including all the UN troops looking for pretty much everyone else. Many of these people were actually hiding in the park itself.

The last time northern white rhinos had been seen alive was during an aerial survey of Garamba in March 2006, when two adult males, a single adult female and a young animal of indeterminate sex were spotted, albeit briefly. As far as anyone could tell, there were just four left.

We had absolutely no doubt that this trip really would be our last chance to see what was probably the most critically endangered animal in the world.

Once upon a time, a few million years ago, there was a rhino that split in two. It didn't split like an amoeba, of course, literally tearing itself in half and wandering off in two different directions. It split in two in the evolutionary sense.

The two rhinos eventually grew into separate subspecies. One became the northern white rhino (speak quickly and you'll say 'northern right wino' – at least you will now that I've pointed it out) and the other became the southern white rhino.

To the untutored eye (and, to be perfectly frank, to the tutored eye as well) the two subspecies look identical. Stand a northern white rhino next to a southern white rhino and most people would be hard-pushed to tell them apart. Read the scientific literature and you'll discover that the northern white tends to hold its head a little higher than its southern counterpart, and its body proportions are slightly different, but that's just splitting hairs.

'The northern white rhino is basically the southern white rhino with a different accent,' as Stephen put it. True, but it's a little more than that – their genetic differences are sufficiently great for them to be considered biologically separate.

One thing you'll notice about both white rhinos is that they're not actually white. A rhino will often be roughly the same colour as the local soil (it rolls around in it a lot), but even if you were to put one through a car wash it still wouldn't be white. It wouldn't even be stone white, or champagne white, or whatever else paint manufacturers call every possible shade of off-white. It's more of a dull grey-brown colour.

Despite what you might think, this isn't because zoologists are either colour-blind or stupid. It's because they are illiterate. It comes from a mistranslation of the Dutch word 'wijde', which means 'wide' and refers to the rhino's mouth. This was misread as the Afrikaans word 'wit', which means 'white'. And so the wide-mouthed rhino became the white rhino.

No one has a clue if this is actually true or not, incidentally, but it's a good story and gets told around campfires the length and breadth of Africa almost every night.

What we do know is that the white rhino's mouth is, indeed, wide. It is designed for grazing, for eating short grass, whereas its African cousin, the black rhino, has a prehensile upper lip designed for browsing. The white rhino is like a lawnmower, the black rhino is like a pair of secateurs, and their lips are the best way to tell them apart.

Now, the white rhino is a bit of a paradox, because it is both the rarest and the commonest of all the world's rhinos. The two subspecies have had very different fortunes. The northerner set up home in the crossfire of a war zone – giving some credibility to the saying 'It's grim up north' – while the southerner settled for a relatively easier life hiding from hunters and poachers, rather than dodging rebels' bullets.

When the southern white rhino was first described by western scientists, in 1817, it was incredibly common. Lots of explorers and travellers wandering around Africa at the time were so impressed by its commonness they made a point of writing about it. But the good times came to an abrupt end pretty quickly. Tens of thousands, if not hundreds of thousands, were killed by sports hunters, poachers and even the early explorers themselves. By the 1880s, conservationists feared the worst.

But a tiny population survived by hiding in a remote corner of Hluhluwe-Imfolozi Game Reserve, which is north of Durban in South Africa. All the stops were pulled out to protect these last few survivors – perhaps a couple of dozen animals altogether – and the southern white rhino became one of the greatest conservation success stories of all time.

There are now more than 17,480 southern whites in the wild in Africa, and another 750 or so in captivity around the world. This is nowhere near as many as there once were, of course, but at least now they are out of immediate danger. It just shows what can be achieved with a good plan, political will, dedicated people on the ground, and plenty of money.

But there is a slight catch. Part of the conservation plan includes trophy hunting. Under government licence, hunters have been allowed to shoot a small number of elderly male rhinos – for a hefty price – every year since the late 1960s.

The white rhino is a bit of a paradox, because it is both the rarest and the commonest of all the world's rhinos. The two subspecies have had very different fortunes.

It sounds ridiculous, shooting an animal you are trying to protect, but there's no denying that it has worked. By raising desperately needed funds and giving local communities (and landowners – many of the rhinos are on private land) an incentive to look after them, trophy hunting has played an important role in southern white rhino conservation.

Never in a million years could I shoot a rhino myself – or begin to understand the mentality of the people who do. I couldn't even wring the neck of a dying, one-legged chicken. But I try to be realistic and, begrudgingly, I do agree with most conservation groups that trophy hunting has been a necessary evil in saving the southern white rhino from extinction (assuming, of course, that the hunting is properly managed, the population is large enough and the profits are injected back into conservation efforts).

Killing individual animals for the greater good of the species is a tough call, but in some cases there is no alternative. Unfortunately, making wildlife pay for itself is sometimes the only way to make most people consider it worth saving.

Stephen arrived in Africa in customary style. When his plane came in to land at Nairobi's Jomo Kenyatta Airport, as soon as the wheels hit the ground the brakes screeched and he was thrown forward into the headrest of the seat in front (actually, I'm probably exaggerating – in First Class, apparently, the headrest of the seat in front would have been too far away for him to make physical contact).

Anyway, his plane made a squealing, swervy landing.

'Sorry about that,' said the pilot, after he'd wrestled back control of his Boeing 777. 'There was an aardvark on the runway and I didn't want to hurt it.'

There is something rather special about stepping out of a plane onto African soil. Anyone who has done it will know what I mean. There is a particular smell, a sense of anticipation and an overwhelming feeling of space. Douglas Adams described his first impression perfectly: 'The sky over Kenya is simply much bigger than it is anywhere else.'

We were in East Africa to visit Ol Pejeta Conservancy, a non-profit rhino sanctuary in the shadow of Mount Kenya and a few hours' drive from Nairobi. The rhinos in this 36,500-hectare (90,000-acre) fenced enclosure are protected round-the-clock. Anti-poaching patrols aim to see each individual (there were 78 black rhinos and nine white rhinos at the time of our visit) at least once every four or five days. If one goes missing, reinforcements – more rangers, a surveillance aircraft and even two bloodhounds – are brought in to step up the search until the disappearing perissodactyl is found.

More importantly, Ol Pej, as it's called by the locals, had been preparing itself for a small party of northern white rhinos. The original plan was to evacuate the last survivors from the war zone in Garamba National Park and put them into this rhino health farm for safe-keeping. The plan has since changed, but more of that later.

First we had an appointment to see a southern white rhino, to get Stephen in the mood.

With the help of Batian Craig, the Wildlife and Security Manager, we found one fairly quickly. We stopped the car and cut the engine to look at it properly through binoculars. It was busy feeding and had its back to us. It seemed a little incongruous for such a monstrously huge animal to be doing such a gentle activity as grazing, rather like watching a road digger doing a bit of weeding.

Very slowly, Batian opened the driver's door.

'We're not going to get out, are we?' asked Stephen, looking a little alarmed. 'Aren't there lots of lions here, too?'

'Yes,' said Batian, starting to whisper. 'But there's nothing to worry about.'

Anyone can walk in lion country, of course, but the professionals do it without being eaten. I remember going on a survival course in South Africa many years ago, and the game ranger in charge gave us this nugget of advice: 'If we stumble upon a lion,' he said, 'we'll get out of the area by moving slowly backwards. We will not run. If we run, we have a hundred per cent chance of being killed.'

I told Stephen, but he just glared at me.

We slipped out of the car as quietly as possible, closing the doors without shutting them properly, and started creeping towards the rhino.

'Just listen to Dixon and the other rangers,' said Batian. 'Do what they say. If something happens, don't suddenly bolt or you will leave somebody in the… in the… you know what.'

'It looks remarkably prehistoric,' whispered Stephen, who was suddenly rising to the occasion. 'It wouldn't look out of place wandering alongside a woolly mammoth or a sabre-toothed tiger.'

We crept forward, very quietly, very slowly, constantly stopping, crouching and shifting our position. Gently cropping the grass, the rhino seemed to be completely undisturbed by our approach. But then it stopped eating and looked up. We froze. It started to chew a little more thoughtfully (it was hard to tell if it was regarding us with grave suspicion or without a care in the world) and then resumed the eating position.

'This is insanity,' said Stephen. 'I've been brought up all my life to believe that rhinos are amongst the most dangerous and bad-tempered animals on the face of the earth and here we are closer to one than I'd normally get to a German Shepherd.'

Nervously, we set off again. At last we made it to a small clump of trees about 20 metres (66 feet) away and watched quietly from there. The rhino was so big it was like stalking a Cherokee Jeep.

The rhino looked up again. This time it lifted its head, clearly sniffing the air. Its tubular ears swivelled, like mini parabolic reflectors, trying to pick up the slightest sound. We hardly dared to breathe. Rhinos have poor eyesight, but this one was definitely looking at us with one eye, and then swung its head to the side to look at us with the other.

We stepped out from behind the clump.

'Should we be going any closer?' asked Stephen.

The rhino turned and walked straight towards us.

'Oh my God!' said Stephen. 'It's coming.'

The ranger signalled that it was okay and stood in front of us like a Secret Service bodyguard diving in front of the President to take the full force of an assassin's bullet.

'Oh my God!' said Stephen again, as the rhino came nearly to within touching distance. 'Surely, this isn't right?'

I heard chuckling and turned around to see Dixon and the other rangers doubled-up with laughter.

'Good grief!' chuckled Stephen. 'You swines!'

We'd been tricked. It turned out to be a bottle-fed, hand-reared rhino, called Max. The three-and-a-half-year-old male southern white must have been the tamest rhino in Africa.

'That was a complete con,' said Stephen. 'There we were, tiptoeing around, the most frightened people in Africa, and all the time it was tamer than a labrador!'

We patted Max on the head, introduced ourselves, and took some photographs. A storm was gathering and the sky was a threatening, dark blue. A rainbow appeared above Max's head. It was an incredible, once-in-a-lifetime photo opportunity.

So there I was, lying on the ground no more than 3 metres (10 feet) away from a two-tonne southern white rhino, photographing it with a wide-angle lens, when my mobile phone rang (reception in much of the developing world is considerably better than, for example, along the M4 into London).

It was the moment I'd been waiting for and dreaming about for years. I'd imagined all the possible scenarios:

'Hello, I can't talk right now, I'm kayaking with a humpback whale... Hello, I can't talk right now, I'm getting ready to snorkel with a whale shark... Hello,

Top
A baboon not
showing its bottom.

Above
And here's a picture of
a tree-climbing lion.

Opposite
Mark with several
tonnes of the tamest
rhino in Africa.

I can't talk right now, I'm stalking an Alaskan brown bear... Hello, I can't talk right now, I'm climbing a Scot's pine to look inside an eagle's nest'... etc.

Anyway, it actually happened. The phone rang. Max snapped to attention and listened intently to my ringtone (which happened to be the vocalisations of a pod of killer whales in British Columbia – something he probably hadn't heard many times before). He was still watching me suspiciously as I answered the call.

'Hello, I can't talk right now, I'm lying on the ground next to a two-tonne rhino.'

'That's nice,' said John, a globe-trotting friend from the BBC Natural History Unit in Bristol. 'I just wondered if you can remember the name of that Asian restaurant we went to in Clifton the other day.'

We said goodbye to Max, walked back to the Land Rover without being eaten by lions, and headed out across the savannah towards a specially built enclosure called a boma.

Going on safari with Stephen is like going to the Grand Prix with Murray Walker. He gives a running commentary.

We drove past some Grant's gazelles ('or are they Thompson's gazelles?' asked Stephen), past some giraffes ('with their heads in the clouds'), past some warthogs ('I like warthogs'), past an enormous troop of baboons ('baboons have blue bottoms, you know') and past an ostrich ('with knobbly knees like that I'm not surprised they bury their heads in the sand').

And so the commentary continued until we arrived at the boma.

We were with a lady who has done more for the last surviving northern white rhinos than anyone else on the planet. I first met Kes Hillman-Smith when Douglas and I visited Garamba National Park in 1989. Douglas described her at the time as: 'a formidable woman, who looks as if she has just walked off the screen of a slightly naughty adventure movie.' Twenty years later, she hadn't changed a bit.

Kes used to live with her husband, Fraser, and their two young children, in a house they built themselves on the banks of the Garamba River. The house was largely open to the elements – when it rained they simply lowered tarpaulins over the spaces where windows weren't. It was regularly full of animals, including a young hippo that used to chew on the pot plants in the living room, rats that used to eat the soap in the bathroom and termites that were gradually nibbling away at the support poles of the entire house. The garden was a veritable menagerie – having survived all the snakes and elephants, their pet dog was eventually eaten by a crocodile.

I asked Kes if her children were still alive.

'Yes, of course they are!' she said, laughing. 'They still love the bush. One is working in northern Kenya and the other is a pilot flying for safari lodges.'

Opposite
Rhino horn is worth
more than US$1,500
per kilo on the black
market.

Kes and the family were forced to leave their home in Garamba, because of all the troubles. It was getting too dangerous even for them. They hadn't been back since 2006.

We walked around the boma and there, standing on its own in one corner, was a rhino. It was listening to the radio.

'That's Barack,' said Kes.

'You're kidding! Barack?' asked Stephen, to confirm what he thought he'd just heard. He had been following the US Presidential elections very closely during our travels in Kenya.

Barack was a 14-year-old blind southern white rhino, living in comfortable retirement at Ol Pej. He had few pleasures in life except for sweet sugar cane, which he chewed all day long, and the radio. While we were there he happened to be listening to a school broadcast teaching children (and, presumably, rhinos) about the colours of the rainbow.

'He likes talk shows most,' said Kes. 'He's not really into music.'

The rest of the boma was eerily empty. Kes had hoped that this would be the heart of the last-ditch effort to save the northern white rhino from extinction. But the chances of finding any survivors, let alone catching them, were getting slimmer with every passing day.

Stephen and I watched as she strolled around the boma, looking visibly upset. Kes had devoted most of her life to the northern white rhino and was on first-name terms with the last of the subspecies. She told us afterwards that, as she walked around the deserted boma, she had a terrible feeling in the pit of her stomach that it was game over.

While we were in Kenya, I introduced Stephen to a couple of old friends. I can't tell you their names, because they are undercover agents and need to keep a low profile. I know it sounds a bit cloak and dagger, but revealing their identities really would put their lives at risk.

They work for the Lusaka Agreement Task Force, which is a dreadful name for an absolutely brilliant organisation established in the late 1990s to fight illegal wildlife trade across Africa's borders. My two friends work in a highly dangerous world of undercover operations, crime syndicates, informants, intelligence gathering, gunfights and double-agents. Talking to them is like watching *The Bourne Identity* – except, instead of working for the CIA, they risk their lives to protect endangered wildlife.

After a lot of gentle persuasion, they kindly agreed to show us a haul of confis-

The rhino's great misfortune is that it carries a fortune on its nose.

cated rhino horns. We were led to a darkened vault at a secret location and came face to face with horns representing the deaths of dozens of black and white rhinos.

'How can you be sure these horns are real?' asked Stephen.

One of the agents picked up the nearest horn and threw it hard against the stone floor, making us jump.

'If it smashes, it's fake,' he said, 'and if it doesn't, it's real.'

The horn bounced high into the air, nearly hitting Stephen in the groin, and landed in a corner of the vault. It didn't smash.

The heaviest horn in the vault weighed 5.02 kilograms (11.07 pounds).

'That would be worth at least US$8,000 on the black market,' said my friend.

We told him about our plans to go to the DRC to look for the last remaining northern white rhinos.

'Those rhinos couldn't have chosen a worse place to live,' he said, clearly in despair. 'Trouble and violence means poaching. Rhino horns fund rebel activity, so the two are intimately linked. And, of course, the poaching itself is made easier by the ready availability of weapons and the inability of weak governments to worry about wildlife. To be honest, I don't think the northern whites stand a chance.'

As recently as the 1960s, rhinos roamed across virtually all of sub-Saharan Africa. But by the early 1990s, 95 per cent of them had been killed for their horns.

Opposite
Stephen comes face
to face with rhino
horns confiscated
from poachers.

The slaughter was so merciless that it's a wonder any survived at all.

Yet they are still being killed today.

Generally speaking, the horn from rhinos killed in East Africa tends to end up in the Middle East, while the horn from those killed in southern Africa and Asia ends up in the Far East.

In Yemen and Oman it is carved into ornamental dagger handles, called jambiyas, which symbolise the status and masculinity of their owners. The demand was so high by the 1970s and '80s that one horn dealer alone reportedly produced 6,000 rhino-horn dagger handles in a single year. Fortunately, it has declined since then and more are being made from buffalo horn, plastic or other substitutes (although those made of rhino horn are still regarded as the 'Rolexes' and 'Porsches' of the jambiya world).

In the Far East, the horn is ground into powder to make Traditional Chinese Medicine, as a cure for just about everything from poisoning, snakebite and suppressing fever to devil possession, blurry vision and rectal bleeding (incidentally, the idea that rhino horn is an aphrodisiac is a complete myth, originally spread by uninformed westerners). It's seen as a kind of wonder drug, with magical properties, so no wonder it's so popular.

'The rhino's great misfortune,' commented Stephen, 'is that it carries a fortune on its nose.'

'Exactly. The horn is its Achilles heel,' said the agent, proving that he was a grammatical guru, too. 'And the rarer the rhinos become,' he continued, 'the more valuable the horn and the greater the demand. It's like pouring petrol onto an open fire.'

By the early 1990s, 95 per cent of Africa's rhinos had been killed for their horns. The slaughter was so merciless that it's a wonder any survived at all.

I explained to Stephen that, to make matters even worse, most of the rhino goes to waste. The poachers kill an animal weighing several tonnes for a horn weighing just a few kilos.

'Don't they use any other part of the animal?' he asked.

'Only very rarely,' explained the agent, 'and then for rather odd purposes. Some people hang a bottle of rhino urine in the doorway, for example, to keep away evil spirits.'

'Imagine trying to get a rhino to pee into a bottle,' said Stephen, who often joked when he was shocked or upset. I think it's a defence mechanism.

To add insult to injury, tests in western laboratories have found no evidence whatsoever for the claimed medical properties of rhino horn. There is no reason why it should be considered special, because it is made out of nothing more auspicious than keratin, which is the main constituent of hair, fingernails, claws and hooves. Unfortunately, though, practitioners of Traditional Chinese Medicine have successfully persuaded a lot of people that the uniqueness of rhino horn has no substitute.

The thing is this. If everyone wants to believe in voodoo, reiki or vitamin C tablets, that's absolutely fine. But if they believe in a product that has been shown to be useless, is traded illegally and kills endangered animals in the process, then that's not fine at all.

I'd been in East Africa the year before, working undercover with my two friends and other agents from the Lusaka Agreement Task Force. It was a fairly daunting experience that illustrates the astonishing efforts being made to protect rhinos and the region's other wildlife.

On one particular undercover operation, we were just a short drive from several popular tourist lodges. There were four of us, sitting at a rickety wooden table in a run-down café on the border between Kenya and Tanzania, in the shadow of Mount Kilimanjaro. Next to me was a senior undercover agent. Heavily scarred from many previous encounters with poachers, he had a pistol tucked into the back of his trousers, hidden under his shirt.

Two men sat opposite. They were members of the Luo tribe and were acting as brokers for some Maasai warriors who wanted to sell ivory weighing about 150 kilograms (330 pounds). I don't know if they were armed.

I was posing as an ivory dealer. We had told them, in a mixture of English and Swahili, that I was a South African, working for the UN in Sudan, and was using my diplomatic privileges to smuggle ivory out of the country. They seemed convinced.

We talked for an hour and a half. They wanted to do the deal in the bush, about 35 kilometres (22 miles) away, after dark. But we refused. It was too dangerous – in the dark it would be impossible to evaluate how heavily they were armed and how many other men were hiding in the bushes. We made up a story about being tired after the long journey from Nairobi and, eventually, they relented. They would call us first thing in the morning and arrange an alternative time to meet (mobile phones have transformed ivory dealing in this part of Africa).

I was up and ready at 5am the next morning, waiting for the call. It never came. Eleven hours later I was still waiting, in my grubby, £5-a-night so-called hotel room, trying to resist calling them to find out what was happening for fear of raising suspicion.

Another undercover agent had already been working on this bust for more than a week, posing as a scout for ivory buyers such as myself. A hundred and fifty kilograms of ivory represents up to ten dead elephants, so this would be no small haul and we couldn't afford to muck it up (great care is taken to ensure that

I was posing as an ivory dealer. Next to me was an undercover agent, heavily scarred from many previous encounters with poachers. He had a pistol tucked into the back of his trousers.

the elephants are already dead and are not being killed on demand).

The proposed deal was going to be fairly typical. We would be taken to the poachers and their ivory to weigh and inspect the pieces. If we were satisfied, we would pay the poachers about £500 (big money for a couple of Maasai) and the brokers about £1,000 (they wanted £2,400 for making the introduction but knew we would pay less than half that amount).

Then it was dark. I was still sitting in my room at about 7.15pm when there was a knock on the door. It was the senior undercover agent and two of his colleagues from the Kenya Wildlife Service, who were providing essential back-up. The brokers had finally made contact. There was no power in the hotel, so we sat in darkness and discussed the latest conversation. The situation, apparently, had changed. Instead of two Maasai poachers, there were now six. And they were still insisting on doing the exchange in thick bush, in the middle of nowhere, later that night.

The undercover agents were on edge, pacing around the room. They were making me nervous.

We called them back and, after a long discussion, agreed to inspect the ivory at first light the following morning. But there was no ivory. The poachers were there when we arrived but, for some reason, were convinced that we were all being watched. The deal was off.

I was devastated, but the agents took it in their stride. It's all part of the job. They would reopen negotiations and go back to that run-down café on the Kenya–Tanzania border to start all over again.

They did succeed, eventually, in arresting all the poachers and both of the brokers. But they weren't particularly happy with this outcome.

Catching poachers is *relatively* easy with the help of motivated, well-trained and well-armed anti-poaching patrols and undercover agents. But the challenge is to tackle the people in the middle and, especially, at the top of the hierarchy. Known in the trade as the 'untouchables', they have their own intelligence (the poaching equivalent of the CIA or MI5) and are surrounded by lawyers. They will kill anyone who gets in their way – and frequently do.

Interpol estimates that global illegal trade in wildlife is worth US$6–10 billion annually – second only to drugs trafficking. But fighting this wildlife crime is unbelievably difficult. There isn't enough money, time or human resources to do it properly. Investigations take too long, shipments aren't checked properly, fraudulent documents are overlooked, wildlife legislation is out of date, border staff are poorly trained, poorly equipped and underpaid, and penalties are not sufficient to act as deterrents.

I've been on anti-poaching patrols, involving gun battles and machete fights, when we've arrested the poachers successfully but they've been back in the bush, poaching again, a few weeks later. In some cases, the patrols and the poachers were actually on first-name terms.

So the rangers and undercover agents risk their lives while the vast majority of those involved in poaching get away scot-free.

Stephen and I had a few dangers of our own to worry about.

We were pinning our hopes on joining one final search for the northern white rhino, but increasing talk of rebel activity in and around Garamba National Park made the prospect seem seriously risky.

I spoke to a senior member of the UN Peacekeeping Force, which was 17,000-strong at the time. I was on a satellite phone in Uganda and he was on a satellite phone in the eastern Democratic Republic of Congo, so the line was frustratingly crackly and intermittent. It was difficult to hear exactly what he was saying. But I could just make out enough to ring alarm bells: 'situation getting worse', 'Garamba extremely unstable', 'thousands of people on the move' and 'dangerous to travel' gave me the crucial headlines.

Opposite
Elephant ivory confiscated from poachers.

I discussed the call with Stephen.

'My God,' he said. 'We don't realise how lucky we are living in Britain, do we? We moan about the weather and the trains and bloody Dan Brown's Da Vinci whatsit, but can you imagine all the things we'd have to moan about if we lived in the DRC?'

We sat down to discuss our plans and, sensing rebellion in the ranks, I began by letting Stephen know what he'd be missing if we didn't go.

Garamba National Park is a very special place. One of the first national parks to be established in Africa (it would have been the first – but Virunga, to the south, just pipped it to the post), this vast wilderness of undulating savannah grassland, rivers, swamps, woodland and rocky hills is considered so important that it has been declared a World Heritage Site. Home to no fewer than 138 different mammal species, and more birds, reptiles and other wildlife than anyone has properly counted, it is as wild as wild can be.

The northern white rhino has always been the jewel in its crown. Losing it would be like Buckingham Palace losing the Queen – suddenly, the place would seem considerably less important. It's hard enough protecting a national park that is home to one of the rarest animals on the planet, let alone one that has failed to protect one of the rarest animals on the planet. Losing the rhinos would spell disaster for the whole park, so there was an awful lot at stake.

'Yes, but… call me an old-fashioned coward, if you like,' said Stephen.

'You're an old-fashioned coward,' I said, trying (but failing) to lighten the mood.

He gave me the kind of glare he normally reserves for sycophantic journalists and incompetent hotel check-in clerks.

'But,' he continued, 'I find myself questioning the wisdom of going into a war zone on the off chance of finding four animals that are virtually identical to one I have already seen in a perfectly peaceful part of Kenya.'

'I know this will sound strange,' I replied, 'but I just feel that we'd be letting the rhinos down, not to mention the rangers who are risking their lives every day that they refuse to abandon Garamba. They need all the help they can get. If their home is so perilous that we daren't even visit, what chance do they have? I believe we have a duty to tell the world what is happening.'

'But then you also believe you should give up drinking vanilla lattes and watching *The X Factor*,' said Stephen. 'Anyway, can't we tell the world what is happening from a comfortable hotel across the border in Uganda?'

He did have a point. I didn't admit it at the time but, in my heart, I knew he was probably right.

'I've always wanted to see chimps,' enthused Stephen. 'Especially if it involves delaying our travels into a war zone.'

For better or for worse, we continued heading west in the vague direction of the DRC, leaving Kenya and crossing the border into Uganda.

The first thing we did was to drop in to see the relatives – the noisy, boisterous, furry side of the family, otherwise known as chimpanzees. Chimps are, of course, only collateral relatives – nth cousins, n times removed – but they are the closest relatives we've got.

The chimpanzees, gorillas and orang-utans are all great apes. So are we. The distinction we have put between ourselves and the others is blurred, to say the least.

Humans and chimps are particularly close – we have more in common, genetically, than chimps do with either gorillas or orang-utans. We descended from a common ancestor (sadly, no longer with us) and were in the same ancestral line for the first 99.99999 per cent of our history. In fact, you could argue that there are really three species of chimp: the common chimpanzee, the bonobo or pygmy chimp, and the human. If we were to apply the same classification principles to us as we do to other animals, we would all belong to the same genus – let alone the same family.

Incidentally, given those three choices, I think I'd like to be a bonobo. We don't know all that much about this principally vegetarian, female-dominated great ape, but what we do know is greatly appealing. It is a good-looking animal, with a slender body, a neat haircut (it has a central parting on top) and natty sideburns. But, best of all, it lives a hippie lifestyle, making love not war and resolving conflict with sex instead of violence.

The main difference between us and the other great apes is that they are all endangered and we are not. You might even say that they are all endangered primarily *because* we are not.

During the past century alone, chimpanzee numbers have plummeted from more than two million to as few as 100,000. We've been logging their forest homes, hunting the adults for bushmeat and capturing their babies for the international pet trade.

We are definitely the black sheep of the family.

Anyway, an old friend of mine, Lilly Ajarova, happened to be in charge of the Ngamba Island Chimpanzee Sanctuary and had invited us to meet some of the animals in her care.

As we set out across Africa's biggest lake, and sailed over the equator, Stephen seemed relieved.

'I've always wanted to see chimps,' he enthused. 'Especially if it involves delaying our travels into a war zone.'

We had worked hard for this visit. Before leaving the UK, Lilly had insisted that we endure an awfully long list of injections. She warned us that we wouldn't be allowed ashore without written medical proof that we had been vaccinated recently against hepatitis A, hepatitis B, meningococcal meningitis, polio, tetanus and yellow fever. We also had to provide proof of immunity to measles, as well as letters from our doctors stating that we'd had Mantoux tests and were definitely TB negative.

But Stephen was worried. He had developed a bad cold.

Lilly met us at the wooden jetty and, before we'd even unloaded our bags, he asked her the inevitable question.

'I don't have measles, I don't have TB, I don't have hepatitis,' he said. 'But in the last day or so I have developed the mother and father, brother and sister, aunt and uncle of all colds. I have a really terrible cold. Is that going to be a problem?'

Lilly was sympathetic, but emphatic.

'Absolutely. I'm very sorry, Stephen, but we can't let you get close to a chimpanzee. Because we are so similar, the diseases we have can be very contagious to them and, of course, what they have can be very contagious to us.'

Stephen looked crestfallen.

It was such bad luck. Impervious to a rogues' gallery of many of the worst and most evil diseases on the planet, but scuppered by the common cold, he promised to keep his distance from all things chimp.

I couldn't help thinking that it should have been the other way round – I should have had the cold instead. Stephen really wanted to spend a couple of days in the company of chimps, but I didn't. To be perfectly honest, I had mixed feelings about the visit because I've never been able to get as excited about chimps as I do about almost all other animals.

I think I know why. It's because they are so similar to us.

Don't get me wrong – it's not that I don't like people. Some of my best friends are people. It's just that chimpanzees share too many of our more unpleasant characteristics. They gang up on one another, indulge in office politics, beat up and bully weaker individuals, lie, gossip and bear grudges. They even take part in tribal warfare.

Ngamba's introductory 'Visitor Safety Information' did not encourage me to change my opinion: 'In the event of any chimpanzee escaping,' it warned, 'everyone on the island should move to a designated area near the lake… and if the chimpanzee approaches you, enter the water.' Then it went on to say: 'Some of our chimpanzees throw stones… the effect of people scattering when a stone is thrown increases the stone-thrower's confidence.'

Part of the problem is that I was once in a forest surrounded by a troop of chimpanzees while they were having an argument. It was incredibly intimidating. They were fighting, shouting, screaming and crashing through the under-

Above
Stephen and his cold stay on the human side of the fence, while Mark and the crew are allowed onto the chimp side of the fence.

Opposite
Mark learning to like chimps.

growth all around me. They are huge animals – an adult male has several times the upper body strength of a man – and have been known to attack people.

Chimps aren't all bad, of course. They have long-lasting friendships, remember favours, enjoy being tickled (they share the same ticklish parts of the body as we do – like under the armpits), show incredible compassion and kindness, and mourn the death of family members. They even seem to appreciate natural beauty (they've been known to stare in admiration at a fine-looking sunset) and show empathy towards other animals in trouble.

And, of course, it's impossible not to admire their ability to surprise and impress us with their countless skills – not to mention their intelligence (if that's the right word – it's a bit patronising of us to presume to judge their intelligence, as if our own is any kind of standard by which to measure).

Imagine if every animal in the world had its own survival instruction book. Impalas, warthogs and fish eagles would have simple pamphlets of no more than a few pages each. But the chimp instruction book would be a veritable tome, equivalent to several volumes the size of the *Encyclopaedia Britannica*. There is so much to being a chimp that they don't just learn by trial and error – they have proper lessons in which they are actively taught by their mothers and other experienced members of the troop. Their tutors are incredibly tolerant, waiting

patiently as their students make mistakes and gradually, day by day, learn the tasks in hand.

It takes a youngster nearly a decade to acquire most of the skills, knowledge and competence to be a fully qualified, professional chimpanzee. Some skills, such as cooperative hunting or opening certain types of nut, can take several decades to be taught properly.

Just think about everything they need to learn. They use twigs to fish termites out of their mounds; they use rocks as missiles (throwing them at potential predators, or people they don't like) and branches as clubs; they make sponges to soak

Opposite

It's so hard not to be anthropomorphic when talking about chimps.

up water from inaccessible tree holes; they open nuts with a Heath-Robinson hammer and anvil; and they make comfortable cushions with large leaves.

In recent years, in Senegal, there have been reports of them using sharp sticks as spears, especially to catch bushbabies.

Actually, I've just realised that one reason I have a completely irrational bias against chimpanzees is because they kill other mammals for food. I'm not a vegetarian myself, so I'm being astonishingly hypocritical, but why can't they be like bonobos and eat mainly fruit? Instead, they hunt everything from flying squirrels to baboons. I think it's a kind of unreconstructed species prejudice: it's acceptable for lions and tigers to kill other animals, because they are predators and they need to do it to survive. But a chimp is one of us. I haven't thought this preposterous idea through properly – but it's clearly been in my sub-conscious for years.

It's so hard not to be anthropomorphic. I'll never forget reading about an observation Jane Goodall made during her study of the famous chimpanzees in Gombe Stream National Park, in Tanzania. She noticed that young chimps with very affectionate and supportive mothers tend to grow up as calm and confident individuals. But those raised by careless and stressed mothers are more likely to develop a hyperactive, impatient and nervous character. How human is that?

Ngamba Island is divided into two unequal parts. A tiny portion of its 40 hectares (100 acres) is reserved for conservationists. The other 98 per cent is wild and belongs to the chimps. It's all natural rainforest and there is plenty of room to roam.

Lilly took us to meet some of the rescued orphans. We had a tin bucket full of food and threw bananas and carrots to the chimps on the other side of the electric fence.

'Hello!' said Stephen, as I threw a carrot to a huge male chimpanzee.

'Oooooh-uuh, ooooh-uuh, ho-uh, ho-uh, ha-uh, ha-uh, ha-ha-ha-ha!' said the chimp.

The carrot fell a couple of metres short of the fence. As we watched, the chimp picked up a stick, poked it through the wire, and dragged the carrot to within arm's reach.

'Our own ancestors must have started off doing things like that,' said Stephen, hugely impressed. 'We just got a little bit further. They haven't invented mobile phones yet, have they? Or broadband. But they're pretty close. Clever thing!'

Several other chimps were waving their arms in the air.

'They've got their hands up,' laughed Stephen. 'They're like school children, who know the answer, aren't they? Please Sir! Sir! Over here! Me! Me, Sir!'

'Do you know all their names?' I asked Lilly.

She did, and started introducing us to them as if they were old friends.

'That's Bahati, over by the tree, and there's Baluku chasing Nakku in the bushes behind.'

She told us about some of the 45 orphans in her care. More than half of them came from the DRC, where they had been rescued from traders working in the live pet trade. They looked healthy and happy, with plenty of space, good food (they even had porridge for dinner) and a choice of sleeping platforms and hammocks.

There had, though, been one unsatisfied customer. A male called Sunday once made a bid for freedom by stealing a fishing boat (the fisherman was still in it – he leapt into the water). The daring chimp had obviously been planning and researching his escape for some time because, as he floated off into the sunset, he tried to pull the cord to start the engine. He was returned to the island none the worse for wear and has lived there, without incident, ever since.

One daring chimp made a bid for freedom by stealing a fishing boat. He had obviously been planning his escape for some time because, as he floated off into the sunset, he tried to pull the cord to start the engine.

The next day we met Afrika and Mac, two of the youngest chimps on Ngamba. Afrika's mother had been killed for bushmeat. She was just a few months old when she was found, lying on her side and squashed into a tiny wooden cage. Mac had a similar story. But they had spent the past year being rehabilitated – learning a little bit about how to be chimps – and were ready to begin their return to the wild.

We happened to be there on the day they were being introduced to some of the older members of the Ngamba community.

Stephen watched from a safe distance as we took the two orphans into the chimp side of the island.

'Good luck, non-cold people,' he called from the other side of the fence.

I was carrying Afrika, who was climbing all over my head and shoulders, nibbling my thumb, swinging from my arms and playing like a human toddler.

'You lucky beggar,' said Stephen.

Lilly looked worried.

'You never know what's going to happen,' she said. 'This is the most nerve-wracking part of the whole rehabilitation process. Sometimes the adults reject the babies and even hurt them. One nearly killed a baby just like Afrika and Mac, by banging the poor thing against the ground.'

The introduction was organised like a military operation. Pasa and Ikuru, two adult chimps, were ready and waiting in a separate enclosure on the other side of a trap door. Pacing and hooting, they were getting impatient.

Lilly gently put Mac down onto the ground and told me to do the same with Afrika. The two young chimps looked nervous and clung to our legs.

The trap door opened and Pasa and Ikuru came racing towards us.

We held our breath.

The enormous adults paused in front of the two wide-eyed youngsters and looked them up and down. Gently, they put their arms on their shoulders and gave them huge hugs. The four animals rolled around together, held hands, and then hugged again.

'Oh my God!' said Lilly, who was almost in tears. 'I've never seen anything like it. We couldn't have hoped for more.'

I was trying to be strong, but could feel the tears welling.

'For a man who claims not to like chimps, you seem to have had a change of heart,' called Stephen, in a wavering voice.

I had.

Every morning in this corner of Africa starts with popping a malaria tablet. I take mine religiously, without fail. I'm a little paranoid, because I nearly died from the disease many years ago (it would be tedious to relate all the details, but not half as tedious as it was to suffer them at the time).

Malaria is actually quite interesting (an understatement for the millions of people who die from it every year). It is transmitted via the saliva of female – never male – mosquitoes. Most of the time they feed on nectar. But nectar doesn't contain enough protein for them to produce and lay eggs, so, once in a while, after dark, they go out and look for a good blood meal to build up their strength. Personally, I wouldn't begrudge them a tiny drop of blood to help them lay a few eggs. But there is a catch, because their saliva contains a little microbe, called *Plasmodium*, which wheedles its way into your bloodstream – and that is what makes you decidedly ill.

'Taken your Malarone?' asked Stephen, as he sat down opposite me for breakfast. We had an unspoken agreement to remind one another every day.

'Yep. You?'

'I couldn't find my Malarone, so I've taken Toblerone instead.'

We were in the open-air dining room of Bukima Lodge, in the middle of the Bwindi Impenetrable Forest in the southwestern corner of Uganda. Looking over Stephen's shoulder, I could see a vast expanse of misty, mountainous jungle stretching out below us.

'Did you sleep okay?' asked Stephen.

'Yes, thanks,' I replied. 'I sleep much better listening to the sounds of the African night than I do at home.'

'I don't,' said Stephen. 'The jungle wildlife sounded like a thousand people testing their mobile ringtones: brrr-brrr, ooh-ooh, rattle-rattle, bing-bing, ting-tong, dat-dat. And goodness knows what was making a sing-sing-dock-dock-ping-ping sound right outside my bedroom window.'

'Oh dear,' I sympathised. 'Why don't you…'

'And what the hell is that?' he interrupted.

A bird – I never found out what it was – had been screaming its incessant metallic bleep-bleep call since before Stephen had sat down.

'Surely the bloody thing must have charged by now,' he said, a little grumpily.

'Ah well. It'll be worth it when we get into the forest.'

'Surely,' he said, 'the whole point of an impenetrable forest is that it's impenetrable? And yet we are going to penetrate it.'

I laughed.

'How far do you think we'll have to walk to find them?'

'It depends which family we are allotted. It could be as little as an hour's trek

Opposite
On the gorilla trek – before Mark and Stephen realised how much sweating and panting, crawling and clambering along slippery mountain tracks there was still to come.

away, if we're really lucky, or up to eleven hours if we're not.'

'Eleven hours? Eleven hours? Are you kidding? Eleven hours! Oh my God.'

We had come to a tiny island of 331 square kilometres (128 square miles) of equatorial rainforest, surrounded by a sea of banana and tea plantations, close to the border with the DRC.

Bwindi is home to nearly half of the world's remaining 700–750 mountain gorillas. The other half live in the Virunga Volcanoes, which straddle the borders of the DRC, Rwanda and Uganda, just 25 kilometres (15.5 miles) to the south.

Douglas and I visited them in The Country Formerly Known as Zaire. My main memory of that particular encounter was our larger-than-average gorilla-watching kit. I can't remember exactly why, but it consisted of the basic stuff – jeans, T-shirt, waterproofs and a load of cameras – plus an immense store of dirty laundry, a suit and shoes for Douglas to meet his French publisher in Paris, a dozen computer magazines, a thesaurus, half the collected works of Dickens and a large wooden model of a Komodo dragon. It all belonged to Douglas, of course.

There were no other gorilla-watching tourists in Zaire at the time. There aren't many there now, either. Unhappily, the gorillas have been caught in a vortex of human conflict and misery and are forced to share their home with a motley collection of rebels from both the DRC and Rwanda.

They made headline news in July 2007, when seven of the 12-member Rugendo family were killed in cold blood. Images of grieving villagers carrying Senkwekwe, a 227-kilogram (500-pound) silverback gorilla, on a makeshift bamboo stretcher were seen around the world.

The gorillas had not been killed by poachers, which would have been bad enough, but were executed – some even shot in the back of the head. Poachers would have removed the heads and hands to sell as souvenirs to tourists (there was once a grisly tourist trade in poached gorilla heads and hands – and a small number of uninformed or uncaring tourists still buy such gruesome artefacts) and they would have kidnapped the infants. But the bodies were just left where they fell.

There was no shortage of suspects. The gorillas share the DRC portion of the Virunga Volcanoes with tens of thousands of heavily armed soldiers engaged in a three-way guerrilla war between two rival militias and the Congolese army. It's also home to poachers and hordes of illegal charcoal producers, and it is bordered by subsistence farmers and vast refugee camps overflowing with families fleeing the bloodshed. Most likely, the killings were a warning to local conservationists trying to prevent the commercial destruction of the rainforest by charcoal-makers, who chop down the park's trees.

But if the gorillas are hugely vulnerable, so are the rangers trying to protect them. They are exposed to just as many dangers, if not more, as they try to continue their work no matter how much rebel activity there is in the region. Several hundred gorilla rangers have been killed in the line of duty in recent years.

Soon after the Rugendo executions, many of the rangers were forcibly ejected from the park by the notorious rebel leader, Laurent Nkunda. The 53 rangers suddenly found themselves without food or water, dodging rebel bullets in a war zone, trying to make their way on foot to safety.

Nkunda took control of the region during an offensive to seize strategic land near the Ugandan border. The tall, slender ethnic Tutsi, leader of the National Congress for the Defence of the People, recognised that gorillas sometimes draw more global attention than people. He was actually quoted as saying: 'For us, the gorillas are worth more than diamonds.' In between waging war against the Congolese army and Hutu militias, the 41-year-old warlord actually organised tours – a kind of guerrilla's gorilla-watching – for journalists and adrenalin-seeking tourists. He was eventually captured, early in 2009, during a joint operation by the Congolese and Rwandan armies.

Even Bwindi, where Stephen and I went to see the gorillas, has had its fair share of troubles. A group of more than a hundred machete-wielding rebels killed eight tourists and two tour guides while on a gorilla-watching holiday there in March 1999. It was a bid by Rwandan Hutus to weaken US and British support for the new

Rwandan government. The murders dealt a crippling blow to Uganda's tourist industry, particularly in Bwindi, although it recovered surprisingly quickly (so many people *really* want to see gorillas that they're prepared to overlook levels of security that would scare away 'normal' tourists in an instant).

A friend of mine was staying at the lodge on the day of the rebel attack. By pure chance, he happened to wake up early and left before the violence erupted. He only heard about it later in the day. It reminds me of the film *Sliding Doors* – how one chance event can affect the rest of your life.

After breakfast, Stephen and I wandered down to join the gathering crowd of gorilla-watchers on the lawns near the park headquarters, for a detailed briefing.

'We recommend you take a walking stick,' the ranger told us. 'Don't touch the gorillas,' he continued. 'And if you need a poo, tell a ranger and he will close shop after you've finished.' That was all fine. But when he said 'If you can't manage the trek you can be carried up the mountain on a stretcher' I glanced over at Stephen and we both started to giggle. It was terribly unprofessional of us and we got

some surly glances from a well-behaved group of German tourists. The ranger carried on regardless: 'If it's all too much, I suggest you go home and get fit and then come back again.' At that point, we lost it altogether and had to turn away.

We had been given the Mubare group – a family of eight gorillas that spend most of their time fairly close to the park headquarters. Despite the giggling, I think the rangers had taken pity on us. The Mubares happened to be the first of four gorilla families (out of about thirty altogether) that have been habituated to receive human visitors. They were formally introduced to people for the first time in 1991.

I had been to Bwindi the year before, to see the Rushegura group, and I asked how they were doing. There were fourteen members when I saw them and apparently, by the time Stephen and I arrived, they had had a few babies and there were seventeen. The only problem was that, in July 2008, they moved out of Uganda and into the DRC. Gorillas are not yet sufficiently advanced in evolutionary terms to have discovered the benefits of passports, currency declaration forms and official bribery, and therefore tend to wander backwards and forwards across the border as and when they feel like it. That's all very well, but their unofficial primitive wanderings were causing havoc with the tourists who had come all the way to Uganda specially to see them.

Opposite
'Believe me, the spirit
is willing, even though
the flesh is a bin liner
full of yoghurt.'

Below
Two great apes meet
(Stephen is the one in
the foreground).

Once the giggling had subsided we set off into the forest, chaperoned by trackers, guides, armed guards and super-human porters (anyone who can carry my 20-kilo/44-pound camera bag up and down the steep slopes of the Impenetrable Forest has to be super-human). Within minutes we were sweating and panting, crawling and clambering our way along slippery, precipitous mountain tracks. The dark, wet Impenetrable Forest is aptly named – it's a riot of green where things grow on top of other things that grow on top of more things in layers of ferns, mosses, creepers and lichens. In places, the forest is so thick you have to hike on solid mats of vegetation that tremble and flex with every step, threatening to break through and dump you into the unseen depths below.

Stephen was struggling even more than I was, and I asked if he was okay.

'Believe me, the spirit is willing,' he said, 'even though the flesh is a bin liner full of yoghurt. Oh heavens.'

The deeper we penetrated the Impenetrable Forest the taller the forest undergrowth became, until every single bit of it was considerably taller than either of us. We hacked and stumbled our way to a clearing and there, on the other side, was an even more impenetrable forest.

'Oh good Lord. Have we got to go in there? Go on without me. It's fine. I'll lie here and die,' said Stephen.

About a couple of hours into the trek, our guides signalled for us to keep quiet. It was a moment or two before I saw anything, but then a slight movement caught my eye. No more than 10 metres (33 feet) away in the thick forest, partially hidden by a tree, was something so big that I hadn't even noticed it. It was a mountain gorilla, or more appropriately a gorilla mountain, standing propped up on his front knuckles. He assumed the shape of a large and muscular sloping ridge tent and was looking straight at us.

Seeing a gorilla in a zoo (or any animal in a zoo, for that matter) is absolutely no preparation for seeing one in the wild. In the seemingly limitless mountainous jungle, the silverback was in his element, clearly master of his own wild world.

'He's belching,' said Stephen, laughing.

It was a belch vocalisation, or BV as primatologists like to call it. When researchers began to spend quality time with gorillas they thought they were just burping. But now we know better. A BV is an effective way of keeping contact in the thick foliage, as the gorillas spread out to feed. Each belch is a way of saying 'I'm over here'.

'The researchers should have another abbreviation,' suggested Stephen, 'called the FV, or fart vocalisation, because I must say they do fart quite a lot. What does that mean, do you think?'

'It probably means they've been eating too many fruits and vegetables,' I replied.

'He's got a pot belly,' observed Stephen, 'just like me.'

The silverback relaxed and lay down, resting his enormous elbow on the ground and his enormous chin on his enormous hand. Best known for impressive displays of strength – hooting, chest pummelling and ripping branches off trees – this particular silverback looked the picture of peace and contentment.

'You know,' whispered Stephen, looking straight into the silverback's wise and knowing eyes, 'the gentler side of gorillas is just as compelling as their huge size and those dramatic displays of strength you keep hearing about.'

'Did you know it's rude to stare?' I asked him.

'What do you mean?'

'Well, you know how we find long, uninterrupted stares a bit intimidating and threatening?'

'Unless it's someone you fancy,' interrupted Stephen.

'Yes, unless it's someone you fancy. But other primates are exactly the same. If you catch a gorilla's eye you are supposed to glance away and then look back, or it'll think you are squaring up for a fight.'

Stephen looked away immediately.

'And another bit of advice is not to stand directly beneath primates in a tree.'

'Why?'

'Because you're basically standing at the bottom of a long-drop toilet.'

We both laughed, in a quiet, gorilla-watching sort of way.

I explained that the dominant male gorilla has a saddle of silver fur on his back.

'Oh, *that's* why it's called a silverback,' said Stephen, sarcastically.

The saddle develops when the male reaches puberty, at about ten or twelve years old, as a badge of maturity (before then he is known, rather appropriately, as a blackback). At the same time, he loses all his chest hair. The development of chest hair in gorillas is the reverse of that in human males – they have hairy chests when they are young and then lose all the hair when they get older.

There were several females in the group (we saw three altogether) and some youngsters. One was so tiny it tripped over Stephen's size-12 feet. Mum seemed completely unconcerned.

It was a dripping wet, misty morning that neither of us will ever forget. The hour went so quickly it felt as if it had only just begun, but one of the trackers signalled that we had five more minutes and then we had to leave.

'Before we go,' said Stephen, 'let's get a picture of us with the gorillas. We can call it *Mzungus in the Mist*.' ('Mzungu' means 'white person' in some African languages.)

Opposite
The gentler side of gorillas is just as compelling as their huge size and those dramatic displays of strength we keep hearing about.

A bit of advice: never stand beneath primates in a tree, because you're basically standing at the bottom of a long-drop toilet.

We hacked and stumbled our way to a clearing and there, on the other side, was an even more impenetrable forest.

We stopped halfway back to the lodge to admire the view. Stephen was bright red.

'I know, I know,' he said when I told him. 'I'm glowing like a radioactive tomato. It's part physical exertion and part radiant bliss. But it was worth every sobbing, gasping, aching step of horror, sweat, wheezing, and – frankly – humiliation to get to see those gorillas. It's been unbelievable. Wonderful.'

The business of gorilla tourism is obviously a vexed one. I know people who have wanted to visit the gorillas for years, but have been worried that tourism must be causing disturbance or exposing the animals to deadly diseases to which they have no immunity.

But in truth the gorillas probably wouldn't be there at all without tourism. It is the one thing that can guarantee their survival, by making them worth more alive than dead.

It is all very carefully monitored and controlled. Each habituated gorilla family can be visited only once a day, for a maximum of one hour, by a party of no more than eight people (all of whom have been approved fit – well, relatively fit – and healthy). Each person pays US$500 for the privilege and, when you include all the additional money everyone spends on flights, hire cars, food and lodging, it soon adds up. So the gorillas are able to generate several hundred million dollars every year. Much goes to central government coffers, of course,

Opposite
Bwindi Impenetrable
Forest: home to
nearly half of the
world's remaining
mountain gorillas.

some goes to the local communities (or, at least, it is *supposed* to go to local communities – though it doesn't always arrive) and the rest helps to pay to look after the gorillas themselves (as well as other parks in Uganda and Rwanda).

I believe we have a special responsibility to make gorilla conservation work in any way we can. Think of it like this. We are the rich, successful members of the primate family. We are the ones who made good. We should be looking after our less well-off relatives.

We were running out of time, so I made another call to my UN contact in the Democratic Republic of Congo. It was a better satellite link than before and this is roughly how the conversation went:

Me: 'How is the situation in the Garamba region at the moment?'

Him: 'Absolutely terrible.'

Me: 'Why? What's happening?'

Him: 'There are lots of violent attacks on civilians, nearly a quarter of a million refugees are heading for the border and Garamba itself is becoming more dangerous by the day.'

Me: 'So if we do decide to come, what would be the main risk?'

Him: 'Apart from getting caught in the crossfire you have a good chance of being kidnapped, especially if you're travelling with a high-profile celebrity and a film crew. You'd be an obvious target. And, without a doubt, the rebels would know you were there.'

Me: 'So is your advice not to come?'

Him: 'Absolutely. No doubt whatsoever. I very strongly advise you not to come.'

And that was it. My long-held dream of revisiting one of the rarest rhinos in the world had just collapsed.

I went to find Stephen and we wandered down to sit by the river. Staring across to the other side – across the border between Uganda and the DRC – we knew that this was as close to the northern white rhinos as we were ever going to get.

> 'Apart from getting caught in the crossfire you have a good chance of being kidnapped, especially if you're travelling with a high-profile celebrity and a film crew.'

We returned to Kenya in sombre mood and the next morning went straight to Nairobi National Park.

I used to live right next to the park, in the mid-1980s, when I worked for the United Nations Environment Programme. I didn't enjoy working for the UN, to be honest (too much red tape, too many meetings, too little progress), but

I adored Nairobi. It was a fun time to be there, with few tourists and relatively few security problems (although they were just starting – there was an in-joke at the time that you had to check before you shut a window in case you trapped somebody's fingers).

There was a fence along three sides of the world's most thrilling and untamed city park, to keep wildlife out of Nairobi itself, but in those days it was on its last legs in many places and absent altogether in others. So we often had animals in the garden. Warthogs and baboons were almost resident, but we occasionally had lions, and a leopard sometimes sunbathed on the garage roof.

I used to go on a mini game drive every evening after work and frequently saw black rhinos. They were often standing in front of the famous Kenyatta International Conference Centre, the most iconic building on the Nairobi skyline just 6 or 7 kilometres (4 miles) away.

Nairobi National Park has been one of the most successful rhino sanctuaries in East Africa. In fact, there were no fewer than 65 in the park when Stephen and I were there. We were joining park staff to help move a crash of rhinos to Ol Jogi Ranch, not a million miles from our old friend Max in Ol Pejeta Conservancy.

(I've always wanted to say 'a crash of rhinos' but never thought I'd have the opportunity, until now. It's one of the better collective nouns for animals – and depressingly appropriate given what's happening to rhino populations. Some other good ones include: a dissimulation of birds, a murder of crows, a troubling of goldfish, a kaleidoscope of butterflies, a smack of jellyfish and a quiver of cobras.)

One of the best ways to conserve rhinos is to move them around a lot. The individual animals don't like being moved around a lot, of course, but the population as a whole benefits enormously. Surplus animals are moved from one place to another, to prevent numbers getting unnaturally high and to set up new breeding populations while there is still time. It worked for the southern white rhino and now it's working pretty well for the black rhino.

Kenya's black rhino population plummeted from 20,000 in the 1970s to fewer than 350 by the early 1990s – as a direct result of intensive poaching. Now there are 577 and counting.

We arrived just in time for a long and serious briefing, followed by a prayer, blessing the rhinos, and us, and anyone else within shouting distance. There must have been fifty or sixty people preparing for the translocation altogether.

The briefing had only just finished when a helicopter rose above the trees. It was like one of the HueyCobra choppers in *Apocalypse Now*, except that this was a small six-seater owned by the Kenya Wildlife Service. Everyone scrambled into an assortment of khaki vehicles and we were off.

This was the plan. The helicopter pilot, along with the chief vet and rhino

There was a one-tonne rhino staggering about like a drunk at closing time. It staggered this way, lurched that way, wobbled back again, and then dropped to the ground.

Opposite
Nairobi National Park: in search of a suitable rhino.

darter, was going to find a suitable rhino. The vet would fire a tranquiliser dart, from a hovering height of about 6 or 7 metres (20–23 feet), to sedate the rhino – and the rest of us would leap into action.

We quickly discovered that the journey to the capture site requires a fast driver, a sense of humour and a good grip.

'Aaagh! Holy mackerel!' shouted Stephen. 'People pay a lot of money for this kind of thing at A-A-Alton Towers.'

We screeched to a halt.

'Oooph!' said Stephen, lowering his voice to a scream. 'What in the name of twenty arses is going on? Why are we reversing?'

Ten minutes of racing in the manner of the Paris-Dakar rally later, we screeched to a halt once again.

'That was one of the most terrifying drives I've ever had,' said Stephen, climbing out of the Land Rover. 'Absolutely terrifying. But at least we're here.'

At first glance 'here' appeared to be a rhino-less middle of nowhere. On closer inspection, it turned out to be just that – a rhino-less middle of nowhere. We were waiting for further instructions from the helicopter. This time, it was with a nagging feeling that another fast journey was firmly on the cards.

Suddenly, the convoy was back on the move and, as predicted, it was fast. But this time, just to keep things interesting, it was hellish fast.

'I think it's loosening the screws in my arm,' yelled Stephen. 'I think my bone is about to start coming out. Aaaagh!'

We screeched to another halt and, unexpectedly, arrived just in time to see something extraordinary.

There was a one-tonne rhino staggering about like a drunk at closing time. It staggered this way, lurched that way, wobbled back again, and then dropped to the ground.

The moment it fell, we all abandoned our cars and ran across the savannah towards the giant grey lump. We were in a race against time (it's critically important that the rhino is unconscious for as little time as possible) and there was such a sense of urgency that, for a moment, I felt like an extra in a scene from *ER*. The rhino was lying on its side, panting and quivering slightly, while hordes of people rushed around doing all kinds of important things. This was clearly a group of experts who knew exactly what they were doing.

Someone gently put a little ointment into the rhino's eyes, to keep them moist, and then placed a cloth over them to keep out the dust. Another person poured water all over its body, to keep it cool. Several rangers were working together, taking measurements with a long tape measure. One man had the job of sticking his finger up the rhino's nose, to make sure it was breathing properly,

Above
Good news at last – Kenya's black rhino population is increasing.

Opposite top
Drilling a hole into the rhino's horn for a radio transmitter to be fitted.

Opposite
There's only one way to get an animal the size of a VW Beetle into a wooden crate – you have to wake it up.

while someone else cut a neat little notch out of each ear, to make it recognisable from a distance – like pinning a name-tag to its chest. And all the time the rhino was receiving a seemingly endless stream of injections.

One man had a huge thermometer. We had a sneaking suspicion where that was about to go and, sure enough, it did.

'I don't know why,' said Stephen, 'but it makes me want to cry when I see all this attention being given to an animal like this, this great mighty beast that doesn't give a damn for us. It sort of goes some way to make up for what the poachers are doing.'

The top of the horn was sawn off (just the pointy bit – to stop the rhino hurting itself, or one of its human helpers, when it woke up) and then a 2cm (3/4-inch) hole was drilled into the base for a radio transmitter to be fitted by the person in charge of radio transmitters.

Ten minutes later, we were ready.

There's only one way to get an animal the size of a VW Beetle into a wooden crate – you have to wake it up. But first we had to prepare for the inevitable. A rope was tied around its head and horn, and another around its backside, ready to pull. A dozen of us stood next to the rhino, with our hands firmly on its back and side, ready to push. Everyone was preparing to pull and push as if their lives depended on it, which they probably did.

Then the vet injected the quivering hump with a kind of anti-sedative, to bring it round.

We waited for something to happen. Nothing. He started flicking the rhino's ear. Still nothing. I relaxed. Just as I let my guard down, it sprang to life. One second it was lying down, fast asleep, the next it was standing up and wide awake.

This may be stating the obvious, but when a black rhino wakes up to find itself tied up in rope and surrounded by people pushing and pulling, it's not particularly pleased about it. Black rhinos are famously irritable – and this one was doubly so.

How on earth it ended up inside the crate I will never know. I remember lots of shouting and shoving, and the sound of the door slamming shut, but that's about it. The rest is a big blur. Admittedly, the poor animal wasn't particularly happy to be in the crate, either, and rammed the inside so hard it split at the seams, but it would all be worth it in the end.

We caught and processed two more rhinos during the course of the morning and then drove them in convoy – with a police escort in case we were ambushed – on the five-hour journey north. There, in the safe surroundings of Ol Jogi, they were released into their new home.

The next day, Stephen and I stood on the top of a hill surveying the scene and listening to the distinctive bleeps of their radio transmitters. They were out there, somewhere, in the peaceful vastness of the African bush, though we couldn't actually see them.

I had mixed feelings. The rhinos translocated to these fenced sanctuaries will be made as safe as humanly possible. Their new homes are immense – the size of English counties in some cases – but they are still fenced. And the rhinos themselves will have to receive round-the-clock protection. So, in one way, it's all very artificial. They're not wild in the sense that rhinos living in a place like Garamba are truly wild.

But they are wild-ish. And if we're at the point where we have to choose between wild-ish and extinction, I know which I would choose.

Soon after leaving Kenya we received news that an intensive search by the brave rangers hanging on in the crossfire found absolutely no evidence of northern

Meanwhile,
the formalities
are under way
to declare the
northern white
rhino extinct in
the wild.

white rhinos surviving in Garamba.

We had gone in search of one of the rarest animals on the planet. But even if we'd managed to get to their home in the war zone, we would have been too late.

There is, however, one last tiny sliver of hope.

The northern white rhino may be gone from Garamba, but it hangs on by a thread in captivity. There are three in San Diego Wild Animal Park – two females and a male – which were caught in the wild many years ago. One of the females is infertile, and the other hasn't been interested in the male's advances for longer than he can remember, so this population is not breeding. But thanks to the life's work of a fanatical Czech northern white rhino collector, there are seven at Dvur Králové Zoo, in the Czech Republic (actually, there are seven and a half, because the pure-bred animals share their enclosure with a hybrid called Arthur, whose mother was a northerner but whose father was a southerner). But they haven't had a calf for nearly a decade.

Now there is a plan to move four of the Czech seven to that boma at the Ol Pejeta Conservancy, in Kenya. Conservationists are hoping against all hope that the wide expanse of African sky, and a last chance to stand on African soil, might encourage the rhinos to breed. It's a long shot, to say the least, but in the conservation business we simply can't afford to give up hope.

Meanwhile, the formalities are under way to declare the northern white rhino extinct in the wild.

3

BITS OF OTHER ANIMALS

It started with a kiss. Well, not exactly a kiss, but a box of chocolates. We'd been advised to bring an edible offering to ease our way through customs and, sure enough, one box of assorted Belgian chocolates and five minutes later, seven of us and our thirty eight bags were being waved through to the outside world by a man with bits of truffle stuck in his teeth.

We had arrived in Madagascar.

Many travellers have commented that Madagascar is unlike anywhere else in the world. And they're right. It's hard to be more insightful than that – at least, it's hard to be more insightful without using an awful lot of trite and unimaginative clichés. You can't say 'Madagascar is like somewhere-or-other' because, quite simply, it isn't.

Part African and part Southeast Asian, it's the kind of place that grabs you by the scruff of the neck and shakes you about until you fall head-over-heels in love with its unique and consummate charm. It happened to me and it's happened to everyone else I know who's been there. There aren't many places you can say that about.

Despite its proximity to the African mainland, the country's first settlers came from entirely the opposite direction – mainly Indonesia and Malaysia – less than 2,000 years ago. Then others came from Africa, Arabia and elsewhere in the Indian Ocean. The French turned up much later (Madagascar was officially

Opposite
Baby ring-tailed lemur: no word has been invented to describe cuteness on such a grandiose scale.

Opposite top
With their own soft, singsong language, and a happy blend of racial diversity and cultural uniformity, the people of Madagascar are uniquely Madagascan.

You can't say
'Madagascar is
like somewhere-
or-other' because,
quite simply,
it isn't.

declared a French colony in 1896 and wrested back full independence in 1960) and left behind an indelible colonial stamp that lurks around every corner, adding its own unique flavour to the mix like vanilla in a cappuccino. There are French cafés serving coffee and croissants in the capital, men playing *boules* in village squares and, best of all, badly driven Citroën 2CVs and Renault 4s pretty much everywhere.

Yet everyone seems to have been absorbed into this eclectic mix with such alacrity that Madagascar has accomplished an incredibly rare and happy blend of racial diversity and cultural uniformity. The Malagasy don't have the effervescence of Southeast Asians, the ebullience of Africans or the Gallic ways of the French. With their own soft, singsong language, they are uniquely 'Madagascan' (not the correct word – it should be 'Malagasy' – but I like it). And while Madagascar is among the poorer countries of the world, its people seem to be some of the happiest. Call me a gullible westerner, but they're certainly some of the friendliest.

Here is a country where there are traditional healers and sorcerers in Malagasy villages, and yet finely dressed transsexual ladyboys touting for business in the big city; where people email one another to arrange a meeting under an upside-down baobab tree, where they plan to place sacred offerings; and where the best restaurants serve tender mouthwatering steaks with good wine from around the world, while roadside stalls serve stir-fried locusts with illegal (and quite hazardous) home-made rum.

I love it.

What's not to like about a country whose people passionately and unerringly believe in magic, elect a snappily dressed yoghurt baron for president, and live alongside animals that look as if they have just arrived from outer space?

(Sadly, Madagascar's reputation as an otherworldly tropical paradise was knocked just a couple of months after our visit. A serious breakdown in law and order was followed by violent protests and a kind of military coup. The army forced out the elected president, Marc Ravalomanana, and installed the opposition leader, Andry Rajoelina, in his place. One of the many repercussions has been a dramatic rise in criminal networks plundering the country's national parks for precious hardwoods and wildlife.)

If a spaceship were to land on earth, the creature most likely to emerge from its cargo doors is an aye-aye. One of the strangest animals on the planet, Douglas Adams reckoned it looks as if it has been assembled from bits of other animals. It has a sort of cat's body, a bat's ears, a beaver's teeth, a long bushy tail like that of a squirrel on steroids, and enormous, bright yellowy-orange eyes even more beady than those of ET. It's a real-life work of art.

The aye-aye was probably the strangest animal on our endangered species list, and was certainly one of the hardest to find.

'It looks like someone has tried to turn a bat into a cat,' Stephen explained to a group of British tourists who asked for his autograph in Antananarivo, Madagascar's capital. 'And then they stuck a few extra gadgets on it for good measure.'

The best of all its gadgets, fulfilling something of the role of a Swiss Army knife, is a skeletally thin middle finger rather like a long dead twig. Little more than skin, tendons and bone, it looks more like a contraption for zapping creatures from another world. Little wonder some Malagasy people believe that if an aye-aye points one of these long middle fingers at them, they are going to die.

The aye-aye baffled taxonomists for years. It's such an anatomical jumble that they couldn't make up their minds what it was and, at first, classified it as a rodent. It was an understandable mistake. With small cheek teeth, no canines and a single pair of enormous incisors that never stop growing, some kind of weird and wonderful rodent would be a logical first guess.

Now we know better. It's actually a lemur – albeit such an unusual one that it has been dignified with a zoological family of its very own (known in the scientific

world as Daubentoniidae). It's a nice way of classifying such an enigma because, as Gerald Durrell shrewdly observed, 'an aye-aye is, quite simply, an aye-aye'.

It doesn't zap extraterrestrials, of course, but what it does do with its long middle finger is almost as implausible. It taps wood. The aye-aye comes out after dark and taps branches and tree trunks as it moves nimbly about the treetops. Using its outsized, leathery ears (which are capable of moving to and fro independently like radar dishes), it listens intently for the faintest whisper of juicy wood-boring grubs that might be hiding inside. As soon as it detects one it starts to gnaw a hole with its front teeth, sending wood shavings flying all over the place. Then it inserts its middle finger, with the delicacy and precision of a surgeon's probe, and extracts the unfortunate grub from its hidey-hole like a sausage on a stick. It chews off the head first and then spoons out the delicious contents of the still-wriggling body with its middle finger.

Few other animals (let alone people) can do 'percussive foraging', as this is called, so young aye-ayes have to undertake a long apprenticeship to get it right. From their first few clumsy attempts to passing their final exams takes about ten years.

Aye-ayes have an important role to play in the ecological framework of the forest: they fill a specialised ecological niche that would otherwise be left untouched. They have evolved to fulfil a role that in other parts of the world is undertaken by woodpeckers and squirrels – both of which are absent from Madagascar.

Opposite
E.T. eat your heart out.

Aye-ayes also have a positive approach to sexual equality. The females wear the trousers in their world, having first pick of all the best food and exerting dominance over all the males. When a female is on heat she advertises the fact, with a loud and distinctive call, and as many as half a dozen males come running. They tussle with one another and can get quite possessive, even pulling successful rivals off the female while they're mating. The female loves all the attention and, when she's mated with as many suitors as she likes, scuttles away through the trees to do the same thing all over again somewhere else.

It's a lot of fuss and fornication to produce a single baby aye-aye, weighing no more than 100 grams (4 ounces), some six months later. But it's worth it. A baby aye-aye will never win a beauty contest – it would look awesomely unlovely in a passport photograph – but there's no denying that it's the cutest, most adorable little creature from outer space you'll ever see.

The aye-aye's skeletally thin middle finger looks like a contraption for zapping creatures from another world.

Douglas Adams and I dreamed up the idea for *Last Chance to See* while camping in a dilapidated hut in the middle of the rainforest on a great green hump of an island called Nosy Mangabé.

That was in 1985, when this idyllic tropical island, just off the northeastern coast of Madagascar, was believed to be the last place on earth where aye-ayes could be found (or more usually not found). Nine of them had been released there some twenty years before, as a precautionary measure at a time when they were believed to be pretty much extinct everywhere else in Madagascar.

Although no one knew it at the time, aye-ayes still had a few secret hideaways on the mainland and it's since been discovered that they weren't quite so rare after all – just very good at hiding.

In those days, getting to Nosy Mangabé was quite a palaver. I remember we spent months arranging special government permission and, even when we were within sight of the island, it took hours to find something resembling a boat to take us there.

'Only once have I seen a boat significantly worse than the one which took us over to Nosy Mangabé,' Douglas said later, 'and that was the boat which, a few days later, took us back. It was basically full of sea.'

I remember trying to negotiate a price for the seven-kilometre (4½-mile) trip across open sea with Douglas anxiously interrupting to point out that the thing we were about to charter was so old and dilapidated it was almost indistinguishable from driftwood.

We shared the island with an American photographer, who had already been there for several months. He was on a proper expedition to get something no one else had managed to get – a picture of an aye-aye in the wild. But he dampened our enthusiasm with tales of tramping through the jungle, night after night, mostly in the pouring rain, in the vague hope of seeing an aye-aye let alone photographing one.

So far, he hadn't had any luck.

We only had three nights (since aye-ayes are nocturnal they don't make daytime appointments) and it was raining heavily, so our visit seemed more than a little futile. But, on the second night, soaked to the skin and with our torches fading fast, Douglas and I actually saw an aye-aye on a branch no more than 50 metres (55 yards) from the hut.

We rushed back, whooping and cheering and analysing every tantalising moment of our ten-second encounter, and burst through the door to tell our friend the American photographer the good news.

He just stood there in shocked silence.

'What do you mean?' he asked, eventually. 'What do you mean you've seen an aye-aye? Are you sure? Where? Near the hut? Just now?' He suddenly looked pale and dropped down to the floor in a grief-stricken heap. 'Oh my God.'

We tried to be more considerate, fighting not to tell him in intimate detail how 'our' aye-aye had strolled right out into the open on a branch immediately above our heads and then stopped to stare at us with those hypnotic aye-aye eyes before ambling off into thick foliage on the other side of the clearing. We struggled not to tell him that it was one of the most exciting moments of our lives, or that he could have got a front-cover shot.

We just rummaged around in our bags, looking for something edible to rustle up for supper.

I heard later that our American friend never did see an aye-aye on Nosy Mangabé and left, several months later, without his world exclusive.

Some twenty years after that, Stephen and I had a plethora of seaworthy boats to choose from when we rolled up at the remote town of Maroantsetra. We picked a comfortable fibreglass motor launch and travelled along the Antainambalana River, out into the Baie d'Antongil, and past several rusty shipwrecks to a divine sandy cove in the southwestern corner of the island.

If you had to be stranded on a desert island then this would be the one to go for. Stepping onto Nosy Mangabé is like stepping onto the set of *The Beach*. With beautiful sandy coves, waterfall grottos, extravagant trees complete with huge buttress roots and hung with strangler figs and orchids, it is cloaked in lowland rainforest from the water's edge to its 331-metre (1,100-foot) peak.

But all sense of our intrepidness melted into the soft, golden sand in an in-

stant. In our eagerness to get ashore, we almost tripped over an elderly tourist sunbathing on the beach. And there were other tourists in 'I Love Madagascar' T-shirts, or something similar, noisily eating lunch in a wooden shelter among the trees.

It was one of many moments during my travels with Stephen when I realised just how much had changed since visiting the same wild, idyllic, remote, undisturbed places with Douglas. They just aren't quite so wild, idyllic, remote or undisturbed any more.

But I believe we're living in the best possible period for watching wildlife in the history – and future – of the planet.

Think about it. If you were to go back in time – just one hundred years or so – you'd be joining perilous and expensive expeditions lasting several months or even years in an effort to watch little-known wildlife in difficult-to-visit far-flung corners of the world.

But nowadays, especially since wide-bodied 'jumbos' took off in 1970 and travelling by plane has become faster, more comfortable, safer and cheaper, almost everywhere is within easy reach. Admittedly, vast tracts of Siberian wilderness are still a bit of a challenge and swathes of the nature traveller's map have been gouged out by political instability. But few places are truly inaccessible.

A few weeks before filming in Madagascar I had been standing in a snowstorm high up in the Canadian Arctic – just 48 hours after leaving my home in Bristol. I could close my front door after breakfast on Monday and be cruising along the Antarctic Peninsula by late evening on Thursday.

Alternatively, if you were to go forwards in time – perhaps as little as fifty years – there would almost certainly be less wildlife to watch and, worse still, you wouldn't be able to see it over the shoulders of all the other people who got there first.

I've been travelling extensively for a quarter of a century, returning to many wildlife hotspots over the years, and my overwhelming impression is of everything being more and more organised and of ever-increasing numbers of people. Where once there was an empty patch of ground now there is a campsite, where there was a campsite now there is a small hotel, and where there was a small hotel now there is a big one.

I remember the days when I'd moan if I saw a couple of other vehicles in Tanzania's Ngorongoro Crater, for instance, but nowadays there can be as many as fifty four-wheel-drives and mini-buses parked around the public picnic site alone. When I first started exploring South Africa's Cape Peninsula National Park, in the late 1980s, it was a haven of peace and tranquillity; now it is swamped by more than 1.3 million visitors every year and, if you're not careful, you can spend more time queuing behind coaches full of foreigners than watching local wildlife.

> Where once there was an empty patch of ground now there is a campsite, where there was a campsite now there is a small hotel, and where there was a small hotel now there is a big one.

Below
Things that go slither and crawl in the night (from left to right): panther chameleon, Madagascar tree boa, rot-hole tree frog and leaf-tailed gecko.

Even Mount Everest is getting crowded. The weather dictates a very narrow window of opportunity, but it's still shocking to think that more than fifty people sometimes reach the top in a single day.

If current trends continue, it's only a matter of time before many of the world's nature hotspots are completely ruined – if they're not already.

So if I had a time-machine and could live on earth during any period in the last four billion years or so, I probably wouldn't use it. Admittedly, I'd love to sit in a hide and watch *Archaeopteryx* fluttering about in ancient trees or go cage-diving with a 15-metre (50-foot) megalodon shark in prehistoric seas. But despite a few tourists sunbathing on what was once a wild and deserted beach, I'd rather hang about in the dawn of the 21st century.

After all, Nosy Mangabé is still bursting with wildlife.

We couldn't resist dumping our bags in the sand and exploring straight away. We'd barely stepped into the forest before finding a small troop of white-fronted brown lemurs, munching fruit in the treetops; they were so inquisitive it was hard to tell who was supposed to be watching whom. Then with the help of our guide, Paul, we poked around in the tangled undergrowth and found a panther chameleon, two beautifully camouflaged and perfectly motionless leaf-tailed geckos and a Madagascar tree boa a metre (three feet) long.

Suddenly, it was getting dark and as the sun disappeared below the horizon we heard an unearthly, raucous call straight out of *The Blair Witch Project*. We stopped and looked at one another.

'OUCH! Shit.' Slap.

'What now?'

'There was something climbing up my leg.'

'That is without a shadow of a doubt a herd of pigs being stabbed to death by an evil Malagasy ghost,' said a wide-eyed Stephen.

Paul laughed and motioned towards the other end of the island. 'Black and white ruffed lemurs,' he assured us, 'just settling down for the night.'

We had a bite to eat, deposited our bags into various tents dotted around the forest, took a swig out of Stephen's bottle of vodka (never far away when we were camping), grabbed some powerful torches and set off into the night.

Almost immediately, we found another chameleon: a pygmy chameleon. It wasn't quite what we had come to Nosy Mangabé to look for, but this is the *crème de la crème* of chameleons – the Holy Grail for chameleon-watchers.

'Can I hold it?' asked Stephen. That was usually his first question whenever we got close to any animal smaller than a Border collie. I never found out if the enquiry was a veiled 'will I hurt it if I hold it?' or 'will it hurt me if I hold it?'.

In this case, I'm sure, it was the former. The pygmy chameleon is one of the smallest chameleons in the world. Small but perfectly formed. 'Good grief!' Stephen enthused, as it climbed onto the tip of his forefinger, 'it's hardly there it's so small.' It was as well made as a proper-sized chameleon, with fused toes, pinhole eyelids, individually rotating eyes and a long curly tail, but was less than half the length of Stephen's finger.

He gently put it back among the leaf litter.

Stephen may be brilliant at many things, but he's not especially good at keeping quiet. In thick rainforest he tends to stagger and stumble instead of walk, neatly placing his full two-metre (six-foot five-inch) frame onto every snappable twig, and not surprisingly he's rarely short of a few things to say.

'Okay, Stephen, we need to be as quiet as possible now,' I whispered.

'Okay,' came the slightly miffed reply.

'That means no talking.'

'Okay.'

'Not even whispering.'

Silence.

We walked deeper into the dark forest.

'AAAGH! WHAT THE BLOODY HELL WAS THAT?' shouted Stephen.

'What?'

'Something brushed against my arm.'

'It was probably just a moth. Sshhh.'

'Okay.'

Stagger, stumble, crack. Mutter, groan.

'Sshhh.'

'Sorry. Sorry. God, this is a nightmare,' said Stephen, exasperated.

'It's impossible to walk quietly through thick jungle. How the hell are we supposed to… OUCH! Shit.' Slap.

'What now?'

'There was something climbing up my leg.'

And so it went on.

We lurched and hacked our way through the jungle, and the dark, shining our torches up into the treetops in the vague hope of seeing a pair of tell-tale eyes staring back, but saw absolutely nothing. To be fair to Stephen, while aye-ayes normally stay well and truly hidden and are notoriously difficult to find, they can also be remarkably bold and fearless and aren't likely to be all that bothered by a bit of stumbling and slapping. There are even stories of them walking right up to flabbergasted naturalists and sniffing their boots, or strolling nonchalantly through village streets.

We thought we heard something aye-aye-like at one point (a sort of *cree-cree-cree* sound and some rustling in the upper canopy), but we couldn't actually catch sight of anything we could even pretend was an aye-aye. After a few hours we gave up and headed back to camp.

There was a hedgehog tenrec snuffling about in the grass right outside my tent. Not a hedgehog, but a hedgehog tenrec. This is another Malagasy speciality, which looks spookily like its namesake. Its ancestors were probably the first mammals to arrive in Madagascar, millions of years ago.

Stephen crept up behind me and I told him what it was. He didn't believe a word of it.

'No it's not – it's a hedgehog,' he said with the authority of a man who's spent a bit of time in the jungle. 'Even I know that.'

'Honestly, it's a tenrec – it nicked the idea, complete with stiff spines, from true hedgehogs on the mainland.'

'Why?'

'Well, it's probably filling a very similar niche. It's a great example of convergent evolution.'

'How long did it take scientists to come up with its name?' asked Stephen.

'What do you mean?'

'Well, why isn't it called a "fiverec" or a "sevenrec"? How many potential names did they try before they hit upon the perfect "tenrec" do you think?'

We dumped the torches, grabbed the vodka and headed down to the beach to lie on the sand and stare at the breathtakingly clear night sky.

Time to contemplate.

Madagascar had once been a human-free refuge for lemurs and a hotchpotch of other weird and wonderful wildlife off the coast of mainland Africa, and

We lurched and hacked our way through the jungle, and the dark, shining our torches up into the treetops in the vague hope of seeing a pair of tell-tale eyes staring back, but saw absolutely nothing.

now Nosy Mangabé is a (relatively) human-free refuge off the coast of mainland Madagascar. The main difference is simply that the refuges are getting smaller and smaller. It's the same in so many parts of the world.

I said something along these lines to Stephen, who was lying on the sand a few metres away, but he didn't answer. So I lay back and listened to the sounds of the Nosy Mangabé night: white-fronted brown lemurs squabbling in their nocturnal roost, owls calling to one another somewhere in the distant forest across the bay, a motley collection of indistinguishable frogs and insects, and a British actor and comedian lightly snoring.

When Madagascar decided to slip away from the ancient mega-continent of Gondwana some 160 million years ago, it unwittingly made a good tactical move. (It was still attached to India at the time, but that was a temporary hindrance – the two countries separated about eighty million years later.) The new island, roughly the size of France and escorted by a flotilla of isles and islets, travelled several hundred kilometres east before settling off the coast of Southern Africa. There, while the rest of the world grappled with the emergence of *Homo sapiens*, it was able to develop completely unscathed. And while all the less fortunate creatures left behind on the African mainland ultimately faced a barrage of competition from the likes of monkeys, lions and woodpeckers, the inhabitants of Madagascar had the fourth largest island all to themselves.

Some plants and animals happened to be in the right place at the right time when Madagascar made its escape, and by sheer chance they got away too. In the years since, others have made their own way across the Mozambique Channel, though scientists are still bickering about exactly how they did it. Was there an ancient land bridge that has long since disappeared? Has the sea level changed? Or did they raft across on clumps of floating vegetation that had been washed out to sea from large rivers on the mainland? It sounds like an unlikely film plot, but the general consensus seems to be that the floating vegetation theory is most probably true. It's known in the scientific world as 'sweepstake dispersal'.

Evolution couldn't have been happier as it set to work on this life raft from a different time. It produced a highly imaginative collection of strange and exotic plants and animals to fill the mini-continent's rich ecological niches and in no evolutionary time at all successfully produced one of the most unusual and varied assemblages of wildlife anywhere on earth.

This is what makes Madagascar so thrilling and stimulating (and important) from a wildlife point of view: virtually everything that lives there doesn't exist

anywhere else. In fact, more than eight out of every ten species inhabiting the 1,600-kilometre (1,000-mile) long island is absolutely unique.

The African mainland is so close – and yet so far away in evolutionary terms. There are no elephants, no rhinos, no giraffes, no antelopes, no lions or leopards, and no hyenas. And no lots of other things. Madagascar's wildlife is remarkable for its uniqueness (or endemism, to use the proper term) rather than its diversity.

If Charles Darwin had stopped off in Madagascar, instead of the Galápagos Islands, he would almost certainly have reached exactly the same conclusions about evolution and the progression of life.

Visiting this chip off the old Gondwana block is rather like landing on another planet. The plants and animals are vaguely familiar – they resemble monkeys, hedgehogs and civets, for example – yet they are actually lemurs, tenrecs and fanalokas. What's happened is that in Madagascar evolution has come up with different solutions to the same problems elsewhere in the world.

The complete absence of people was, of course, a huge advantage. Madagascar had already disappeared over the horizon by the time we started causing havoc almost everywhere else in the world. But the good times came to an abrupt end when people showed up from distant nations skirting the Indian Ocean.

Unfortunately, though not surprisingly, these people decided to stay.

They found a wildlife wonderland almost entirely covered in forest. There were gigantic, ostrich-like elephant birds that laid eggs big enough to have fed everyone in a Malagasy village with a double omelette each. They discovered false aardvarks, dwarf hippos and giant lemurs nearly as big as themselves, and a host of other wildlife startlingly different from most of the creatures they had ever encountered before.

The outcome of this human invasion was perhaps a foregone conclusion. The elephant birds, false aardvarks, dwarf hippos, giant lemurs and many other Malagasy specialities became extinct. Nowadays, they live on only in scientists' notebooks, museums and Malagasy legend.

Madagascar is still stuffed full of wildlife goodies, but what's left is disappearing fast. And the situation is getting worse. In the two decades since Douglas and I arrived to look for aye-ayes, the country's human population has doubled from roughly ten million to more than twenty million – and that means yet more pressure on the country's natural resources.

Worst of all, the forest that once clothed Madagascar like a protective coat is disappearing astonishingly fast, being chopped and burned down to provide more elbow room for agriculture. I remember flying down the east coast with Douglas over an almost continuous swathe of rainforest that stretched as far as the eye could see. Sitting next to Stephen little more than twenty years later, staring out of the window at the same stretch of coast, I could barely believe how little of it was left. Just a few isolated pockets of forest had survived intact.

It's not hard to see why Madagascar is now one of the highest conservation priorities on earth.

Stephen bounded triumphantly into breakfast, looking better than he had done for days.

'I did such a deliciously professional, firm poo this morning,' he announced to the world in his finest Blackadder voice, 'I nearly called you to come and have a look!'

I was exceedingly jealous.

We'd all had upset stomachs since arriving in Berenty, a three-hour pothole slalom from Fort Dauphin at the extreme southern tip of Madagascar. The cameraman, Sam, was feeling particularly shoddy and was still struggling to divide his time more or less equally between the loo and his camera.

But Stephen was suddenly back on top form and thoroughly enjoying a return to life in the fast lane. Best of all, he was being text-bombed by the rich and famous with the good news that, while we had been fighting over our limited supply of toilet paper, Barack Obama had won the US Presidential election.

We finished our banana-and-coffee breakfast, gathered our kit and set off to meet researcher Josia Razafindramanana.

Opposite
This red-fronted brown lemur had never seen so many mobile phones.

I felt sorry for her immediately. I have to spell my name to strangers at least three times a day, which I estimate takes about a minute or so. Over the course of a year that's 365 minutes, or six hours. So far, in fifty years, I've lost about 37 working days as a result. Josia Razafindramanana has lost many more, I imagined sympathetically, and she's considerably younger than me. Normal people don't take this kind of thing into account.

Out of interest, her name means 'granddaughter of somebody rich'. Mine basically means 'once lived in Cheshire'.

Josia was forever on the verge of giggling. With the look of a naughty child at the back of the class, trying not to laugh, she was one of those happy, smiley people who raise the spirits of everyone around them. From the moment she clapped eyes on us until the day we said goodbye, she was either giggling or stifling a giggle. I liked her immensely. She positively burst out laughing when we started bickering about who had taken the last Imodium out of the BBC Medical Pack, and was in stitches when we complained about the heat.

'You're never going to survive midday!' she howled, wiping the tears from her eyes. 'It'll be more than 40°C.'

Berenty is one of Madagascar's most-visited reserves. It's a slightly surreal place, with bright-red sandy roads, white picket fences and the kind of chalets you'd expect to find on Chesil Beach. Located on a bank of the Mandrare River, it is home to natural gallery forest and spiny forest and yet plonked in the middle of a gargantuan sisal plantation.

Whether you like watching wildlife around white picket fences or not, it's one of the best places in Madagascar for guaranteed lemur sightings.

When Douglas Adams and I were there, in 1985, scientists had identified and named a grand total of 21 species of lemur living in Madagascar. It was around that time that interest in Malagasy wildlife really blossomed and, since then, a great many new species have been discovered. The list has more than quadrupled in the years since, with an impressive 88 species known to date, and I'm sure there are more yet to be found.

We had come to Berenty to see three of them, and first on our 'wish list' was Verreaux's sifaka.

Goodness knows how you're supposed to pronounce that. It's yet more evidence that zoologists really do get drunk before they name new species. Why not call it the black-faced dark-capped silky-furred yellow-eyed lemur, or at least something a little more descriptive and easier to enunciate?

To be fair, based on my limited experience, no one in Madagascar can agree on how most words should be pronounced. They all seem to have several 'correct' pronunciations, depending on whom you happen to ask. One problem is the confusion between French, the official language, and English. Take the word 'Malagasy', for example. In French, it is pronounced 'Mal-gash'; but in English, it's pronounced 'Mal-er-gassy'. That doesn't really explain the problem with most animal names, though, which tend to cause the most bewilderment.

So how about Verreaux's sifaka? As far as I can tell, the correct way to say it is 'Verreaux' as in 'plateaux'. However, if you believe one of the guides I asked in Berenty, it's actually 'very-ers shi-fukka'. The Americans say it is 'ver-oxy shee-fuk'. And, according to the pilot who flew us from Antananarivo to Fort Dauphin, it should be 'ver-ows sif-arka'.

Anyway, the black-faced dark-capped silky-furred yellow-eyed lemur, or VS for short, is famous for dancing.

We'd been waiting on the edge of the forest, with the temperature rising and our shirts drowning in sweat, for at least a couple of hours. We were hoping to catch a glimpse of a VS leaving the safety of the trees and dancing across the open patch of land in front of us to the forest on the other side.

But Stephen was huffing and puffing. He looked hot and uncomfortable, and

was getting bored. It was understandable, really. As far as he knew, we were waiting for a fairly unremarkable-looking lemur to dash across the clearing and disappear among the trees. He'd rather have had a more leisurely breakfast followed by a gentle morning planning his escape from hot and dusty Berenty, which he didn't particularly like.

I decided to demonstrate the spectacle we were hoping to see. I balanced on tiptoe and hopped sideways across the open patch of red sand, like a ballet dancer doing a *grande jété*. Holding my arms high above my head for balance, I twisted 180 degrees in midair ready for another bout of sideways hopping towards the forest, but fell heavily onto an exposed tree root with an 'oomph!' and a lot of pain. Several weeks later, my rib was still so painful I wanted to cling to the ceiling every time I sneezed.

Stephen wasn't all that impressed. But as I dusted myself off, Josia called in a stage whisper from the edge of the forest.

'They're coming!'

She had been watching a small troop of seven sifakas, taking a long time to prepare themselves for their regular morning dash across the sandy plain, and one was about to go.

It was all over in less than a minute. The sifaka dropped to the ground, looked at us, hesitated for a moment, then stood up on its hind legs, locked its ankles together, thrust its stomach out, lifted its arms and tail into the air and skipped and hopped its way across to the other side. It looked like a competitor in a sack race. Even Stephen agreed that it had been worth the wait.

'That's the most preposterous way of getting around I've ever seen in my life,' he laughed.

As soon as the sifakas had disappeared we were joined by a troop of ring-tailed lemurs.

With their distinctive black-and-white coats, soft-toy cuddliness and air of swaggering arrogance, ring-tailed lemurs were hard to miss around Berenty. This particular troop was sixteen-strong and included several babies, which were riding on their mothers' backs like wide-eyed miniature jockeys. 'Cute' wasn't the word; in fact no word has been invented to describe cuteness on such a grandiose scale. I'm already sounding a bit soppy and sentimental, so just look at the picture (page 119) and you'll see what I mean.

The highlight of the morning was a stink-fight between two males. I used to have stink-fights with my brother Adam, when we were kids and shared a bedroom together, but male ring-tailed lemurs do it professionally. It's a way of establishing rank. Our two males ran their bushy tails over hidden scent glands on their wrists, to make them as smelly as possible, and then waved them about in one another's faces. Eventually, one of them (presumably the least smelly) backed off, but by then we were all in heaps of laughter. Zoologists aren't supposed to giggle at their subjects (we're supposed to retain an air of detached scientific professionalism), but it was ridiculously funny.

Josia eventually dragged us away to help with her research on brown lemurs. We just had enough time before moving on.

There were about fifty troops of brown lemurs in Berenty and each troop had to be marked with a harmless coloured dye as part of an ongoing study into their population dynamics. I was issued with a bunch of bananas while Stephen was armed with a syringe. The plan was for me to tempt them in close enough for him to fire the dye. I'm sorry to report that he was pretty hopeless, despite recently being trained to shoot a .44 Magnum for *Stephen Fry in America*. The lemurs continued to eat their bananas, innocently oblivious to the clouds of purple dye being squirted to their left, to their right, over their heads and in front of their feet. We were crouching on the ground, almost within touching distance of the targets, so it didn't exactly require shooting to Olympic standard.

The more he missed, the more the rest of us struggled to keep straight faces and the more tense and nervous poor Stephen became. Eventually, two little spots of dye hit the back of one of the females, then a single spot hit the tail of another. Before you could say '*Dirty Harry*' (repeatedly, for 45 minutes), Stephen had marked a grand total of three brown lemurs.

'That'll do,' said Josia, slightly exasperated. 'We only need to mark a few from each troop.'

'Great!' said Stephen enthusiastically, suddenly proud of progress so far. 'I've got the hang of it now. Let's go and find another troop.'

There was a long pause as Josia caught the eye of one of her research students.

'Erm, it's okay thanks,' she said. 'We'll take over from here.'

Superstition is central to life in Madagascar. I'm not talking about walking around ladders instead of underneath them, tossing spilt salt over your left shoulder or avoiding the number thirteen. The Malagasy version is a more specialist form of superstition that is so complex and all-encompassing it has an enormous impact on the way many people live their lives.

It begins with a great belief in the power of dead ancestors. This isn't so much a morbid obsession with death – it's more a rather convoluted celebration of life. Dead people are considered to be potent forces that continue to look after their descendants and share in everyday family affairs. Their wishes dictate the behav-

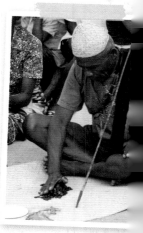

Above
Failing to hit brown lemurs with purple dye from point-blank range.

Opposite
Forget walking around ladders or tossing spilt salt over your left shoulder – superstition in Madagascar is nothing short of professional.

iour of living family members and any calamities in the household are usually blamed on their anger.

Central to these beliefs is a complicated network of taboos, called 'fady'.

In Madagascar, things you would hardly even notice elsewhere in the world are supposed to bring bad luck. And an inordinate number of routine day-to-day tasks are frowned upon, or downright forbidden. There are few places in the world where it is possible to offend so many people so easily without even realising you're doing it.

There are so many potential *faux pas*. For instance, you mustn't sing while you are eating (admittedly, not a major problem for most of us) or you will grow long teeth; you must never hand an egg directly to another person (it must be placed on the ground first); you mustn't hold a funeral on a Tuesday or there will be another death in the village; and you must always use a spade with a loose handle to dig a grave (to keep a loose connection between the living and the dead). These fady (the plural is the same as the singular) vary from place to place, family to family and even from person to person, making them even more indecipherable for bumbling, uninformed westerners.

Fady has a big impact on wildlife and conservation, too. Sometimes it is beneficial (killing certain animals or chopping down sacred trees is prohibited) but more often it is detrimental.

Perhaps not surprisingly, the aye-aye is central to many superstitious beliefs. In a few areas it is thought to embody ancestral spirits and bring good luck, but for the most part it is considered at best a harbinger of evil and at worst an omen of death.

Its otherworldly appearance probably doesn't help. Nor can its rather alarming repertoire of weird and wonderful calls: grunts, screams and whimpers, as well as eerie sounds that can only be described as 'fuffs' and 'hai-hais' (it's one of those animals that helpfully calls out its own name, like a cuckoo or a curlew, but not like a pygmy puff-back flycatcher).

Some people believe that if an aye-aye points its middle finger at you, or strolls through your village, you or someone close to you is going to die. Others go so far as to claim that aye-ayes sneak into houses through their thatched roofs and murder the sleeping occupants, using those long middle fingers to puncture their victims' hearts. A few people in the far north actually believe that aye-ayes eat people.

This may seem a little absurd – laughable even – in the comfort and safety of the western world. But it's serious stuff in Madagascar. There have even been cases of entire villages being burnt down, and rebuilt, after an aye-aye has dared to set foot somewhere inside.

Fady aren't good from an aye-aye's point of view either, because the only way to prevent bad luck prevailing is to kill the offending aye-aye. Incidents of such killings are reported every year.

Then there is the problem of disposing of the body. In some villages, if someone finds and kills an aye-aye near his house, he thoughtfully removes the bad luck from his own family by putting the corpse in his neighbour's back garden. Then the neighbour does the same thing, to try and avoid something awful happening to his family, until the carcass ends up on the village outskirts. But it's still too close for comfort, so someone hangs the dead animal (or just its head or tail) from a pole, in the hope that passing travellers will carry the evil and ill-fortune away with them.

Such is the ingrained fear of this harmless nocturnal lemur that 'aye-aye' was once reputed to be the cry of alarm uttered if the Malagasy saw one of these enigmatic animals.

Sadly, these days, hardly anyone ever does.

We were so tired by the time we'd flown to Morondava and driven most of the way to Kirindy Forest, near the west coast, that we had resorted to negotiating with our hapless driver over how much longer we had to go.

'How long do you reckon before we get there?' asked Stephen.

'Oh, about an hour.'

'Do you mean exactly an hour or a little under an hour?' I asked.

'Um, probably a little under I would guess.'

'So that means 45 minutes or actually nearer to half an hour then,' cajoled Stephen.

'In fact, if we keep up this speed and don't make any more stops it'll be more like 15 minutes,' I confirmed.

'Less than 15 minutes. Great. We're nearly there then.' Stephen's voice had a sense of finality to it and drew a firm line under the negotiations. We'd be there in ten minutes, which made us both much happier. The driver just sighed.

I think it was Indiana Jones, when someone accused him of getting old and struggling to keep up, who observed that 'it's not the years – it's the mileage.' Exactly. It's the relentless packing and unpacking, the driving and flying, waking up to a different ceiling every morning and adapting to different food and ways of life that really takes it out of you.

On this particular morning, I'm pretty sure Stephen was feeling the same weary way.

We were sitting in silence (unusual for us) in the back of a Land Rover, watching

Their pot bellies are adorned with sparse and ridiculously stubby and twisty branches, making them look as if they are having a particularly bad hair day.

the world go by. Another early start, another airport, another flight, another back-breaking drive on so-called roads that wouldn't even pass for roads in other parts of the world, and yet another bloody adventure.

Sometimes, just sometimes, it would be nice to have nowhere to go and nothing to do.

We made a brief stop at Baobab Alley, two parallel lines of baobab trees that neatly lived up to their name. We bought a couple of Cokes from a man with an unlikely bright orange fridge fired by kerosene (bear in mind that this was in the middle of nowhere), and wandered in admiration among the trees.

There is an old saying that one day God gave each animal a tree to plant and the hyena accidentally planted his, the baobab, upside down. That's exactly what these Grandidier's baobabs, to give them their full and proper name, looked like. They are quite unlike trees in lesser parts of the world. For a start, they have massively swollen trunks that act like huge sponges and store vast amounts of water, and give them the shape of giant Chianti bottles. Then their pot bellies are adorned with sparse and ridiculously stubby and twisty branches, making them look as if they are having a particularly bad hair day. And to complete the look their freaky, flaky bark has a distinctive reddish hue.

Baobabs are emblematic of Madagascar and are often protected by fady (and because the wood is neither strong enough for building nor particularly good for burning). Most of the surrounding forest had been cleared, but these few baobabs in Baobab Alley survived. With luck, they will live for hundreds or even thousands of years.

By the time we arrived at Kirindy itself, it was well and truly dark. There were a few wooden huts in a clearing in the forest and some tents in amongst the trees, but no sign of a toilet.

'The forest is our toilet', pronounced Stephen in the manner of Ray Mears. 'But I'd hold it in as long as you can, if I were you.'

'You seem surprisingly happy,' I said. It was a relief. Stephen and tents are rarely a happy mix.

'There's only one word that would make me really happy,' he replied. 'And that's "broadband". I suppose a century ago it would have been "pigeon loft". But sadly we have neither here. Just forest. And tents.'

In fact, Kirindy was probably the part of the trip we'd been looking forward to the most. An area of dry deciduous forest, it is not as rich as the eastern rainforest but is home to more endemic and endangered species than anywhere else we'd been so far. And they are all animals with remarkably exotic-sounding names: hog-nosed snakes, narrow-striped mongooses, pale fork-marked lemurs and straw-coloured fruit bats among them.

Our first quest was the giant jumping rat – the kind of animal that would require a wild imagination, a completely free rein and a bottle of vodka if you were designing it from scratch. We barely had time for a swig of vodka (or several swigs in Stephen's case, as the reality of yet more camping suddenly dawned) before jumping back into the car and heading off into the darkness. Like aye-ayes, giant jumping rats only come out at night.

'What the hell am I doing?' asked Stephen of the world at large. 'I could be sipping a glass of chilled Cloudy Bay Sauvignon Blanc and eating *moules marinières* at a candlelit table in my favourite restaurant in London, before an entertaining and relaxing evening at the theatre and a good night's sleep in my own exceedingly comfortable bed. But, instead, I am excruciatingly hot and covered in dust, I've been travelling all day, I haven't eaten for as long as I can remember, and now I'm racing along a dirt track in the dark with a bunch of people talking about transects and vositses, to look for a dim-witted giant rat that jumps. Good grief. What was I thinking? And what is a vositse, anyway?'

'That's the Malagasy word for "giant jumping rat",' I answered, trying not to provoke a debate about the expediency of our little adventure. 'And, besides, how do you know that it's dim-witted?'

'Um, because I read about it on the internet last night' came the slightly embarrassed reply.

'But you're not supposed to be reading up about anything. That's the whole point – it's all meant to be surprising and fresh so you learn about it as we go. It's supposed to be a journey of discovery.'

'Well, I was interested.'

'Mmmm.'

'Sorry. I won't do it again.'

'That's what you said in the Amazon. And Uganda.'

'Ah well, I didn't read all that much.'

'Ha. Okay. What's the scientific name of the giant jumping rat, then?'

'Well, actually, I do know that. It's *Hypogeomys antimena*.'

'There we are, you see. Typical. Go on, what does it look like?'

'Um, let me think. It's browny-grey, roughly the size of a small cat and looks a bit like a rabbit with a horse's head. Oh, and it has a very chunky, bare tail. And big feet and huge ears.'

'Oh God. You have been swotting, haven't you? Right, here's another one. Where does it live?'

'Ah, I know that. It lives only in a tiny patch of dry deciduous forest in and around Kirindy Forest, which is where we are now, and nowhere else in the world. And there are only about 30,000 of them left.'

He hesitated for a moment.

'Or did you mean where does it live *within the forest*? In which case, the answer is that it lives in a complex network of underground tunnels, with as many as six entrance holes, a bit like a badger sett. *'And'* (he emphasised the word to irritate, aggravate and exasperate as much as possible) 'it plugs the entrances with a barrier of soil to keep out Madagascar ground boas and other predators. Am I right?'

'Yes.'

'Sorry.'

We lapsed into a sulky silence.

It was all a bit embarrassing because we'd been joined by an old friend of mine, British ornithologist and conservationist Richard Lewis, who didn't know what to think, where to look or what to say. I hadn't seen Richard for years, and this was the first time he'd met Stephen – and all he'd seen so far was an argument.

I explained that we were tired, and it was the mileage, and that he shouldn't worry.

Richard and I first met in 1989, when I'd visited Mauritius with Douglas Adams to search for the endangered Mauritius kestrel. (Actually, we'd gone to look for the slightly less endangered Rodrigues fruit bat, which of course is a mammal, but with a 'why are you going off to the stupid island of Rodrigues to look for some ridiculous fruit bat?' Richard persuaded us to stay on Mauritius and spend quality time with his beloved birds.) Richard is well known in the conservation

Opposite
Stephen 'can I hold it?'
Fry with his next victim.

The giant jumping rat stared back in disbelief, peering through a jungle of stiff white whiskers like someone sneaking a look through a net curtain.

world for bringing birds back from the brink of extinction, and for reckless driving. In the twenty years since our first meeting, he had married a Malagasy woman, had two children, saved a few more endangered birds, settled in Antananarivo, and learnt how to drive a little more slowly.

We stopped the car and followed him, with a small team of local researchers, deep into the forest. We picked and clambered our way to a little opening between the trees and stood in front of a big hole. Immediately outside the hole was a metal box, containing a rustling sound. And sure enough, inside the box was a giant jumping rat. One of the researchers pulled it out, carefully.

'Can I hold it?' asked Stephen.

He could, and did, and held it up for all to see. The giant jumping rat stared back in disbelief, peering through a jungle of stiff white whiskers like someone sneaking a look through a net curtain. I begrudgingly confirmed, at Stephen's insistence, that it looked exactly as he had described, watched in admiration as the rat tried to bite his thumb, and then stood back to let the researchers take a few measurements before letting it go.

The next morning we were up and about earlier than expected. The Malagasy have no respect for lie-ins – and for that I blame the wildlife as much as the people. Dawn was still two hours away when the drivers decided to have a

car door-slamming competition, then an engine-revving contest, and finally a hearty singsong right in the middle of camp. There were birds calling noisily, never-to-be-identified mammals snuffling and shuffling in the undergrowth around my tent and a never-ending cacophony of insects humming, drumming and thrumming.

I gave up, and got up, when I heard people running around shouting 'fossa! fossa! fossa!'. That was one sound I did want to hear. The fossa is the largest carnivore in Madagascar and it's an animal I hadn't really expected to encounter during our trip. Looking like a cross between a puma and a mongoose (actually, it's more like an Egyptian carving of a sacred cat), there's nothing else quite like it. Since it's not particularly common, comes out mostly at night and generally likes to keep itself to itself, it is a hard animal to see. Like almost everything else we had come across so far, it is endemic to Madagascar.

I struggled out of my tent and immediately clapped eyes on a flash of honey-coloured athletic-looking body with a small head and an inordinately long tail racing across camp. I sprinted across the clearing, almost bumping into Stephen coming the other way, and we caught up with the fossa on the edge of the forest on the far side. It stopped suddenly and we came to a skidding halt no more than 5 metres (16 feet) away. It gave us a disdainful sideways glance and, with no hint of concern, did a rather condescending sniff before trotting off among the trees, silent as a light breeze.

In fact, we saw as much wildlife around our camp in Kirindy as you're likely to see in an entire national park.

That night we heard the most extraordinary shrieking and screaming noise coming from high up in the forest canopy. We left our tents and tiptoed through the darkness, expecting to find a young researcher being ripped to shreds by a yet-to-be-described species of giant carnivorous lemur.

'I can see something,' whispered Stephen, slightly alarmed.

'Where?'

'Over there next to that big tree. Oh my God, it moved. It's huge. It's about the size of a bear.'

We crept forwards.

'Ssshh!' said the thing about the size of a bear. It was a primate – a young re-searcher, sitting on a deckchair and pouring hot coffee from a flask.

'Ssshh!' she said again.

'Sorry.'

She gave us the same sideways glance as the fossa had done earlier in the day. Then she shone a torch up into the treetop and peered through a pair of binoculars.

We both looked up.

There was the very same fossa (I recognised a distinctive cut across its nose) with another fossa, twisted together on a thick branch. They looked too big to be so high above the ground. And they were quite clearly mating. Very noisily.

'How long have you been watching them?' I whispered to the researcher.

'Hours,' she answered, monosyllabically.

'Hours?' asked Stephen.

'From dusk until dawn. I watch them all night.' She sounded cross. Actually, since it was too dark to see her face (I wouldn't recognise her in a police line-up) it was impossible to tell if she really was cross, or simply busy, or just shy.

'Really? All night?' I asked.

'All night, every night.'

'How long have you been doing that?' asked Stephen.

'Sssssshhhhh!' she said.

She was definitely cross.

We took another peek into the canopy, feeling guilty in case merely looking at the fossas might make her even more cross, said a few whispered goodbyes and carefully picked our way back to camp.

We couldn't have stayed too long, anyway, because we had an appointment with two rather more friendly primates: a Madame Berthe's mouse lemur and a Madame Berthe's mouse lemur researcher, called Melanie ('not Mel').

Found only in Kirindy Forest, and nowhere else on earth, this record-breaking lemur is the smallest of all the world's primates. It was named after a famous Malagasy primatologist (famous in the world of primatology, at least) after being discovered for the first time just a few years ago.

Melanie had caught one as part of her study, to take essential measurements, and had kindly invited us to help release it back into the forest.

We peered into its little box. Two inoffensive brown eyes peered innocently back. The mouse lemur lived up to its name – it was so small it could have sat comfortably inside an egg cup. In fact, it could have perched on my finger. Its head was more orange than brown and it had white streaks down its nose, like face-paint left over from a children's party. And its little ears twitched as Stephen ooh-ed and aah-ed with every little movement. I've never heard the big man ooh and aah so much over anything, before or since.

Melanie gently rested the box on a branch and the rare Madame Berthe's mouse lemur slowly and cautiously inched its way towards the exit, and freedom. After what seemed like an eternity, since we were involuntarily holding our breath, it plucked up the courage to stand on the branch and look at us with those adorable hypnotic eyes. What it lacked in size it made up for with animal charisma.

'Ooh!' said Stephen.

Suddenly, the diminutive lemur made a dash for it. It ran up the branch, pausing briefly to look at us one more time, before leaping a good 2 metres (6½ feet) to another branch and disappearing into the darkness.

'Aah!' said Stephen.

The world's smallest primate had captured the heart of one of the world's biggest. I think if we'd seen a baby Madame Berthe's mouse lemur (which is reputed to be an energetic little furball, climbing and jumping all over the place and swinging, Tarzan-like, from its mother's tail) Stephen would have exploded with excitement.

That night I lay awake in my tent, imagining our mouse lemur skipping and jumping around the twigs and branches of its forest home. I pictured it lying in wait for passing moths (it catches moths – even ones bigger than itself – by leaping into the darkness and seizing them in its mouth in midair), and fell asleep hoping it would be safe.

I've added it to my imaginary list of truly special animals that give me a huge amount of pleasure just knowing they're out there. Now that I am back in England, watching the rain on a grey Monday morning, all I have to do is to cast my mind back to that Lilliputian lemur ... and I will survive until Tuesday.

It was a four-hour drive from Antananarivo to Analamazaotra, or Perinet as it's more commonly called. But in those four hours we had more near misses than a lifetime of drunken air traffic controlling.

The general rule of thumb when driving in Madagascar is that if you don't clip someone or something with your wing mirror, as you pass each other in the street, you're not driving close enough. The Malagasy would think nothing of squeezing three or four lanes into a typical one-way street in Britain.

It's remarkable how quickly we got used to it.

Driving anywhere outside the highly regulated, nanny-stated western world gives you a false sense of security. I wouldn't dream of speeding in Britain with bald tyres and intermittent brakes and without wearing a seat belt. But somehow it seems less dangerous when you're thousands of kilometres from home.

'It's just the way we do it here in Madagascar' was a common explanation.

But overtaking on blind bends, with steep drops on either side, in torrential rain with fork lightning, in a vehicle that swerves towards the oncoming traffic without any help from the driver is just as dangerous in Madagascar as it is anywhere else in the world. Of course it is.

The world's smallest primate had captured the heart of one of the world's biggest.

So it was a truly horrible car journey to Perinet. Thrown around like a couple of test dummies in a Maserati crash laboratory, on the fastest road in the country, both Stephen and I felt car-sick most of the way.

We started talking about death.

'It's a mystery we're not dead already,' observed Stephen.

'I can think of better ways to go,' I replied.

'How about being eaten by a lion?' he asked. 'Do you think if I got eaten by a lion people would laugh? They'd be sad, of course. At least, I hope they'd be sad. But not in the same way as if I'd been killed on a winding mountain road in Madagascar. No one would be able to keep a straight face.'

'Yeah, you're right. Just imagine Ian Hislop and Paul Merton sniggering on *Have I Got News For You*.'

'I know, I know. Every time anyone got eaten by a lion it'd be known as "doing a Stephen Fry".'

'At least people would take notice.'

'What do you mean?' asked Stephen.

'Well, suppose we'd crashed when we were flying back to Tana through that awful thunderstorm the other day' (we'd been caught in a dreadful storm on the way back to Antananarivo – so bad that the Cessna flying with us, and carrying most of our kit, had to make an emergency landing en route). 'None of the rest of us would have got a look-in. The headlines would have read "Stephen Fry killed in fatal plane crash".'

'Maybe we should fly in separate planes, then?' he suggested helpfully.

'Well, that wouldn't help. If our plane crashed and yours didn't the headlines would simply read "Stephen Fry narrowly escapes fatal plane crash".'

'You're right, I suppose. It's one of the big advantages of fame – more people tend to hear about it when you die.'

We stopped talking about dying and tried to focus on living, pretending not to notice the driver as he screamed 'Whoaa!' and laughed hysterically every time we had yet another near miss.

Against all the odds, we made it to Perinet in record time.

We screeched to a halt and the driver's mobile phone rang. Hallelujah! There was reception. After hours of fidgety signal-less torture all the way from Antananarivo, Stephen leapt into action, pulling a selection of mobiles from his various pockets faster than Clint Eastwood could draw a Smith & Wesson. Using both hands and all fingers to text and email simultaneously from them all, he set to work. He was never happier than being in one part of the world while maintaining direct contact with as many people as possible in other parts of the world.

Things just got better and better. Not only was there mobile phone reception, but we were staying in a positively comfortable lodge. Stephen was ecstatic. So was I, to be honest. I'm all for camping and adventure, or even sleeping rough, if that's the only way to see a rare lesser-spotted, ruby-throated, bow-legged something-or-other. But if there's an option to stay in a comfortable lodge instead, and still see the animal in question, I'll go for the lodge every time.

That night we ate a longed-for simple dinner of spaghetti bolognese next to an enormous window overlooking the jungly Andasibe-Mantadia National Park, did our best to drink Madagascar dry of all its best French wine, and stumbled through the dark to our various chalets. We were dead tired. We'd been on the road for more than a month and desperately needed a few nights' good sleep in comfy rooms with cosy beds.

No sooner had I fallen into a deep slumber, or so it seemed, than something on the end of my bed started howling and screeching so loudly I almost leapt out of the window in a half-conscious heart-pumping panic. It sounded like a cross between a police siren and an amateur opera singer. In fact for a moment, while fumbling for the light, I thought I must have been having a dream, in the sea, under water, listening to a yet-to-be-described species of whale with a preposterously loud voice.

As soon as I grasped that there was actually nothing sitting on the end of

the bed, I began to work out what might have woken me. It was a troop of teddy-bear-faced lemurs, called indris. They were yelling their 5am territorial calls from deep within the surrounding jungle. They were as loud as a fire alarm. (It later dawned on me that this was a daily event and, sure enough, comfy room and cosy bed notwithstanding, I was woken in a state of mild distress at five o'clock on the dot every single bloody morning.)

The eerie, wailing sound was definitely a song, rather than a call. While other lemurs mutter, grunt or swear, indris literally sing.

The mother and father sing in duet, with the youngsters joining in the first part of the chorus in a kind of family singsong. The songs spread from one family to another across the forest, until every group in the local vicinity has declared its location to the world at large.

The indri is the largest living lemur. I once heard it described as 'more like a gone-wrong giant panda than a lemur', which is a pretty good way of introducing this animal oddity. Predominantly black and white, it has silky fur, large greenish eyes, round fuzzy ears and long, immensely powerful legs designed to propel it as far as 10 metres (33 feet) from trunk to trunk. It's yet another endangered species to add to Madagascar's notoriously world-beating collection of animals and plants on the edge.

Indris were precisely what we'd come to Perinet to see. There were two habituated troops in this well-studied corner of the montane rainforest, so we got up in the dark and set off in search of one of them.

Clambering up and down the wet, spongy, steep forested slopes, struggling through a thick jungle of ferns on the forest floor and hauling our way past colossal bamboo stems and myriad trees, it was a pretty hard and dirty hike. We decided to head for a vantage point to look for the troop from up on high.

'Do we have to?' asked Stephen. 'I hate vantage points,' he muttered, plonking himself rather stubbornly onto a fallen tree. 'They inevitably involve a steep walk or a climb.'

'But that's the best way to find the indri,' I countered. 'And, besides, there is supposed to be mobile reception somewhere on the top of this ridge.'

That was, I admit, a bit of a lie. But it worked.

'All right,' he said more cheerily, leaping melodramatically from the log faster than you could say 'texting'. 'Let's go.'

We spotted the indri at roughly the same time as one of Stephen's mobiles spluttered into life. Inadvertently, I hadn't lied after all.

There were two adults, a young male and a four-month-old baby, gazing down at their human observers rather benevolently. The baby looked permanently wide-eyed and surprised, as if it were being mercilessly goosed by its older brother. It was leaping, or rather bouncing, from branch to branch like a rubber yo-yo, always returning to pause next to Mum and regain enough confidence and assurance to do it all over again.

Stephen had settled down on another wet and rotting log and, with a half-hearted eye on the baby indri, was tapping enthusiastically into his mobile phone.

'What on earth are you doing?' I asked, clambering back to where he was sitting.

'Just checking emails,' he said, cross that I should ask.

'But we're in the middle of the jungle, surrounded by endangered indris.'

'So?'

'So? So? What do you mean "So?" This is a once-in-a-lifetime opportunity. This is what we risked life and limb on that road from Antananarivo for.'

He ignored me. I didn't have the energy to argue and brushed past him to watch the indris myself. I distinctly heard Stephen mutter 'twat' under his breath. Ah well. Perhaps he had a point. I get so wrapped up in wildlife sometimes that I forget how insufferable I must be to someone who isn't quite so obsessed. To Stephen I must sometimes sound like a man with a side parting and adenoids. I think this time I might have dragged the poor guy away from his natural habitat for a little too long.

Suddenly, we both snapped to attention. Without warning, the indris had started calling from just 5 metres (16 feet) away. It was so loud and so unexpected that we both instinctively covered our ears, as if a car alarm had erupted into life as we were walking past.

We marvelled at the indris for half an hour or so, one of us more enthusiastically than the other, and then turned back towards the car and the lodge.

Stephen was uncharacteristically irritable. Even the forest insects were getting on his nerves.

'What's the point of wasps?' he asked grumpily. 'They're not like bees, are they? Bees are useful because they make honey, so I can respect them and like them,' he continued for the benefit of anyone who cared to listen. 'But wasps. Ugh. If they could at least make sandwich spread or something. And as for flies...'

The next day Stephen was unable to hike. He had a bad knee. He really did have a bad knee, to be fair, although it seemed to flair up as a Pavlovian reaction to the word 'hike'.

The rest of us decided to go anyway, to try and film the rarest lemur in the world – the greater bamboo lemur. With fewer than a hundred survivors left in the wild, this unassuming olive-brown lemur eats virtually nothing but giant bamboo. It's not merely endangered, it is critically endangered. Few people have ever seen one in the wild, but some researchers had offered to take us to see one of their study groups.

We drove to a research camp (just a few tents in the jungle) and then started a long and arduous hike, up and down the forested slopes, literally fighting our way through the tangled undergrowth, slipping and sliding in the mud and counting all the snakes and scorpions we stumbled past along the way. Stephen would have HATED it, in large capital letters.

The whole thing was a complete fiasco. We hiked for seven hours before catching a fleeting glimpse of a single greater bamboo lemur, about 10 metres (33 feet) away through thick foliage. The entire encounter lasted no more than one and a half seconds, during which time it was barely visible, before the rarest lemur in the world bounded off into the impenetrable jungle never to be seen again.

We returned to the lodge. Still filthy and soaked in sweat, with my hair standing on end and a leech ceremoniously clinging to my leg, I went off in search of Stephen. I found him by the pool, reclining in the sunshine and calmly sipping a gin and tonic. He listened sympathetically while I told him my story, gasped at the sight of my still-expanding leech and then told me about his visit to Lemur Island, a 50-metre (160-foot) stroll from the lodge. He'd seen diademed sifakas dancing on the path, fed black-and-white ruffed lemurs by hand, photographed a grey bamboo lemur leaping from tree to tree, and had brown lemurs climbing all over him. And he'd had an ice cream. He was very excited.

'I still don't understand why you have to go on a seven-hour hike not to see one kind of lemur when you can potter down the path by the pool and be surrounded by four other kinds of lemur before mid-morning coffee,' he commented. 'Why do you have to make it all so difficult and complicated?'

We'd gone all the way to Madagascar to see an aye-aye, and we did see one eventually.

We stayed at the promisingly named Aye-aye Hotel to maximise our chances. Within a stone's throw of Mananara airport (though calling the airstrip and ramshackle terminal building an 'airport' is rather like calling Godalming a bustling 'metropolis'), it was a pleasant place to stay. There were lemurs running around the garden, a couple of mangy dogs barking at the brightly coloured Madagascar day geckos on the veranda, and a shockingly large orb web spider hanging over my bed.

Basically a collection of large bamboo huts with holey palm-leaf roofs, the Aye-aye Hotel was run by a delightfully eccentric and overwhelmingly hospitable French lady who took an instant liking to our Director, Tim. She made a great performance of cutting his hair, even though he didn't really want it to be cut ('Oh my God! What on earth has happened?' was Stephen's reaction to seeing

Opposite
Stephen checking emails, ignoring the indris and muttering 'twat' under his breath all at the same time.

Tim shortly afterwards, thinking he'd had an accident). She even laughed at all Tim's jokes (something we hadn't considered trying ourselves).

We rescued Tim, drove a short distance to the river, picked up a boat and took an even shorter trip to the promisingly named Aye-aye Island. At last, the stars were aligned and the signs were good – if we were going to see aye-ayes at all before leaving Madagascar we agreed wholeheartedly that this was going to be the place.

'Of course we will see an aye-aye,' said our local guide Marie-Claire, shocked at our audacity in enquiring about the odds. 'I know exactly where they are. Follow me.'

'When did you last see one?' asked Stephen, suspiciously.

'Last night. And the night before that, and the night before that. I see them every night, except when it rains.'

She led us along a well-worn path to a cluster of coconut palms, and it started to rain. It was only a light drizzle, but it was enough to justify more than a slight sense of despondency.

'They're up there,' Marie-Claire said confidently, pointing into the crown of a tree about 20 metres (65 feet) above our heads.

'Really, can you see them?' I asked, peering through binoculars and feeling a

sudden sense of excitement.

'No, of course I can't! It's not dark yet. They're still asleep.' She didn't actually say 'I thought you were a zoologist' but I could tell by the way she looked at me exactly what she was thinking.

I caught Stephen's eye and he grinned.

Marie-Claire reminded me of Josia, who'd been our guide in Berenty – forever on the verge of giggling. She spent night after night in the gathering gloom on Aye-aye Island, answering a stream of inane questions and pointing into coconut palms – and clearly loved it. Her eyes positively lit up as she told us about the animals we were hoping to see.

We'd barely set up base camp beneath one particular coconut palm, surrounded by delicious-smelling ylang-ylang trees, when the world's largest nocturnal primate suddenly appeared from nowhere and started to groom immediately above our heads. It was hanging upside down by its feet. We watched closely as it scratched and cleaned, then used its long middle finger to rub its eyes, poke something out from one of its ears and, as if for a grand finale, carefully pick its nose.

Then there was another aye-aye, and the two animals started to groom each other. They weren't as large as I remembered. In fact, they were quite weedy at heart, with surprisingly small bodies bulked up with the help of an extraordinarily shaggy, unkempt grey-brown-black coat of coarse hair.

The last light of the day had long gone by the time the aye-ayes had finished their evening ablutions and were on the move, and we found it surprisingly hard to keep up with them. Bumbling around in the darkness with the fading lights of our torches (we'd forgotten to change the batteries since Nosy Mangabé), we were clambering and stumbling our way through the undergrowth of the forest floor while they ran along palm fronds and leapt from tree to tree with gay abandon.

Occasionally, they would stop and tap a coconut with one of those long middle fingers, before gnawing a hole about 3 centimetres (1 inch) in diameter to reach the flesh inside, showering us in gooey coconut milk in the process. At one point they spent a lot of time in a lychee tree, scooping out the pulp of the fruit and licking it off the ends of their fingers.

Once or twice we made too much noise, struggling to coordinate filming in the dark. Every time we disturbed them, albeit briefly, they'd make a loud sniffing sound, just like someone trying to stifle a gigantic sneeze, and move on in disgust.

We lost them, eventually, and despite Tim's protestations headed back to the hotel.

We were halfway through our year-long quest and the aye-aye had been our first real success – our first proper tick. We'd seen everything from pink river dolphins and emerald tree boas to mountain gorillas and tree-climbing lions, but we'd emphatically failed to see the primary animals on our endangered species list. We didn't see Amazonian manatees in the wild on our first trip, to Brazil, and never did stand a chance of finding extinct northern white rhinos in the Democratic Republic of Congo: not only that – we hadn't even managed to enter the DRC to fail to find them.

But the aye-aye was definitely a good sign and we returned to Antananarivo in high spirits. Casting aside centuries of Malagasy folklore and superstition, we convinced ourselves that seeing the animal most shrouded in fear and folklore would bring us good luck for the next trip.

It was our final day and we were heading back to the airport for one last time, reminiscing about our adventure.

'I really want to come back to Madagascar,' I said.

'Me too!' enthused Stephen, 'but I think I'll wait until it's finished.'

'I really want to come back to Madagascar,' I said. 'Me too!' enthused Stephen, 'but I think I'll wait until it's finished.'

Opposite
Only an aye-aye could get away with looking so delightfully shaggy and unkempt.

4

DEAR OLD RALPH

I was on the train to London, where I was going to meet Stephen for lunch, and stared out of the window imagining how the conversation might go…

Opposite
The only bird with a song like an unreleased collection of Pink Floyd studio outtakes.

'A parrot? We're flying nearly 20,000 kilometres (12,000 miles) just to see a parrot?' asks Stephen incredulously. 'Are you sure?'

'Of course I'm sure!' I reply.

'But why? It's on the other side of the world and it's… it's… a parrot. It doesn't sound like the ultimate must-see animal. What's the point? I could go to Beaconsfield or Basingstoke to see a parrot.'

'Ah, but not this kind of parrot. We're going to look for a kakapo, the old night parrot of New Zealand. It's actually the world's largest, fattest and least-able-to-fly parrot.'

'What do you mean "least-able-to-fly"?' he asks, unimpressed and a little tetchy. 'Surely if a bird can't fly, it can't fly? Simple as that.'

'Well, yes, I see what you mean. But the kakapo has forgotten that it has forgotten how to fly. Sometimes, a seriously worried one will run up a tree and launch itself into the air before remembering that its wings don't actually work.'

'So what happens?'

'Well, it flies like a brick and lands in a graceless heap on the ground. Actually, to be fair, with a bit of practice it can do a sort of controlled crash-landing.

At least, that's the rumour – I've never actually seen it myself.'

'And this is definitely a parrot, you say?'

'Yes. But it's so much more than just a parrot. It's part dog, part kitten…'

'Hang on, hang on. How can it be part dog, part kitten? You're just trying to convince me to go to New Zealand to see a parrot.'

'No I'm not.'

'Yes you are.'

'Okay, I am. But what I meant to say was that it's as *affectionate* as a dog and as *playful* as a kitten. And there's more. It can inflate itself with air to become the size and shape of a football; it has a song like an unreleased collection of Pink Floyd studio outtakes; it only comes out at night; and it smells like a musty clarinet case. There's nothing else quite like it.'

'Are you making this stuff up?'

'No, honest.'

'And presumably, it's endangered too – or it wouldn't be on our radar?'

'It's about as endangered as you can possibly get without disappearing off the map altogether. There are just ninety kakapo left, so it's one of the most endangered animals in the world.'

Evolution designed the kakapo in the good old days, before there was anything to eat it. Just a few hundred years ago there were no terrestrial mammals in New Zealand. There were a few species of bats, which are mammals, but – and this is the point – there were no *predatory* mammals.

So the kakapo and all the other birds could run amok.

Life was good.

But it was too good to be true. When the Maori and Europeans arrived, they brought a lot of different animals with them – some on purpose, and some by mistake. Suddenly, the country was full of hungry ferrets, stoats, weasels, rats, cats, dogs, hedgehogs and possums. They couldn't believe their luck – they found a smörgåsbord of tasty birds (New Zealand has more species of flightless birds than any other country) with no idea that anything could possibly want to hurt them, let alone eat them.

In fact, if you were trying to design a vulnerable species you'd be hard pushed to come up with something better than the kakapo: it's incredibly tame and trusting; it spends most of its time on the ground; it's lost the power of flight, because it had nothing to fly away from (flying is hard work and consumes lots of energy so if you don't need to do it why bother?); and it has lost the ability to worry, because there was nothing much to worry about.

I imagined explaining all this to Stephen.

'It sounds as if you're describing the dodo,' he comments. He is beginning

Opposite
Stephen was almost ecstatic at the prospect of flying to the other side of the world, and then another 800 kilometres (500 miles), to see a Chatham Island black robin.

You're just trying to convince me to go to New Zealand to see a parrot.'

'No I'm not.'

'Yes you are.'

to perk up.

'Yes, in many ways the kakapo's story is history repeating itself. It just happens to be a giant parrot instead of a giant pigeon.'

'And both of them happened to be sitting ducks?'

'Exactly. The trouble is that natural selection takes so long to adapt to change it would take forever to evolve a kakapo that is sufficiently nervous and fleet-footed to escape all the predators trying to gobble it up, let alone one that could learn to fly all over again.'

'And the kakapo doesn't have forever.'

'Sadly, not. I remember Douglas commenting that if only we could just tell the kakapo "When you see one of those things with whiskers and little bitey teeth, run like hell" it would all be solved in a moment. But that's not going to happen.'

'Presumably, as with so many endangered species, their only hope of survival is human intervention?'

'Absolutely. And when you look into the large, round, greeny-brown face of a kakapo, and see the look of serenely innocent incomprehension in its eyes, you'll understand why so many people have devoted their lives to making sure it will be all right. I guarantee you will fall in love with it. Besides, New Zealand is your kind of place – with no snakes, good wine and high-speed internet access. So what do you think – will you come?'

Stephen laughs.

'Of course I will! But I'll reserve judgement on whether a smelly flightless parrot is worth flying 20,000 kilometres for. Are we just going to see a kakapo and then coming straight back?'

'Um, not really. I thought we could go and see some other endangered wildlife, too, to give you a broader picture of what's going on in New Zealand.'

'Okay,' says Stephen, suspiciously. 'What else, then?'

'A robin.'

'Good grief. A *robin*?!'

In the event, I had nothing at all to worry about. This is how the conversation actually went…

'Oh the kakapo!' he said. 'I remember reading about the kakapo in the original book – and Douglas used to rave about it all the time. The old night parrot of New Zealand was his favourite animal. I can't wait to see one. When are we going?'

And so, with Stephen almost ecstatic at the prospect of seeing a fat, flightless, nocturnal parrot, let alone a robin, we flew to the other side of the world.

If you have dirty boots, the other side of the world is the best place to get them cleaned. Just tick the appropriate box on your landing card and they'll be whisked away by New Zealand Customs & Immigration for a thorough scrub and polish. We couldn't believe our luck. The airport staff refused to do our dirty laundry as well, understandably, but our boots were returned with a friendly smile a mere twenty minutes later, completely spotless and smelling brand spanking new.

Actually, dirt is taken very seriously in New Zealand and we were gently reprimanded for failing to arrive with clean boots in the first place. No patriotic full-blooded New Zealander would consider arriving in such a mucky state.

It's not about pride or an obsession with cleanliness – it's about a thing called bio-security. Bio-security is as much of an obsession in the land of the kiwi as national security is in the land of the free.

We were confronted with bio-security at almost every turn and, to be honest, it was a bit of a palaver.

Take Codfish Island, for instance. Our ultimate goal was to spend several days on this remote and rugged nature reserve off the southern tip of New Zealand, because it's home to most of the last surviving kakapo. It offered our only real hope of meeting a kakapo in real life.

Quite rightly, we'd been made to jump through interminable diplomatic and administrative hoops to get permission from the Department of Conservation for a visit (Codfish is, after all, the jewel in New Zealand's conservation crown). We did get permission, eventually, but we had one large and final hoop to jump through first: the dreaded bio-security one.

Consequently, all we really saw of our departure point, the sleepy town of Invercargill, was the dauntingly named Southland Quarantine Facility.

It turned out to be a large warehouse, in a quiet part of town. We were led into a sealed room that looked just like the inside of a Hollywood space station.

Stephen and I glanced at one another and started to snigger and giggle.

Heavy doors were closed behind us.

Everyone was very serious and solemn as they told us what to do, which made us giggle even more.

We were sent into a small room in one corner and told to change out of our clothes.

'Oh my God, it's like being back at school,' whispered Stephen. 'Do you think we're going to be caned?'

'Um, I think you went to a slightly different school to mine. It feels to me as if we are being prepared for a trip to the moon.'

The clothes we wanted to take with us to Codfish were washed thoroughly in TriGene (I don't know what it is either – but it sounds seriously hazardous and tremendously important) before being transferred to special Department of Conservation-approved disinfected bags. Our sweet-smelling hiking boots were sprayed with TriGene, too, just to be sure.

Then we had to check all our belongings, in intimate detail, for aliens (not the kind that chase Sigourney Weaver, but alien animals and plants that shouldn't have been travelling with us). Not that you're likely to find a mouse or a rat inside your socks, but you might find a seed. In fact, Stephen did find a surprising number of grass seeds in some of his multicoloured Paul Smith socks (he was at a loss to explain how they got there and went bright red when I made some provocative suggestions).

Finally, we had to answer lots of questions. Did we shower this morning? Have we washed our hair? Have we been on a farm recently?

'Please God will someone just kill me?' Stephen muttered under his breath.

We giggled uncontrollably.

No one else was giggling as we were transferred to a specially disinfected Department of Conservation-approved vehicle and driven straight to the heliport.

By the time we landed on Codfish, we were past giggling and just plain bored with bio-security. And just in case something might have wormed its way into our specially approved disinfected bags between the quarantine facility and the helicopter (or, against all the odds, was stowed away in the helicopter itself) we had to go through the whole process all over again as soon as we touched down.

I'm not mocking the principle behind bio-security, even if sometimes it feels as if all conservationists in New Zealand are just a little bit paranoid. But that's okay because they have something to be paranoid about. They've learnt some very hard lessons from a highly destructive past and are absolutely determined to make amends.

New Zealand's wildlife evolved in complete isolation from the rest of the world (the nearest landmass is Australia, 2,000 kilometres/1,250 miles away across the Tasman Sea), so when people started to settle in New Zealand a thousand years ago it was 'ecologically naïve', to use the technical term. In other words, it was completely unprepared for the onslaught.

The result was a swift and, in some cases, final one.

Several dozen bird species have already become extinct. Among them were some of the weirdest and most astonishing birds ever to have lived on earth: the remarkable sexually dimorphic huia, in which the male had a short, woodpecker-like beak while the female had a long, downward-curving curlew-like beak; Haast's eagle, which was the largest eagle ever to have lived, with a wingspan of

Above
Stephen searches for aliens (not the kind that chase Sigourney Weaver).

3 metres (10 feet) and talons as big as a tiger's; and lots of different moas, giant ostrich-like birds with beaks like secateurs and eggs almost as big as rugby balls.

The fastest extinction in New Zealand – possibly in the entire world – was the Stephen's Island wren, which lived on tiny Stephen's Island, in Cook Strait. It was discovered in 1894, when a new lighthouse keeper arrived on the island for the first time. One of his cats caught a bird he didn't recognise, so he sent the little body to a friend in Wellington, who happened to be a professional ornithologist. By the time the excited friend sent news back that it was a species new to science, the cat had caught another fifteen. And that was it – there were none left.

Stephen's Island wren officially became extinct later the same year. The cat had eaten the first and last of the species, and all the others in between. Its owner, the lighthouse keeper, was the only person ever to have seen one alive.

Nowadays, offshore islands like Stephen's Island, and Codfish, offer the only real hope of saving the endangered wildlife that is left. Conservationists are transferring species that are in trouble on the mainland to these manageable safe havens. They are like bank vaults – places where kakapo and other valuables can be hidden away for safekeeping.

Their isolation means that they can be cleared of predators and other aliens (like the grass seeds in Stephen's socks or, more importantly, the ferrets, stoats, weasels, rats, cats, dogs, hedgehogs and possums that run amok on the mainland) and returned to the pristine state New Zealand once was.

We began our kiwi adventure with one of the oldest animals in the world. It's ancestral lineage dates back 200 million years, no less, which means that it was around pretty much throughout the Age of the Dinosaurs and has outlived all the dinosaurs by 65 million years… and counting. The tabloids would inevitably (though incorrectly) call it the ultimate 'living fossil'.

'But it's just a lizard,' said a rather disappointed Stephen, staring at the olive-green animal lying underneath a bush in Karori Wildlife Sanctuary, just outside Wellington.

'Admittedly, it's an out-of-the-ordinary lizard,' he continued. 'It's got a bigger head than usual and sharp-looking spines along its back. It looks like something out of a Michael Crichton novel. But it's still definitely a lizard. Isn't it?'

Actually, it was a 60-centimetre (2-foot) long tuatara. The spines along its back (which do look as if they were designed for *Jurassic Park*) give it its name: 'tuatara' is a Maori word meaning 'peaks on the back'.

But tuataras aren't lizards for all sorts of reasons.

Opposite & above
A tuatara millions of years old and a greying zoologist catching up.

The best one is that their razor-sharp teeth aren't really teeth as we know them – they are little more than serrations of the jaw.

Another is that the male tuatara doesn't have a penis. No reptile has a penis, to be fair, but most have what's called an intromittent organ that does the job pretty well. Many have two. But the male tuatara is seriously lacking in that department. This isn't why the species is rare – although that would be a logical conclusion – because he mates with the female by squirting sperm from his cloaca into hers (a cloaca is basically an all-purpose hole for peeing, pooing and mating). People who are into this kind of thing call it a 'cloacal kiss'. Yuk.

Tuatara also have a remarkable third eye, on the top of the head. They're not the only animals to have one of these, but it's more pronounced in the tuatara than in most others. You can actually see it in the youngsters, but after about six months it gets covered by opaque scales and largely disappears.

Scientists are still bickering about the function of the third eye. It has its own rudimentary lens, cornea and retina, suggesting that it evolved from a normal eye, but they're all agreed that it wouldn't be much good for seeing. It seems to be associated with the pineal gland – an amazing gland in the brain that produces melatonin to regulate what's called the circadian rhythm. In other words, it probably helps to modulate wake/sleep patterns. It may also have something to

do with hormone production for thermoregulation. Or it might help to absorb ultraviolet rays for the manufacture of vitamin D.

Then again, for all we know, it might be an early electromagnetic tuner for picking up local radio.

There are two different species of tuatara: Brother's Island tuatara, which is by far the rarest, with about 400 survivors; and the common tuatara, with about 55,000. They were once found throughout New Zealand, but couldn't cope with all the rats, stoats and weasels that made short work of their eggs and hatchlings. Some did make it to adulthood but they were caught by humans and sent overseas, where they were highly prized by collectors.

It's a wonder any survived at all.

They became extinct on the mainland some time in the late 1700s, but small populations teetered on the brink in the relative safety of a few predator-free offshore islands. They became the first animals ever to be protected in New Zealand, in 1895, and have been a conservation priority ever since.

The best news is that, thanks to Karori Sanctuary, a few dozen tuatara have just been returned to the mainland for the first time in centuries.

Karori is just under three square kilometres (a square mile) in size and completely predator-free – an ecological oasis where native wildlife can roam without having to worry about aliens. Managed like a high-security prison (except the bad guys are on the outside), it is so secure that even house mice can't break in.

As the sun rose higher, our tuatara moved out from underneath its bush. Tuataras are cold-blooded, which means they spend a lot of time sunbathing to warm their bodies up to a suitable operating temperature.

It was fully alert yet meditative, in an 'I've got all the time in the world' kind of way. It embodied a geological patience that was somehow fitting for a species that hasn't physically changed in millions of years.

'I like tuataras,' said Stephen after a while. 'They spend a lot of time sitting and staring. That's what I'd like to do.'

'You'd be bored in five minutes,' I said. 'Actually, make that one minute.'

'Maybe. But life in the slow lane does appeal sometimes.'

'I know what you mean. There's a theory that it makes you live longer, too. The tuatara does everything slowly and lives for ages.'

'It doesn't seem to be breathing,' said Stephen, suddenly concerned for its wellbeing.

'That's because it isn't – well, not very often anyway. It could get away with breathing about once an hour, if it really fancied a lazy day. And being lazy does have advantages, because this tuatara is likely to outlive all its human protectors. It could easily live long enough to get a telegram from the Queen.'

'Doesn't she send emails these days? Or text messages from her iPhone?'

'Does she have an iPhone?' I asked.

'I think President Obama gave her one. But I doubt if she'll know how to use it. And I doubt very much if sitting and staring really makes you live any longer. Anyway, it would be a waste of time trying. Just imagine if you did sit around and stare a lot, and then died young, it would have been a complete waste of time. It would be a bit like going to church, just in case there is a God and a faint chance of making it into Heaven, and then discovering that it was all a load of baloney. You could have spent your Sunday mornings doing something more productive.'

'Like sitting and staring, perhaps? Even so, I think there is at least a grain of truth in the theory. Animals with low metabolic rates do tend to live longer than those with high ones. Shrews rush around in a complete panic, for instance, like traders on the floor of the Stock Exchange, and they live for a year or two at most; yet dormice spend much of their time fast asleep, or pottering about like retired librarians on an allotment, and they live for five years or more.'

'Oh dear.'

'Why "oh dear"?'

'Well, it makes you think, doesn't it?'

Stephen was still pondering the possible repercussions of his frenetic lifestyle when we noticed a slight movement on a rotting log right in front of us. It was another tuatara, so well camouflaged that we hadn't seen it watching us intently from no more than 3 metres (10 feet) away.

We felt quite shocked. Realising that you are being watched can be a little unnerving.

I remember standing perfectly still in the Amazon jungle earlier in the year, looking around and yet seeing very little. I stood there and imagined all the countless animals of all shapes and sizes that were inevitably watching my every move. It sent a shiver down my spine. I told Stephen what I was thinking and he admitted that he'd felt exactly the same; neither of us mentioned it at the time.

We were met in Karori by Professor Charles Daugherty, from Victoria University, and Sue Keall, who were keen to show us some tuatara eggs. These weren't just any old eggs – they were the first tuatara eggs to have been laid in the wild on mainland New Zealand for over two hundred years.

Charles and Sue took us to a little pink ribbon by the side of a path, and Sue started to pick away at the ground with her bare hands, like a palaeontologist on a delicate dig. After about ten minutes she stopped digging and beckoned us to have a closer look. We crouched down and looked into a short tunnel that led to an underground chamber: there, for all to see, was a clutch of small, extremely rare white eggs.

'Can we touch them?' asked Stephen.

Sue laughed, but gave us permission, and gently we felt the tough, leathery shells.

Female tuatara lay as many as fifteen eggs once every four or five years – not very often – then cover them with soil and wander off to sit and stare. That's her job done (presumably because looking after eggs and hatchlings would mean lots of rushing about and that could shave years off her life).

Charles explained how the temperature of the nest determines the sex of the young tuatara, as it does in many reptiles. If it is warm (22°C or above) they will be male, and if it is cool (21°C or below) they will be female. Who knows what happens if it is between 21°C and 22°C?

Stephen liked this idea immensely and, while the rest of us listened in silence, he waxed lyrical about the likely impact of global warming on the natural sex ratio of tuatara, something about how varying temperature might work if there were three sexes instead of just two, and how different the world would be if the same thing happened in humans.

'Does the pink ribbon mean they are all going to be girls?' he asked excitedly, barely skipping a beat.

'No,' replied Sue. 'It doesn't. It's just a pink ribbon.'

Below
The giant weta is so mild-mannered that holding one is much like holding the lead of an ageing labrador after a heavy meal. Note the tiny blue disc on this one's back – a marker for research purposes.

There are many things to do in Wellington (or 'the city they named after a boot' as Stephen called it): a ride on the funicular railway, for example, or a visit to Te Papa Tongarewa Museum.

Surprisingly few people go to Matiu-Somes Island, an old quarantine station and internment camp in northern Wellington Harbour, specifically to see an oversized insect that looks like a cross between a cockroach and a cricket.

We did. It wouldn't have been Stephen's first choice for a day out, but he agreed to come.

Matiu-Somes is now a scientific and historic reserve – a 25-hectare (62-acre) sanctuary free of rats, possums and all the other introduced mammalian predators that have ravaged most of New Zealand. And it's home to an extraordinary animal called the giant weta, or Cook Strait giant weta to be strictly accurate, which is a scary-looking creepy-crawly about the size of a mouse.

In the ecological scheme of things it actually performs a similar role to that carried out by mice and other rodents in less peculiar parts of the world.

Stephen didn't like the sound of it at all.

'We could have gone to an art gallery or strolled along the harbourfront,' he complained on the twenty-minute ferry ride. 'And you make us go to see an insect the size of a mouse. Good grief.'

There are many different species of weta in New Zealand. Seventy, perhaps. Or maybe a hundred. To be honest, there just aren't enough people studying them to know for sure. It's a lot, anyway, and with their grasshopper-like bodies, long spiny legs and curved tusks, they are all instantly recognisable as such.

The much-feared tree weta is the most famous, or infamous. A tough little animal, it is the pit-bull of the weta world. If it doesn't like the look of you it hisses like a horribly large and dangerous venomous snake; and then, if it really doesn't like the look of you, it will lash out with its spiky legs and give you an exceedingly painful bite.

The Cook Strait giant weta, on the other hand, the one we were going to see, is the labrador of the weta world (it's also the dinosaur of the insect world – but that's another story). The ultimate gentle giant, it is a completely harmless and mild-mannered vegetarian. It rarely dislikes the look of anyone and is far too polite to show its feelings if it does. Like so many animals in New Zealand, it has lost the ability to fly. Sadly, it is so heavy that it has also lost the ability to jump. So all it can do is scuttle.

We were met on the dock by rangers Jo Greenman and Matt Sidaway. Jo and

Matt are among a grand total of three people living on Matiu-Somes (the other is Jo's husband, who commutes to the mainland every day in a little boat).

We hiked to the top of the island, admiring the views across the water towards the city skyline, and Jo introduced us to the concept of weta hotels. These are shallow wooden boxes placed on the forest floor to give wetas comfortable daytime hiding places (they rest during the day and come out at night).

Carefully, we opened the lid of the nearest hotel and peered inside. There were four giant wetas in residence. They scuttled about in a complete panic, as if housekeeping had opened the door without knocking and caught them in the shower.

Jo picked out the largest animal – one of the heaviest insects in the world – and gently placed it on the palm of my hand.

'Don't worry about that long thing,' she said, reading my mind. 'I know it looks like a stinger but it's not. It's a female and that's her ovipositor – her egg-laying device. It won't do you any harm. Though, in fact, the stings of bees and wasps are highly modified ovipositors, so it's an easy mistake to make.'

I held the giant weta in position (not all that difficult – much like holding the lead of an ageing labrador after a heavy meal) while Jo carefully glued a tiny blue disc onto its back. The disc had a number on it (96) and was part of a research project to learn more about giant weta movements and numbers.

Stephen wanted to hold the weta, so I carefully prized its tiny hooked feet from my skin and handed it over.

He gently tapped it on the back.

'It's got very tough armour-plating,' he said.

'That's its exoskeleton,' explained Jo. 'We wear our skeletons on the inside and they wear theirs on the outside – which works pretty well until they need to grow bigger.'

'So how do they do that?'

'Well, when we grow bigger, we get bigger clothes. And that's pretty much what a weta does – except it has to break out of its old jacket, its exoskeleton, and grow a new and bigger one.'

Wetas are tough little animals. Rumour has it that one was held under water for four days and survived (but then rumour also had it that the incompetent chief executives of failed banks weren't going to be allowed any more bonuses, so I'm not sure if this is true).

'How many do you reckon there are on Matiu-Somes?' I asked Jo.

'We're not sure – but if I had to guess I'd say around 15,000,' she replied. 'I know that sounds like a lot compared with a large animal like a kakapo, but it's actually a very small number for a population of insects. We're still worried about its future.'

Opposite
Stephen, overwhelmed with excitement after a day of weta-watching.

Below
Mark, overwhelmed with excitement over the latest mobile phone technology.

There were four giant wetas in residence. They scuttled about in a complete panic, as if housekeeping had opened the door without knocking and caught them in the shower.

Jo had a point – great numbers are no guarantee of survival, no matter what kind of animal you happen to be. A better measure is the level of threat.

Take the North American passenger pigeon, which at one time was probably the commonest bird ever to have lived on earth. It is impossible to give an accurate estimate of the population at its peak, but conservative guesstimates suggest that it may have been as high as 10,000 million in the first half of the 19th century. It is likely that 35–45 per cent of all the birds in North America were passenger pigeons and they lived in huge, densely packed flocks which darkened the sky and could take up to three days to pass overhead.

But colossal numbers were killed for their meat. Sports hunters took an even greater toll: hunting competitions were organised in which more than 30,000 dead birds were needed to claim a prize.

The last passenger pigeon to be seen in the wild was shot by a young boy on 24 March 1900. On 1 September 1914 the last of all the passenger pigeons, affectionately known as Martha, died in captivity in Cincinnati Zoo, USA. They had been hunted to extinction in little more than a hundred years. Quite a lesson.

The Cook Strait giant weta had been extinct on the mainland for over a century (although a small number had just been released into Karori Sanctuary – incidentally, with the insect-eating tuatara, thus bringing about an interesting scenario in which one endangered species is likely to be eating another).

So Matiu-Somes offers a crucial beacon of hope.

Let me pre-empt you here. I'm pretty sure I know what you're thinking. You're thinking: who cares? Who cares if a tuatara does eat the odd weta? In fact, who cares if a tuatara were to eat every single weta? Why go to all this bother to save an insect the size of a mouse? A polar bear, yes; a tiger, of course; an elephant, without a doubt. But a giant weta? Surely, if a flightless, jumpless, spiky-legged grasshopper were to become extinct no one would really care? Would anyone really notice?

Well, before I answer the question, let me tell you a story.

A few years ago the European Space Agency's Chief Scientist, Dr Bernard Foing, called for a Noah's Ark to be established on the moon. He wanted the ark to be a repository for the DNA of every single species of plant and animal, in case something unimaginably awful were to happen to earth (like the planet being destroyed by an asteroid or, worse, environmentally unfriendly George Bush returning as US President).

Presumably, the idea was to send a handful of volunteers to the moon first: their main aim in life would have been to survive long enough to carry all the DNA back down to the brand-new, unadulterated, uncontaminated, unsullied world we wouldn't recognise as home.

But here's the rub: would we really want to take every species with us? Couldn't we leave out the Ebola virus, for example? Come to think of it, couldn't we leave out all the viruses responsible for common colds? Perhaps one of the volunteers could accidentally break the vials containing malarial mosquito and tsetse fly DNA?

And who is going to make such difficult decisions?

If it were up to one of my neighbours, she'd leave out all spider DNA; a friend would exclude venomous snakes; and I'd be tempted to forbid any DNA linked to horses (I know this will upset lots of people, and I'm really sorry, but I'm scared of anything with hooves and a mane – I'm in seventh heaven swimming with sharks but nothing would persuade me to climb on to the back of a cantankerous horse).

Indeed, if we're striving for perfection, why stop there? Perhaps we could be selective about the human gene pool, too? We could remove all the genes that make company directors advocate the use of more than one layer of packaging for their products; any newspaper editor who thinks a blue-eyed stripeless white tiger born in captivity is worthy of news but tiger conservation is not; anyone in Bangkok involved in training orang-utans to kick-box; and everyone responsible for Britain's transport policy.

Above & opposite
Visiting Peter Jackson, the man behind the *Lord of the Rings* trilogy, and his mind-boggling collection of Lancaster bombers.

The potential list is endless.

But of course we can't do that. It would be the biological equivalent of ethnic cleansing.

The point is this: if you buy into conservation then it's all or nothing. You can't just elect to save the nicest animals, or the biggest, or the cutest. You have to save the lot. Or at least try to.

Do you remember the old game called *Pickasticks*, in which you would drop a handful of giant wooden toothpicks into a pile and then try to pull them out, one by one, without disturbing the others? Sometimes you could do it, but very often you would disturb another stick or, worse still, the whole lot would collapse. Well, interfering with a complex food web is rather like playing a game of *Pickasticks*, except with higher stakes. If you let an animal like the giant weta become extinct, its disappearance will inevitably have an impact on all the other wildlife in the ecosystem: it's just that no one can predict if that impact will be quite subtle or nothing short of disastrous.

There are plenty of other reasons for saving the giant weta, of course, but more of those later.

After months of immersion in my world of tents and tuataras, wilderness and wetas, Stephen introduced me to a little bit of his world.

While we were in Wellington, we spent a day with Academy Award-winning film director, producer and screenwriter Peter Jackson.

I was expecting the man I'd seen in magazines and on televised award ceremonies – short, long-haired, bearded and, well, quite portly. But instead the man behind the *Lord of the Rings* trilogy was short, long-haired, bearded and as thin as a rake.

'I changed my diet from hamburgers to yoghurt and muesli and it seemed to work,' he told us, quite simply.

He arrived wearing his trademark knee-length shorts, long socks and hiking boots. He looked more like a zoologist about to rugby tackle a New Zealand fur seal in order to take a stool sample, than a film director, and was about as far removed from my idea of Hollywood as it was possible to get.

He is a kiwi to the core and has resisted the inevitable pressures and temptations to leave his native country for Tinseltown. He filmed *The Lord of the Rings* in New Zealand and wanted British countryside to represent the fictional Middle-earth. And he found perfectly unspoilt 'British' habitats right on his own doorstep.

'Why would I want to film anywhere else?' he laughed. 'You can drive for half an hour in New Zealand and you will pass through Surrey woodland, Dorset heathland, Cairngorms pine forest and even Exmoor or Dartmoor. The Britishness of the countryside here is hard to miss.'

Americanness is everywhere, too, apparently. When the *Lord of the Rings* films were still a figment of his imagination, he filmed *The Frighteners* (starring Michael J. Fox) in his treasured home country, cleverly convincing an unsuspecting world that the central character – a psychic architect – was communicating with ghosts in a Midwestern town in the United States.

Peter is an avid collector and he was keen to show us one of his favourite collections.

Most of us have a back bedroom or a garden shed for our hobbies. He has a squadron of aircraft hangars and workshops. We passed through a small office and entered a huge open warehouse the size of Heathrow Airport. Okay, that's a bit of an exaggeration, but it was at least the size of a big part of Heathrow Airport. And, besides, it led to another even bigger warehouse, then another, and another.

They were all chock-full of F.E.2s, B.E.2s and more than enough other World War I planes to rival most world-class museum collections. Some were original and had been painstakingly and caringly restored, while others were absolutely perfect replicas built from scratch.

Many were still in bits and they languished among a battery of tanks, machine guns, bombs, armoured cars, buses and enough other paraphernalia to equip a small army. Make that a big army.

Shrink the whole lot down to Airfix model size and his collection would still have been many times bigger than the one my brother and I amassed at home when we were kids – and we spent all our pocket money on the collection, which was the envy of all our friends.

There were people everywhere, too, tinkering with bits of wood, tightening bolts and poring over complex plans. Peter Jackson's hobby employs more than fifty staff.

Finally, we entered the biggest aircraft hangar of the lot. This was where work and pleasure began to overlap.

We walked past a few Sopwith Camels and a couple of Vickers F.B.12s (at least, I think that's what he said) and there, like a scene from *The Dam Busters*, was a squadron of Lancaster bombers.

Actually, they really were about to appear in a scene from *The Dam Busters*, and were clearly his pride and joy. Peter was working on a remake of the original 1955 film, for which Stephen had already written the script, and I listened quietly as they discussed their joint venture like a couple of eager and enthusiastic schoolboys with a new computer game.

Later in the day we went to visit Peter's film production company, which happens to be called *Weta*.

'You must like wetas a lot to name your company after them,' I suggested. 'Why not something a little more charismatic and inspiring – like *Kakapo*?'

'I don't like wetas at all,' he shuddered.

'In fact, I'm scared stiff of them. I have a friend who once drank a glass of water that had been sitting on his bedside table in the dark. There was a weta in the water and he swallowed it whole. I can't think of anything worse.'

He visibly winced.

'But I must admit I do like the fact that the weta looks as if it is from another world. That appeals to me a lot.'

(We later discovered that he had been quietly funding the weta project in the Karori Wildlife Sanctuary.)

We pulled up outside the *Weta* offices and Peter suddenly vanished. We found him hiding behind a bush: he'd spotted a *Lord of the Rings* tour bus, spilling its slightly obsessive fans onto the pavement just a few metres away. Little did they know that their idol, the man responsible for the second, eighth and fifteenth highest-grossing films of all time, not to mention their two-week tour of *Lord of*

Above
New Zealand's answer to a native mammal.

the Rings film locations, had been almost within touching distance.

We spent a happy few hours discussing what seemed to be an eternal list of new projects in the pipeline, including a forthcoming film of Alice Sebold's book *The Lovely Bones* and a joint project with Steven Spielberg to make a film of *The Adventures of Tintin.*

Then I asked what, to me, was the obvious question.

'How do you fit it all in?'

Peter looked nonplussed.

'What do you mean?' he asked.

'Well, you've achieved more in the film industry than almost anyone else alive. You have a young family and huge, all-engrossing hobbies. And you still have time to spend a relaxing day with us. You make it all seem so easy. How do you fit more hours into a typical day than the rest of us? What's the secret?'

He shuffled from one foot to the other, looking surprisingly shy.

'I don't really know,' he said.

'But you're two years younger than me,' I persisted. 'I work really hard, I play hard, I'm never really idle, and yet you're making me feel as if I've frittered the past fifty years away.'

'Oh dear, sorry,' he said with a smile. 'I suppose if you want to do something bad enough you just make time.'

He laughed.

Stephen laughed too.

Super-achievement is such a normal way of life for them, I don't think they had a clue what I was talking about.

Even the national bird of New Zealand, the kiwi, is in danger.

'Not only is it the national bird,' Stephen pointed out, 'it is also an honorary mammal and, in relation to body size, it lays the largest egg – an eye-watering six times larger than a chicken's egg. I looked it up in Kiwipedia (pun intended).'

'Why is it an honorary mammal?' I asked sarcastically, testing his knowledge.

Stephen smiled, knowing exactly what I was up to.

'Because it fills a similar niche to badgers and hedgehogs back home,' he said. 'Because it has distinctive cat-like whiskers at the base of its bill to help it navigate at night. And because, unlike most other birds, it has a highly developed sense of smell – it literally sniffs out its food with proper nostrils at the end of the bill.'

'And what does it eat?'

Kiwis only come out at night and aren't the easiest birds to find. The best way, as we quickly discovered, was with the help of an English setter called Percy.

'Um, I know, I know. Don't tell me. It eats grubs and worms, which it finds in between all the bits of leaf litter.'

Stephen's swotting had become an ongoing joke between us. The original idea was for me to be telling him about all the wildlife we encountered, or for a local expert to tell us both, but he had decided early on in our travels that he didn't like being kept in the dark. He wanted to be an expert, too.

As always, he had speed-read Wikipedia the night before – and was able to remember and recite every single word.

Kiwis only come out at night and aren't the easiest birds to find. The best way, as we quickly discovered, was with the help of an English setter called Percy.

Percy lived in Trounson Kauri Park, a beautiful forest of huge native conifers, called kauris, tucked away in a far distant corner of North Island. He lived there with his owner and trainer, James Fraser.

James is a freelance kiwi-tracker, Percy is a freelance kiwi-tracking dog and Trounson is home to the North Island brown kiwi.

This happens to be the most resilient and common of the five different species of kiwi (though it's probably a little misleading to say 'common' since the population has declined by more than ninety per cent in the past century).

We met James and Percy early one morning at the entrance to a wooden

Opposite
In Trounson Kauri Park with James, a freelance kiwi-tracker, and a freelance kiwi.

Below
Percy, the freelance kiwi-tracking dog.

boardwalk that winds its way through the marshy, fern-rich kauri forest.

Percy was raring to go. Running backwards and forwards, sideways one way and then sideways the other way, with his tightly muzzled nose almost touching the ground and his tail pointing high into the air, he covered more ground than the rest of us put together.

Within half an hour he had found something. From a distance it looked a bit like a compost heap – a mound of vegetation about a metre (three feet) high.

There were three large holes around the base. Percy stuck his head inside one, James stuck his head inside another and so I stuck my head inside the third. I switched on my head-torch and peered into the gloom. There, just around the corner and no more than 30 centimetres (1 foot) away from the end of my nose, was a big ball of brown feathers. It was a kiwi. I couldn't see its head or beak, but it was definitely a kiwi.

James saw it, too, but decided that it was too difficult to reach. We would have to find another. With Stephen's help, we tugged and pulled Percy out of his hole and set off again into the forest.

James and Percy ran ahead and, in no time at all, we could hear a bark and a shout. We leapt off the boardwalk, ran through the mud and ferns and found them both with their heads deep inside another mound of vegetation piled over a tangle of tree roots.

Just as we skidded to a halt, James pulled a big brown ball of feathers and mud out of the burrow by its legs.

'Can I hold it?' I asked.

Stephen looked a bit shocked – that was his question and he was just about to ask it.

James showed me what to do: hold the surprisingly calm bird upside down, by the legs, and then lift it up with my other arm. It was easy. There was no kicking, no pecking and virtually no struggling.

It was about the size of a chicken, but several times heavier. While the bones of most birds are light and hollow to help them fly, kiwi bones are heavy and filled with marrow to help them walk and run. It had a ring on one leg and James examined it closely: it had been banded as an adult in 1997 and hadn't been seen since.

Its feathers were unlike any feathers I had seen before. They looked unkempt, more like a bundle of shaggy loose hair, as if they hadn't been preened in years. And there were no obvious wings. After an evolutionary lifetime of predator-free bliss, like so many birds in New Zealand the kiwi has lost the ability to fly. All that remains of its wings are two rather pathetic vestigial stumps with claws on the end.

'Is it a male or a female?' asked Stephen.

'This one is a female,' said James. 'They are bigger than the males. Her mate will be around here somewhere, though. They tend to spend their whole lives together as a monogamous couple.'

'You mean no flings with other kiwis?'

'No! Kiwi relationships can last for twenty years or more, though I have to admit we have observed the occasional divorce or two.'

'I think the secret to their marital bliss is not spending too much time together,' I added. 'They keep in touch, by calling while they are out and about, but only meet up every two or three days.'

'Keeps the relationship fresh,' confirmed Stephen.

Suddenly the kiwi made a sound like someone trying to stifle a sneeze. Its whole body shuddered, and surprised me so much I nearly dropped it.

James laughed.

'It's just clearing its nostrils,' he said. 'It has to blow through them once in a while, to get rid of all the soil it has sniffed in while feeding.'

I stared into the eyes of the big brown ball, as it lay peacefully on my arm, and gently stroked its feathers. It stared back and blinked.

I'll never forget the way that kiwi looked at me. It was a look of absolute innocence and incomprehension – one that we were to see many more times during our wildlife encounters in New Zealand.

Halfway through the trip we had a day off in Queenstown, the adventure capital of the world.

Now, Stephen is not averse to a bit of exercise. Throughout our travels, he always took a seven-kilometre (four-mile) walk before breakfast, often in the dark and long before the rest of us had even thought about getting up (unless, of course, we were in a jungle or on the savannah and so his chances of being eaten alive by an anaconda or a lion were greater than the chances of dying from being unfit).

But there's no denying one simple fact: he's not really one for adventure sports.

'How about a bit of mountain biking?' I suggested, hopefully.

'I would rather suck turds from a dead octopus than go mountain biking,' he groaned.

'Or river boarding?'

'What the hell is river boarding? Whatever it is, I don't like the sound of it – it's bound to involve getting wet.'

'Okay, let's try paragliding.'

'Ha! If I were to go paragliding I guarantee that I will not be alone in my pants.'

'All right. I know. Why don't we go abseiling?'

'Nature makes all kinds of humans – and I am definitely not the kind to go jumping off cliffs,' said Stephen, in a voice that was drawing the conversation to a close. 'I need to be in a first-class restaurant within striking distance of a lavatory.'

'Okay. Let's do lunch.'

'Excellent idea. Decision made. It's a bit early, but shall we go straight away?'

We sat at a table in the window of a lovely restaurant overlooking Lake Wakatipu, watching the world go by.

Unfortunately, the world went by pretty damn quickly – mainly on rollerblades, skateboards and mountain bikes.

'Just think,' said Stephen sarcastically. 'Some people go to the theatre and have dinner with friends, when they could be building up a phenomenal sweat and chafing the insides of their thighs on a bloody mountain bike. I'm sorry, but what is wrong with these people?'

He stared out of the window in utter despair.

'They just don't seem to be able to sit still. And they're giving me indigestion.'

So we wined and dined and moaned our day off in Queenstown, until we'd run out of time for a last-minute bungee-jump or the chance to sit astride an inflatable yellow banana and be towed behind a speedboat.

But the next day we had an adventure of our own. We explored Fiordland, a vast and breathtaking tract of mountainous terrain in the southwest corner of South Island.

Admittedly, we didn't explore it on a mountain bike or on foot, as most New Zealanders tend to do. But then much of Fiordland has never been explored at ground level: there are few roads and even those peter out quickly in the foothills.

Instead, we explored it from a four-seater Eurocopter AS350 – one of those little helicopters with a bubble cockpit that makes you feel as if you are sitting inside a fish-bowl.

We were incredibly lucky: it was a perfect crystal-clear day. The view from the fish-bowl, as our pilot Richard Black wheeled and turned through the unbelievably staggering scenery, was almost too dreamy to be real. We circled rugged mountain tops reaching high into fluffy white clouds, swooped along green U-shaped valleys carved out by million-year-old glaciers, cruised down immense rivers, hovered in front of thunderous waterfalls that dropped hundreds of metres down weather-scuffed cliff faces, and simply marvelled at the sheer splendour of it all.

I remember Douglas Adams described Fiordland as like 'the whole of Norway scrunched up a bit, hurtled ten thousand miles round the world and filled with birds'.

Stephen and I struggled to add our own impressions of the panorama stretched out below us, but mere words didn't seem to do it justice.

'To try to describe Fiordland would be about as futile as throwing an orang-utan at a charging rhino,' Stephen offered.

'It's like something Salvador Dalí would dream up,' I tried. 'Those snow and ice formations look like enormous great cathedrals built by a mad architect.'

'If this is New Zealand, just imagine what Old Zealand must have been like.'

Stephen muttered something about having to stand on a chair to get height at his home in Norfolk, and Richard laughed at our futile attempts. This was effectively his office and he'd seen it all and heard it all before.

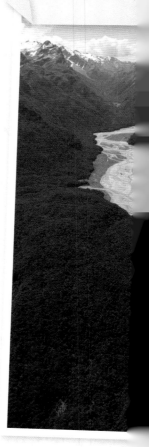

To try to describe Fiordland would be about as futile as throwing an orang-utan at a charging rhino.

His solution was to stick to mere facts. Like every New Zealander, he loved record-breaking detail and gave us a running commentary about the highest, the lowest, the longest and the shortest.

'That's the 27th-largest lake in New Zealand,' he said matter-of-factly, nodding towards a veritable seascape to our left.

'And that over there,' he continued, 'is the 11th-tallest mountain in Fiordland.'

The undisputed winner of all the records we heard during our travels in New Zealand, incidentally, was this little snippet: 'This is the place where freshwater and saltwater run closer together in a residential area than anywhere else in the world.' It doesn't get much better than that.

While exploring Fiordland, we made a brief stop at a place called Kakapo Castle, which used to be the display ground of one of the last surviving kakapo in the whole of mainland New Zealand. Perched high on a precipitous ridge, with a view to die for, it was a fitting site for the kakapo's final stand.

Before New Zealand was inhabited by people, Fiordland was home to hundreds of thousands of kakapo.

But then Pandora's box of mammalian predators was emptied into the innocent land, and suddenly there were tens of thousands.

Then there were thousands, then hundreds. Then there were dozens.

Just two years before Douglas and I visited Kakapo Castle in 1989 there were no kakapo left at all – no kakapo anywhere on mainland New Zealand.

Stephen and I paid homage to that long-lost kakapo and climbed back into our helicopter to see some more of one of the most breathtaking, awe-inspiring and humbling parts of the world either of us had ever seen. We peered out of the fish-bowl goggle-eyed and lapsed into silent contemplation.

We were still engrossed in the surreal world around us when Richard rummaged in a bag behind his seat (holding the joystick between his knees, and

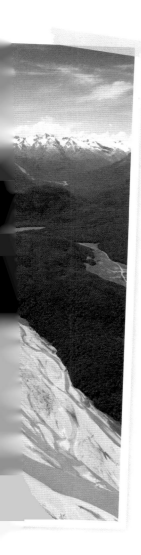

conspicuously not looking where we were going, as all the best helicopter pilots seem to do) and produced an iPod. He plugged it into a socket on the control panel and Pink Floyd's *Dark Side of the Moon* erupted into our headsets.

I glanced at Stephen and we both burst into spontaneous applause. Suddenly, we were in an imaginary spacecraft, wheeling and turning over a fantasy make-believe world.

We landed all too soon, at a place called Milford Sound, and the two of us fell out of the cockpit, laughing and whooping and cheering.

We'd just had one of the best possible hours on God's good earth.

The Godfather of the kakapo world is a tough old-timer called Richard Henry Junior.

His namesake, the original Richard Henry, pioneered kakapo conservation in the 1890s and was the first person to shout from the rooftops that the old night parrot of New Zealand needed help. It was Henry who had the brilliant idea of moving a handful of survivors to island havens for safekeeping – an idea that has become the mainstay of endangered species conservation in New Zealand and a blueprint for conservation efforts on islands as far afield as Mauritius and the Galápagos.

Henry was years ahead of his time, but, thank goodness, a charismatic biologist called Don Merton had taken up the cudgel to continue his work.

And so it was, in 1975, at the end of a long day's search for the last surviving kakapo on mainland New Zealand, that Don found himself precariously balanced on a narrow terrace high above the Gulliver River, in Fiordland. He was with some kakapo-trackers and their kakapo-tracking dogs and, against all the odds, they had picked up the scent of a real-life surviving kakapo.

In fact, they had cornered the kakapo, a male, against the edge of a cliff. The kakapo glanced down towards the valley floor 1,000 metres (3,300 feet) below, trying to remember whether or not it could fly, and wondering whether to give it a try. As it teetered on the brink, Don looked at the kakapo and read its mind. He threw himself towards the precipice, in a goalie's dive, and caught the surprised bird with both hands.

It proved to be a timely save. The bird was named Richard Henry and, almost prophetically, turned out to be the last known surviving kakapo on the mainland.

For a flightless parrot, Richard Henry has done an impressive amount of travelling. He was initially placed on Maud Island, for safekeeping, where he spent a happy seven years. Then he was transferred to Little Barrier Island, where Douglas Adams and I actually heard him booming in 1989. Six years after we 'met', he was sent back to Maud for another six years and became enamoured with a female kakapo (originally from Stewart Island) called Flossie. Then, nearing the end of his island odyssey, he spent a couple of years on Chalky Island.

Finally, in 2004, he was taken to his retirement home on Codfish, where he still lives – more than three decades after being rescued in Fiordland by Don's goalie dive.

He is thought to be more than a hundred years old now and, though he is partially blind, seems to be in good health. He has three offspring from his time with Flossie and they all live together on the same island. Maybe, between them, they will be able to perpetuate the precious genes of the mainland race.

'A little-known aspect of the birds of New Zealand is that they all appear to have been named by ten-year-olds,' observed Stephen one day.

'I'll give you some examples at random,' he said. 'The kakapo (our hero bird, of course), the kokako, the kaka, the takahe, the cocky-poo. Okay, I made the last one up, but did you ever hear a list of bird names more guaranteed to make a ten-year-old (and me) laugh? How about calling one of them a kaka-kokikakapoopookakakokikokipoo? In Britain all we've been able to come up with is "tit". Which is pretty good but nothing like as good as kakakokikaka-poopookakakokikokipoo. It's another aspect of New Zealand bird life that I hope will appeal to the younger generation and maybe get them interested in conservation, too.'

We were making a brief stop to look for a distant relative of the kakapo, a notorious mountain-dwelling parrot called the kea, which chose its own name. In fact, it calls it out loud and clear – a raucous 'keee-aa, keee-aa, keee-aa' – which is great for identification purposes and saves ornithologists all the bother of coming up with a name themselves. It hasn't yet learnt to say its scientific name, *Nestor notabilis*, but these things take time.

The kea is widely lauded as the most intelligent bird in the world. You're probably expecting me to say, at this point, that it's the Stephen Fry of the bird world. But I won't. Stephen always maintains that, despite never-ending claims to the contrary, he's not unnaturally intelligent – he's merely fortunate enough to have an outstandingly retentive memory. It's an interesting theory, with which I wholeheartedly disagree. He is exceedingly intelligent *and* has an outstandingly retentive memory.

The kea calls out its name loud and clear – a raucous 'keee-aa, keee-aa keee-aa'. It hasn't yet learnt to say its scientific name *Nestor notabilis*, but these things take time.

The kea isn't only intelligent, though. It is also charismatic, curious, bold, destructive and reckless. And it's one of the few large birds in New Zealand that hasn't forgotten how to fly.

If you ever want to see one, go to a busy public place. They tend to loiter around ski resorts, alpine picnic sites and car parks, partly because these offer an easy source of junk food and partly because that's where they can get up to most mischief.

Open windows, boot lids and rucksacks provide them with an endless source of pleasure. They carry away any unguarded items of clothing or jewellery and hide them behind rocks, where they sort them in order of size so meticulously that it's hard to believe they don't suffer from obsessive compulsive disorder.

You couldn't take a kea on an aeroplane as hand luggage because its beak would be considered a dangerous weapon. Like a cross between a pair of pliers, a screwdriver and a can opener, it is implausibly powerful and manipulative. And it has claws to match.

So perhaps it's not surprising that keas make excellent car thieves. They don't steal entire cars, of course, but only for the simple reason that they can't reach the pedals. Instead, they steal bits of cars: they are particularly adept at peeling off rubber wiper blades and door seals. They do it with such determination and regularity that it's hard not to imagine them hoarding enough bits to build their own hybrid cars somewhere in the mountains. Just a couple of hubcaps and a wing mirror and they're done…

They can open all manner of containers. A popular pastime among people living in the wilder parts of New Zealand, where there is little else to do, is to try and design a kea-proof container. No one has done it yet, needless to say, so clearly it's a pastime that will keep them busy for many years to come.

Ski huts are a particular favourite with naughty keas. They wait for unwary skiers to leave their doors or windows open, then dive inside to shred all the mats, mattresses and pillows. They enjoy a bit of skiing themselves, too, using the steepest chalet roofs as their ski runs.

At one ski chalet a gang of keas famously posted a sentry outside the main door. Every time it looked as if someone was about to leave, the sentry alerted the others and they started kicking snow from the roof over the door. The skier got covered in snow and all the keas rolled about cackling.

Did I mention, by the way, that the kea is another endangered species? Did I really need to? This is New Zealand, after all.

We went to see them at a car park by the entrance to the 1.3-kilometre (0.8-mile) long Homer Tunnel. Several of the surprisingly large birds surrounded our car as soon as we pulled up, like the people who force you to have your windscreen cleaned before you've come to a complete stop at red traffic lights.

Much like the adrenalin junkies in nearby Queenstown, the keas in the car park didn't stand still. Peering and poking, ducking and diving, they behaved like armed magpies on steroids. One even tobogganed down the windscreen of the car next to us – twice.

They were gorgeous birds, basically olive-green with bright flashes of red, yellow and orange, and awfully endearing.

After watching them for a while, we were struck by the fact that only a couple were really badly behaved. They were the mischief-makers, while the others watched from the sidelines and egged them on.

One of the ring-leaders stole a man's baseball cap from the passenger seat of a bright red Vauxhall Astra and, while it was being chased across the car park by the rightful owner, his wife and their daughter, all the other keas just turned the other way. If they could have shuffled their feet, twiddled their thumbs or whistled nonchalantly that's exactly what they would have done. They looked about as innocent as juvenile delinquents caught smoking behind the bike shed.

The thief meanwhile, perched on a high rock with the baseball cap in its beak, stared back with a disdainful look that said 'Oh yeah, and what are you going to do about it?'

We watched them for absolutely ages.

There was just one problem: we still had the 'effing robin' (Stephen's words, not mine) to see before our final destination in kakapo country. Stephen was convinced that it was going to be an anticlimax.

'Stopping off to see the kea first is a bit like seeing a really good movie,' he said, 'and then being forced to fly 800 kilometres (500 miles) to sit through all the adverts.'

But I was confident. There is much more to the Chatham Island robin than I'd led him to believe.

We flew to the Chatham Islands in an old Convair CV-580 that looked as if it had been built by the first inhabitants of this isolated archipelago some 500 years earlier.

We were checked in by Chris, a vivacious and no-nonsense woman with a brightly coloured cravat; she would have made an outstanding drama teacher. Our bags were loaded onto the plane by Chris, too, this time without the cravat but with a support belt (one of those harnesses to stop the discs in your back, or your intestines, from popping out when they're not supposed to). And Chris was our flight attendant, complete with a navy blue flight attendant's jacket.

We were among a handful of passengers squashed in between piles of old crayfish boxes, which were hidden under expansive sheets of bright blue tarpaulin like bodies travelling back from a war zone.

Chris shouted safety instructions above the ear-splitting noise of the two turbo-prop engines and then made us tea and coffee (the flight had been delayed for nearly half an hour while we all helped her search for the kettle, which had gone missing).

It was the beginning of our fourth month travelling together and, by the time we landed, I think Stephen and I must have morphed into one another.

As soon as we stepped into the ramshackle little airport on the main island, the first thing I did was to check to see if there was mobile reception. There wasn't. I glanced over at Stephen to see if he'd had any luck with his arsenal of mobiles, and caught him peering through binoculars at some Chatham Island oystercatchers on the runway.

'There's no mobile reception,' I said.

'Ah well,' he replied, indifferently. 'It's only for a few days. Anyway, are those Chatham Island oystercatchers on the runway?'

He glanced away from his binoculars and gave me a wry smile as we briefly made eye contact.

He looked at the birds again.

'Aren't they among the rarest birds in the world?' he asked. 'I think there may be fewer than a hundred left and they're found nowhere else.'

'How do you know that?'

'Er, um, I don't know. I think I just read it somewhere.'

'You've been swotting on Wikipedia again, haven't you?'

'No I haven't. Well, maybe I had a quick look. I can't really remember.'

Rather alarmingly, as well as morphing into one another temperamentally, we also seemed to be slipping into what Stephen describes as 'involuntary chromatic synchronisation'. To the rest of us this means that, for some weird and inexplicable reason, after months of travelling together we started to wear exactly the same coloured clothes.

We had developed a form of sub-conscious colour coordination, like a newly formed 1980s boy band.

'Do you happen to be menstruating today,' joked Stephen on the morning we flew to the Chathams, implying that we were a couple of girls in sync. We'd both reported for duty wearing navy blue shorts and light green T-shirts. We looked like molly-coddled twins dressed by an overly doting mother.

The Chatham Islands form a tiny archipelago some 800 kilometres (500 miles) east of New Zealand. Barely a dot on the world map, they are home to about 600 hardy souls of mixed European, Maori and Polynesian descent. There are two main islands – Chatham and Pitt – and these are surrounded by several smaller islands, islets, rocks and stacks, spanning a total radius of about 40 kilometres (25 miles).

The Chathams sit slap-bang on the international date line and, indeed, Pitt Island (population 35) is further east than any other inhabited island in the world. This means that a fisherman leaving Pitt today can sail a few kilometres east and suddenly be in tomorrow. Or is it yesterday? We tried it once and got incredibly confused.

Rather than have a time zone that puts them in a permanent parallel universe between today and tomorrow, or yesterday, the islanders have solved the problem with their own unique time zone – not a handy and simple one hour ahead of New Zealand, but a confusing and difficult 45 minutes.

It's a friendly place, with the quiet charm of a secluded Cornish fishing village.

Everyone waves to everyone else.

'Oh my God!' said Stephen, on the one occasion we forgot to wave to a passing Land Rover. 'You know what's going to happen now?'

'No.'

'You've seen the movies. Next time they see us they'll pull out a pump-action shotgun.'

Best of all, the Chathams are among the best places in the world for bird-watching.

Now, before I lose you, I am fully aware that saying 'this is one of the best places in the world for bird-watching' is about as exciting to most normal people as saying 'let me explain the intricacies of Morris dancing' or 'have you tried the new 1.2.14 version of software for small business accounting?'.

So let me explain.

Evolution has worked with reckless abandon in the Chatham Islands. Like a mad professor in a biologically sealed laboratory, far from the madding crowd, it has been able to design new species without interference from the rest of the world.

One in every three birds in this little Garden of Eden in the middle of the South Pacific is found absolutely nowhere else. The Chatham Island oystercatchers at the airport, the Chatham Island warbler feeding in scrub next to the only proper tar-sealed road into town, and the Chatham Island pigeons in the hotel garden are all endemic.

I fear I might be losing you again, but bear in mind that this would probably sound a lot more riveting if the ornithologists studying these unique birds found nowhere else in the world had a little more imagination for diverse and inspiring names. I know 'Chatham Island pigeon' does what it says on the tin, but it's a bit like calling a kitten 'Kitty' or a café 'The Café'.

If I ever discover a new species, I'm going to invite dozens of my best zoology friends to a special naming party and we'll drink lots of champagne and discuss endless possibilities late into the night until we've dreamed up the most original and ingenious name ever thought possible.

Don Merton, the man who saved Richard Henry Junior (the last surviving kakapo on the mainland) with a goalie's dive, joined us in the Chatham Islands. Don is to conservation in New Zealand what Nelson was to naval warfare in Britain. With the air of a vicar and the determination of an Olympic athlete, he has a string of conservation successes under his belt.

It was Don who took Douglas Adams and me to see the kakapo twenty years ago. He hadn't changed a bit: he looked roughly the same age as he did then, was wearing exactly the same glasses and was still smiling. Don never stopped smiling.

He had retired from his old job at the Department of Conservation, but seemed to be as active in the conservation world as ever before.

Don was keen to show us a rather unremarkable little bird: a black robin called – rather unremarkably – the Chatham Island black robin. Never happier than when foraging among leaf litter on the forest floor, hunting for cockroaches, wetas and worms, it is the kind of bird you would be forgiven for overlooking.

Opposite
With Don Merton – the man responsible for saving the Chatham Island black robin and for catching Richard Henry Junior with a goalie's dive.

Below
The Chatham Island black robin came closer to extinction (without falling off the map altogether) than any other animal on the planet.

But it does have two claims to fame. First, the soles of its feet are bright yellow. And, second, it came closer to extinction (without actually vanishing altogether) than any other animal on the planet.

Chatham Island black robins were once found throughout the archipelago. But when cats, rats and mice were introduced, they began to disappear. As if the onslaught of predators wasn't enough, vast tracts of their forest home were cleared and converted to farmland.

Many other Chatham Island birds suffered, too. A mind-boggling one-third of the 64 species that once bred in the islands are now extinct.

Against all the odds, the robins somehow survived. But by 1880 they had retreated to one last stronghold: a tiny, mammal-free, 10-hectare (25-acre) rocky stack called Little Mangere. And that was it. There was nowhere else. Little Mangere was effectively a life raft from a different time – and the clock was ticking.

Let's skip forward a century to 1980, by which time there were just five Chatham Island robins left. Three of them were loners and showed no interest in starting a family. That left just one breeding pair.

Don and his team were galvanised into action and initiated a daring and dramatic rescue operation to try to save the species. It was a long shot and there was no room for mistakes.

All five birds were moved to a larger sanctuary on Little Mangere's big brother, called Mangere Island, from which all the predators had been removed.

'Much of the credit for the success of this last-ditch effort to save the Chatham Island black robin must be given to two particular birds,' Don told us. 'They were the last breeding female, called Old Blue, and her mate, Old Yellow.'

Stephen raised a quizzical eyebrow.

'They were named for the colour of their leg bands,' laughed Don.

This is a famous story in the conservation world, told around campfires from Tiverton to Timbuktu and quoted in endangered species conferences as the reason why, no matter how bad things may seem, we must never give up hope.

It's one of the most remarkable conservation success stories of all time.

But I could see Stephen struggling to accept the improbability of it all. He thought we were winding him up.

'So let me get this straight,' he said to Don. 'This species was so endangered that there was just one breeding pair left?'

'That's right.'

Stephen still wasn't sure.

Don was keen for us to see one of his beloved robins, so we hitched a ride on a cray-fishing boat and sailed 38 kilometres (24 miles) from the main island to Southeast Island.

As soon as we left shore the boat was rising and falling in the heavy swell. So were the remains of last night's shepherd's pie. Much worse and it would have brought to mind emergency flares, Mayday calls and air-sea rescues.

I spent the two-hour journey looking at bottlenose dolphins, Buller's albatrosses, Royal albatrosses and red-billed gulls, while Stephen spent it looking uncomfortably green about the gills.

Every time we hurtled over the crest of a wave, and free-fell down the other side, it felt as if we had been standing in an elevator when the cable had snapped. The only difference was that, instead of being carried away on a stretcher and given a few weeks off work, we were thrown back in and winched up ready for the cable to snap again. And again, and again.

It calmed a little as we approached Southeast Island. By then, the sensation wasn't quite so violent: more like being in a washing machine on the spin cycle.

Having spent much of my working life on all manner of boats in all corners of the globe, I have learned a thing or two about the dreaded *mal de mer*, or seasickness.

Firstly, the Japanese seem to suffer from it more than any other nationality.

Secondly, artists, writers and other creative people tend to suffer more than practical people such as those in the pharmaceutical industry or bricklayers.

Top
The Buller's albatross Stephen didn't see, mainly because he was seasick.

Above
An imaginatively named Chatham Island shore plover.

Thirdly, if you worry about it you are more likely to get sick than if you turn your mind to more pleasant things. In this respect, it's like jet lag: people who are constantly saying 'Ooh, it's 3.30 in the morning at home right now' are the ones who will be tired all the time.

Finally, it's like giggling: if one person starts it's hard not to join in. I was once on a whale-watch trip off the coast of New England, when a humpback whale came right alongside the boat. A man on board vomited over the side and his sick went straight into the whale's blowhole. The whale blew it all out, understandably, and showered everyone on deck in the process. The poor animal left pretty quickly when every single whale-watcher, me included, started to retch.

As soon as Stephen was feeling better, Don led us along the rocky coast of Southeast Island, through some thick bushes and into a shady little forest in the centre.

We'd barely dumped our bags on the forest floor before there was a fluttering in the undergrowth. Suddenly, there was a Chatham Island black robin perched on a thin branch right next to us, bobbing up and down. There was no doubt it had found us, rather than the other way around, and very quickly we were joined by its mate.

Don pulled a bag of wriggling mealworms from his pocket, brought specially for the occasion, and started to entice them in to within no more than a metre (3 feet) or so.

'Ooh,' said Stephen. 'Can I feed them?'

In profile they looked exactly like our European robins and they were pretty much the same size. They even moved in the same way. The only difference was that they were black instead of brown and red-breasted. Close up, they looked exactly like the tame robin that once fell down the chimney of our old house in Luton, all covered in soot, when I was about ten years old.

'They're not related to your robins at all,' said Don. 'Oh no, no, they belong to a completely different genus,' he added, as if the mere suggestion of a similar bird somewhere else in the world was an unforgivable insult to his feathered friends.

'Have you noticed the green- and white-coloured rings on that one?' I asked Stephen.

He was too busy to hear me – gently holding out a mealworm and trying unsuccessfully to coax the robin onto his hand with kissing sounds and a high-pitched 'come on darling, come on, it's okay, come on.'

'We've used coloured rings since the beginning,' said Don, 'ever since Old Blue. She was a wonderful bird, tolerating our endless manipulation of her breeding attempts. She began to breed successfully in 1979, at the grand old age of nine. Thank goodness she lived until she was thirteen, which is extraordinary for a

bird with a normal life expectancy of just six or seven years. If she hadn't lived so long and bred throughout her geriatric years, the Chatham Island black robin would certainly have become extinct.'

'So in a way it was just luck, then?' asked Stephen.

Don is incredibly modest and he started to nod in agreement, so I intervened.

'There was an element of luck, of course. But Don and his team developed some incredibly inventive and pioneering new conservation techniques to make it happen. And now these are being used in other parts of the world to save other endangered birds.'

'And we took a lot of risks, too,' added Don. 'We had to – we had no choice. It was all or nothing. We translocated birds to safer areas within the Chathams, we used Chatham Island tomtits as foster parents for some of the eggs and chicks, and we manipulated the breeding pairs. By 1986, we'd managed to increase the population to 37 birds. The situation was a lot better than it once was, but 37 was still a dangerously low number. And, indeed, there was a major setback the same year when a massive storm wiped out 14 of the robins. That took us back to 23.'

'How many are there now?' I asked.

'Well, now there are more than we can easily count. Which, of course, is a good thing. I would say somewhere between 200 and 250.'

'But because they are descended from just one breeding pair aren't they suffering from some sort of inbreeding? Don't they have genetic abnormalities?' asked Stephen.

'Well, all the Chatham Island black robins alive today are genetically identical,' smiled Don. 'They are virtual clones of one another. But so far it doesn't seem to be a problem.'

'Fingers crossed,' Stephen and I said in unison, as you might expect mollycoddled twins to do.

We burst out laughing.

'Yes,' said Don, smiling and holding two crossed fingers in the air. 'Fingers crossed.'

There was a time when you could tramp deep into the rugged mountainous region of Fiordland, tucked away in the southwestern corner of South Island, pitch a tent on the boggy floor of a steep-sided valley, wait until dark, and listen to one of the greatest live outdoor concerts in the world.

The best way to enjoy the concert was to lie next to your tent, with your eyes closed.

First, you would hear a deep, body-trembling, reverberating bass sound coming from somewhere high up in the mountains. It was like a foghorn, or distant thunder, or someone blowing across the top of a large empty bottle. Or perhaps more like a heartbeat.

It was such a low-frequency sound that it was just on the threshold of what you could actually hear and what you could feel in the pit of your stomach. Boom, boom, boom, it echoed across the valley sides in the darkness.

Sometimes, there would be more booms coming from different corners of the valley slopes.

You'd have been listening to the unearthly mating calls of the old night parrots of New Zealand. Male kakapo, to be precise.

I should explain why I keep saying 'kakapo' instead of 'kakapos', because it annoyed Stephen and so it's probably annoying you. I don't like it, either, when people talk in the singular when they should be talking in the plural (as in 'we saw a family of gorilla' or 'there are three rhino'). But there's a simple explanation: 'kakapo' is a Maori word and they don't use plurals. In fact, there is no 's' in the Maori language at all, so 'kakapos' would be entirely wrong (plus, Douglas and I got told off for saying 'kakapos' in the original *Last Chance to See* and I couldn't bear another onslaught of cantankerous letters).

Anyway, when the breeding season looms, the male kakapo head for the hills. They climb higher and higher, using their short legs and big feet to clamber up the steep slopes, until they reach a really good vantage point. There they search for a suitable rock or tree trunk and dig a shallow depression about a metre (3 feet) across – known as a 'bowl' – in the ground alongside. They are looking for good acoustics: the bowl acts as an amplifier and the rock or tree trunk serves as a reflector.

Then they do a bit of gardening. They clear a couple of pathways, known as 'tracks', by weeding out all the unsightly vegetation with their beaks. Nearly a metre (3 feet) wide and up to 20 metres (66 feet) long, and meticulously maintained, these tracks lead a merry path through the undergrowth right up to the bowl (they are easy to spot because they look much tidier than all the other tracks made by less house-proud animals blundering their way about through the scrub).

There is method in the male kakapo's madness. If it could shower, dress in fine clothes and hang about in bars, it probably would. It would certainly be an easier way to pull the birds. But it can't. So it builds a 'track and bowl system' instead. Every night during the breeding season, most male kakapo are sitting inside their bowls, puffing up enormous air sacs in their chests, lowering their heads, and booming competitively.

As Stephen pointed out one evening, they defy economic law by having a boom in a depression.

They seem to defy physical and biological law, too. Their deep, powerful booms carry over huge distances – possibly as far as 5 kilometres (3 miles) with the help of the wind – but are so incredibly deep that it's really hard to tell where they are coming from. This must be something of a shortcoming in a mating call: the kakapo's booming display is rather like the balcony scene in *Romeo and Juliet*, except Romeo is throwing his voice and hiding.

Douglas Adams described roughly how it might go in human terms: 'Come and get me!' 'Where are you?' 'Come and *get* me!' 'Where the hell are you?' 'Come and get me!' 'Oh, for heaven's sake.' 'Come and get me!' 'Go and stuff yourself.'

It's not that the females aren't willing. When they are in the mood, their sex drive is extremely strong. They have been known to walk 10 kilometres (6 miles) in a single night to visit booming males, and then walk all the way back again in the morning.

The most likely explanation is that, as the females get closer, the males make special 'chinging' sounds to guide them in. After all, the system must work to a degree or there would be no kakapo left at all.

Come to think about it, there are no kakapo left on the mainland. So, sadly, all concerts there have been cancelled until further notice.

If the male kakapo could shower, dress in fine clothes and hang about in bars, it probably would.

However, concerts are still being held on Codfish Island – and we were lucky enough to have tickets. So, two weeks into our three-week trip, we set off on our final adventure: to see and hear a real-life kakapo.

We just had a couple of small health issues to sort out first.

The Rolling Stones played in Invercargill in the early 1960s and reputedly received such a lacklustre reception that they were pelted with tomatoes. Mick Jagger famously stopped singing, lip pouting and hip shaking just long enough to accuse the locals of living in 'the arsehole of the world', and the southernmost town in New Zealand has struggled to recover from the shock ever since.

We didn't see enough of Invercargill to judge, although we certainly felt at home. Many of the streets appeared to be named after British rivers: Tay, Dee, Esk, Don, Thames, Spey and Eye among them. It's best known for having the only indoor arena for track cycling in the country. Oh, and one of its more famous residents was the inventor of the spiral hairpin.

Apart from the Southland Quarantine Facility, the only other part of the city I saw was a doctor's surgery. I'd been feeling ill, and progressively more ill, for several days, so the night before heading for Codfish Island we decided to check that I hadn't got anything too deadly.

The doctor couldn't believe his luck – something a little out of the ordinary, instead of the usual detached retina he sees most often thanks to so many bungee-jumping tourists popping their eyes out on a daily basis.

'Have you been camping or sleeping in rough conditions?' he asked.

'Yes.'

'Ah, good. Here in New Zealand?'

'Yes. But also in Kenya, Uganda and Madagascar. And before that I was in the Australian Outback and Arctic Canada...'

He raised an eyebrow and hesitated in the way doctors hesitate before pulling open a drawer full of sharp instruments.

'Excellent!' he said.

'Have you handled any animals in the past couple of months?'

'Um, yes. Rhinos, chimpanzees, several different snakes and lizards, kangaroo rats, lots of lemurs, giant wetas... oh, and a tuatara.'

'Brilliant!' he said, while raising his eyebrow a little higher as if he were about to open a drawer of even longer and sharper instruments.

'I hope you're not in a hurry,' he added gleefully, while actually opening a drawer full of sharp instruments. 'This could take some time to sort out. Have you ever been diagnosed with malaria, hepatitis, sleeping sickness or bilharzia?'

'Yes.'

'Which?'

'All of them.'

An hour of prodding and probing and blood-sucking later, I was diagnosed with a mild case of malaria, handed a prescription, and sent on my way.

Meanwhile, Stephen seemed to have developed an allergy to New Zealand (or, at least, to certain parts of New Zealand).

We didn't really take much notice the first time it manifested itself. While we were filming wetas on Matiu-Somes Island, in Wellington Harbour, one of the giant insects had urinated on his hand, which promptly came up in a raging red rash.

We still didn't take it too seriously when he developed a distinctly different blotchy red rash right across his neck, after stroking a kiwi in the Kauri Forest.

As soon as the blotchy red rash had disappeared, his other hand was scratched by Sirocco – a humanoid kakapo on Codfish Island – and an eye-catching white welt promptly took its place. But we put that down merely to a general allergy to sleeping in anything resembling rough accommodation and a world without wi-fi.

The morning after my doctor's appointment he came down to breakfast

'Have you ever been diagnosed with malaria, hepatitis, sleeping sickness or bilharzia?'

'Yes.'

'Which?'

'All of them.'

with a bright red bloodshot eye, and we started to piece the puzzle together. The bloodshot eye must have been a reaction to Don's mealworms, or perhaps even to the Chatham Island black robins. We'll never know for sure.

But we agreed that next time he had to fill in one of those forms that asks 'any known allergies?' he'd have to write 'Yes – New Zealand.'

Meanwhile, Stephen was reluctantly turning his mind to what was in store for the next few days. I'd already warned him that the accommodation, or wooden hut, was pretty basic and that we would be sharing.

He was none too pleased.

'If we're roughing it for four nights can we at least take a bottle of vodka with us?' he asked at breakfast. 'In fact, why don't we take more than one? Or better still let's just take some anaesthetic, to knock me out.'

I laughed, but he wasn't joking.

'Will we be the only people on Codfish?' he asked, gradually easing himself in to the reality that we had to go. He was surprisingly excited about the prospect of meeting a kakapo, but unsurprisingly unexcited about the prospect of sleeping in a hut with me in order to do it.

'No, there will be some Department of Conservation rangers and a team of volunteers,' I replied.

'Oh God. Not volunteers. It'll be full of worthy, stringy people in ponytails.

Will we have to sit around a campfire and sing songs and tell stories?'

'Don't be daft. It won't be like that at all.'

'I'd like to talk about how Jesus came into my life…' he mocked in a pseudo-volunteer voice. 'I'm a vegan you know. Oh do pass the rice cakes.'

Codfish Island is a cartographic speck off the extreme southern end of New Zealand. A 1,400-hectare (3,460-acre), bush-covered, predator-free nature reserve, a few kilometres off the wild west coast of Stewart Island, it is the kakapo capital of the world.

During our visit Codfish was home to no fewer than 75 of the last surviving kakapo: 38 breeding females, 6 non-breeding females and 31 males.

Nowhere else in the world had females. It was quite an alarming thought: all the eggs were in one basket, almost literally.

There were another fifteen birds living on Anchor Island, in Dusky Sound, Fiordland, but they were all male (all the females had been moved to the relative safety of Codfish in 2007, during an emergency evacuation launched after a stoat had been spotted on the island).

There were no kakapo in captivity (they don't do well in confined spaces), so that made a grand total of just ninety.

It was a far cry from centuries ago, when kakapo were counted in millions and so common all over New Zealand that people used to claim you could shake a tree and three or four of them would fall out.

Clearly we didn't learn any lessons from the passenger pigeon, after all.

The good news was that the situation had improved, albeit just a little. When Douglas and I went to look for kakapo in 1989, the population had reached an all-time low of just forty birds – and many people had pretty much given up hope.

In the twenty years since then, the population had doubled, plus a little bit.

There should have been six of us going to Codfish – director, cameraman, soundman, assistant producer, Stephen and I. But in the end we were given permission for only four to go. Two had to stay behind.

Stephen generously volunteered to stay, unless they could build a comfortable hotel during the course of the morning. But clearly they couldn't.

So we waved goodbye to Emily (our assistant producer) and Don (the soundman) in Invercargill and the remaining four set off in a Piper Cherokee 6 plane for a beach at Mason Bay, on Stewart Island. We landed on the sand and jumped straight into a waiting helicopter, James Bond-style, for the final leg of the journey.

'It reminds me of being in prison,' said Stephen as we walked into the wooden hut on Codfish that would be our home for the rest of the week. 'What you in for, then?' he asked in a Ronnie Barker voice, as if we were in *Porridge*. 'Did you do it? Which bunk do you want?'

It was actually quite a comfortable hut, with proper beds, mattresses and even pillows. Perhaps I wouldn't need to anaesthetise Stephen after all.

We sorted out our kit and went to the main bunkhouse to meet our fellow castaways. There were nine of them altogether – Chris, Ness, Jo, Errol and Dana were the rangers, and Jake, Norm, Sari and Kristina were the volunteers.

There wasn't a single ponytail in sight. Stephen looked mightily relieved.

At the height of the kakapo breeding season, the bunkhouse and dormitories would be overflowing with more than forty rangers and volunteers. It sounded like a lot, but these were the lucky few: apparently, there was a waiting list of more than 700 people keen to volunteer to help save the old night parrot of New Zealand.

There was a lot to be done and each person had an important role.

Dana, for example, was a crack shot with a rifle and her job was to shoot branches out of the trees to put at all the kakapo feeding stations. Her main target was the rimu tree, a gargantuan conifer endemic to New Zealand, which is the kakapo's favourite source of food on Codfish: they tend to breed only when the rimu produce copious crops of fruit and seeds – every two to five years.

Sari helped to prepare pellets for the 'smart hoppers', which are basically high-tech bird tables designed specifically for kakapo to ensure that each bird gets exactly the right amount of food. The molly-coddled parrots were never allowed to go hungry – nothing in the world of kakapo conservation is left to chance. Then Sari filled her cavernous rucksack with all the food (it was so heavy I could barely lift it off the ground) and set off into the forest to deliver her wares.

Ness, Chris and several of the others had the job of keeping an eagle eye on the birds themselves. They regularly checked for signs of life and activity, though rarely actually got to see any of the birds in their care.

'Sometimes I get to see a male called Nog,' Ness told us. 'He is quite often at his feeding hopper when I approach and lets me get to within a few metres of him. Then he gives me a resigned look as if to say "Oh dear, I'm supposed to run away at this point, aren't I?" And with that he hunches up and begrudgingly waddles off into the forest.'

The strangest and unlikeliest job goes to a Spanish consultant, who visits Codfish for a couple of weeks every year. He comes, if that's the right word, to masturbate the male kakapo. The idea is to collect semen for examination and artificial insemination. It's a job that takes him around the world, working on a wide range of hapless endangered species, but it's one that must be unbelievably difficult to explain at dinner parties.

We talked about him, in particular, discussed the rangers' gruelling rota (one month on and two weeks off throughout the year) and pored over an old weather-beaten map of the island.

The various beaches, outcrops, ravines and paths had some interesting names – dreamed up, we presumed, by people who had spent too much time cut off from the rest of the world. Dirty Habits, Longdrop, Cleavage, Po Zone, Mudwiggle, Eric, Wounded Knee, Humbug, Arnie's Mistake, Far Canal and Hell were some of the best.

But who are we to criticise? If they'd been named by the unimaginative ornithologists who'd already come up with 'Chatham Island pigeon', the map would probably have featured the likes of Big Round Rock, Sandy Beach, Forest Walk and North-west-Corner-of-Codfish-Island-with-a-Tall-Tree Point.

That night at dinner we listened quietly to one of the strangest conversations we'd ever heard.

Above
Dear old Ralph twenty years younger, with Arab the freelance kakapo-tracker.

The rangers and volunteers on Codfish were utterly, wholly, almost obsessively devoted to saving the kakapo. They ate, slept and talked kakapo 24 hours a day (well, they didn't actually eat them – but you know what I mean). Each and every bird was important and they knew all about their likes and dislikes, their movements and their foibles.

All the birds had names – often borrowed from the rangers and volunteers themselves. So it was surprisingly difficult to tell whether the topic of conversation was a kakapo or a person.

'Lisa mated with Basil last night.'

'Ah, that's great. I think he's had his eye on her for quite a while.'

'Is Rachel coming tomorrow? I wonder if she'll remember to bring spare batteries for my head torch.'

'Yes, I'm going to ask her to spend the night with Felix, because I don't think he's feeling very well.'

'Why, what's wrong?'

'He hasn't been booming much the last week or so.'

'Good idea. Is Rachel coming with Lionel? Are they still together?'

'That reminds me – Nora has been visiting Lionel's track-and-bowl system for three nights in a row, which is a good sign.'

'I thought Lionel fancied Ellie.'

'No, not at all. She only has eyes for Luke.'

'Did Ellie have dinner with Chris when they were on the mainland?'

And so it went on.

Every time I caught Stephen's eye across the table we started to chuckle. Goodness knows what everyone at the Department of Conservation must have thought of us. We laughed more during our visit to the other side of the world than we did during all of our other travels put together.

After a while, I couldn't resist joining in the conversation by asking about an old friend of my own.

'How's Ralph?' I asked the table at large.

Ralph was a male kakapo found on Stewart Island, in January 1987, and moved to Codfish the following year. Douglas and I met him in 1989 and I'd often wondered how he had been doing (all right, I admit it, the rangers and volunteers weren't alone in falling under the kakapo's spell).

'Ralph?' laughed Ness, one of the rangers. 'Ralph is hopeless.'

'What do you mean?' I asked, feeling sorry for my old friend, and suddenly rather protective.

'Oh, he's all right,' she added, sensing my reaction. 'He's still here, but he's not all that keen on booming. As far as we know, the last time he mated was in 1999, with

A Spanish consultant collects semen from endangered birds for examination and artificial insemination. It's a job that takes him around the world, but it's one that must be unbelievably difficult to explain at dinner parties.

Suzanne. But then she laid infertile eggs.'

'Maybe he's just past it?' one of the volunteers suggested. 'He has lots of girls around him, but doesn't seem that interested.'

'Or perhaps they are put off by his arthritic leg?' interrupted another.

There were murmurings of agreement around the table.

It seemed as if dear old Ralph was a bit of a lost cause, though I was happy just knowing that he was still alive and all right after all these years.

I shouldn't have been surprised. Kakapo are believed to live to a hundred years or more and may, indeed, be among the longest-lived birds in the world. In fact, none of the kakapo known to scientists has yet died of old age and the chances are that some of the youngsters will outlive the people who are trying to protect them. Perhaps it's because they do everything more slowly than other birds: they are the tuatara of the bird world.

It's hard to explain, but it felt really good to be sharing Codfish with Ralph a second time around.

Then something extraordinary happened. That evening, after supper, Ness set off in the dark for one of her regular night patrols. We saw her again at breakfast, looking tired but clearly overjoyed.

She could hardly contain her excitement and started talking as soon as she burst through the door.

'Guess what? You'll never believe it. I can't believe it myself. It's amazing.'

'What?' we all asked, wondering what on earth had happened.

'It's Ralph. He was booming last night. Not just a feeble pretence at booming, but a real, heartfelt, professional boom. For the first time in… in… goodness knows how long. It's like he's found a whole new lease of life. It's amazing.'

We all agreed that it was indeed absolutely amazing. And, naturally… I took full credit.

That night I was woken by Stephen muttering in the bunk opposite.

'Oh God, I need to have a pee,' he said, to no-one in particular. 'I'm really going to have to have a pee.'

'Oh dear,' I sympathised, half asleep. 'Can't you wait until morning?'

'Nooooo. I've been lying here for an hour, trying to convince myself that I can, but I can't.'

It was pelting with rain outside. Our waterproofs were by the fire in the main hut and the toilet was 100 metres (330 feet) up a dirt track in the forest.

'Do you think he'll be out there?' asked Stephen, nervously.

Above
Mark took full credit for dear old Ralph's new lease of life.

Opposite
Sirocco, the effing man-eating parrot, looking innocent.

'Probably. In fact, isn't that him skrarking now?'

Stephen groaned. He sat on the side of his bed, huffing and puffing and tying up his bootlaces. We both listened to the unmistakable high-pitched screaming and squealing coming from the darkness outside the hut. It sounded like something out of *The Blair Witch Project*.

'Oh God,' said Stephen, again. 'It's going to ambush me. It's definitely going to attack me. Do you think I could pee out of the window?'

'No, you bloody well can't!'

'Maybe I'll just pee in my bed, then.'

'That's what I've been doing.'

'You're kidding?'

'Of course I am! I'm just very careful not to drink too much in the evenings so I don't have to go outside after dark.'

'Why didn't you tell me? Oh God. Now I have to run the effing gauntlet of an effing man-eating parrot.'

He cautiously opened the hut door and peered through a tiny gap into the pouring rain and the gloom.

Opposite
Sirocco looking like a mentally challenged dachshund, Mark looking well and truly ravished, and Stephen looking nervous.

'Right,' he said, melodramatically. 'I'm going. I'm going outside… I may be some time.'

The effing parrot in question was Sirocco, the closest thing to a man-eating parrot you are ever likely to see. An incorrigible 11-year-old, he literally terrorised the camp.

Sirocco had never mated with another kakapo, but had tried many times to mate with people.

The situation had become so bad that the entire compound was fenced to keep him and his over-amorous intentions well and truly out. The main aim was to give all the rangers and volunteers a safe passage up to the toilet, where he had inconveniently set up his track-and-bowl system, and between the dormitories and the bunkhouse.

So his human protectors were imprisoned inside this little fenced enclave, while Sirocco had the run of the whole of the rest of the island.

But it didn't work. Within hours of the fence being finished, he had discovered (or made) a hole underneath – a hole that has yet to be discovered by anyone else. Fence or no fence, he was spending as much time on the inside as he pleased – and that happened to be rather a lot.

We lost count of the number of times he rushed out of the bushes and tried to grab one of us by the leg.

One day Ranger Chris saw me being mauled, or should I say ravished, and called over.

'We need semen from him, to artificially inseminate one of the females, so if he tries to mate with you please can you collect some for us?'

I think he was being serious. What was I supposed to collect the semen in, exactly? One of the pockets in my shorts? A boot? My cupped hands?

Sirocco climbed up my leg, using his beak and claws like mountaineers use axes and crampons, then made his way up my back, and finally was rocking backwards and forwards on my head like a mentally retarded dachshund. His soft, musty-smelling feathers were rubbing against the back of my hair and his claws were digging into my neck.

'Take one for the team!' shouted Stephen, laughing hysterically from a safe distance away.

But it really hurt. He ripped a mole off my head, pierced one of my ears and scratched my cheek. Stephen suddenly noticed blood running down the back of my neck and stopped laughing. He ran over, shouting for Sirocco to stop.

Sirocco took no notice.

'Oh my God!' Stephen shouted to the camera team. 'Stop filming! This is serious. He's really getting hurt. Someone do something. Come on. Quickly.'

> We lost count of the number of times he rushed out of the bushes and tried to grab one of us by the leg.

Jo (Head of Kakapo Operations) heard the kerfuffle and leapt into action, pulling Sirocco off me by the scruff of his neck. She held him firmly on the ground, covered in her fleece and complaining loudly, while we made a dash for it: four grown men running away from an endangered parrot the size of a chicken.

I had a cut on my arm, too. With hindsight, I wish I had done what the Maori do and rubbed ash into the wound. Then I would have a kakapo scar. How cool that would have been.

Born on Codfish in 1997, the son of Zephyr and Felix, Sirocco was the smallest chick of his brood and partially hand-reared from the tender age of just three weeks. That, in a nutshell, was his problem. No one had actually explained to him that he was a kakapo.

Named after the hot wind that comes off the desert in North Africa and blows across southern Europe (what else would you call a parrot living in New Zealand?), he was transferred to Maud Island – and that's when all the trouble began.

One day, when the rangers and volunteers were taking some much-needed time off, he watched them running and jumping off a wooden jetty into the sea. Hating to be left out, he ran along the jetty and jumped into the sea with them.

Opposite
It wasn't so much
a walk as a wade.

That was the moment, as Sirocco calmly did a combination of breaststroke and doggy-paddle back to shore, that his astonished human carers discovered kakapo could swim.

When he was first moved to Codfish, he was introduced to a lovely new home range, with wonderful views, on the other side of the island. It was perfect. Any normal kakapo would have been delighted. But Sirocco didn't like it. He wanted to be with his human friends and kept walking all the way back to the rangers' hut. Time after time, they would catch him and carry him the one-and-a-half-hour trek back to his home on the other side of the island. But by the time they got back, and had a cup of tea, he'd already be outside the hut waiting to greet them.

Last year a TV crew wanted to film Sirocco. They built a special wooden hide to observe him, in the hope that he might behave more naturally if he couldn't see them. They waited in their hide all afternoon and then for most of the night, yet there was no sign of him. They were just about to give up when they heard a slight rustling sound. There was Sirocco, in the corner of the hide, waiting patiently with them.

Watching him from inside the safety of the hut was fun. He was a beautiful mottled green colour and full of life and bluster. We could see why he had his own page on Facebook (though, being a bird, he should really have been on Twitter – he could have rivalled Stephen and Barack Obama in the popularity stakes) and why he had an ever-increasing fan base worldwide. He was a lovable rogue – it was impossible not to fall for his innocent charm.

Several weeks after we left Codfish, though, we heard that it was becoming increasingly difficult for the volunteers to go outside. So he was moved to a secret island hideaway, with a couple of other males for company, to keep him out of trouble.

At least, that's what everyone had hoped…

Sirocco is named after the hot wind that comes off the desert in North Africa and blows across southern Europe (what else would you call a parrot living in New Zealand?).

The rangers and volunteers swore blind that it had been hot and dusty until the day before we arrived on Codfish, but it rained on and off for most of our stay.

We explored the island on foot, partly because that's the best way to experience its rich and beautiful diversity, but mainly because there was no alternative. There were no roads (not such a big issue given that there were no cars either) and even mountain bikes would have struggled through the rivers of mud.

On the first day there was a torrential downpour and everywhere was flooded. Stephen didn't fancy coming for a walk.

'Come on, Stephen, you have to go outside in the rain to experience the real New Zealand,' I cajoled.

'Ah, but you can only experience the real Stephen Fry by watching him stay indoors in the dry,' was his considered reply.

So I went with Ben, our director. The flimsy wooden boardwalk that weaved its way through the forest was under at least a metre (3 feet) of water. Imagine trying to tiptoe your way along a narrow tightrope in the dark and you'll get the idea. It wasn't so much a walk as a wade. And when we fell off the wooden planks (which was often – because they were invisible underwater) it wasn't so much a wade as a swim.

Strong currents almost swept our feet from under us, as creeks became streams and streams became fast-flowing rivers. There was thunder and light-ning, too, which merely added to the mood of this wild and rugged island far from home.

Against all the odds we found some kakapo droppings, which had a surpris-ingly sweet, herbal smell. As far as animal droppings go, they were quite pleasant (if you are that way inclined).

We had hoped to find Jem, an eight-month-old chick that had wisely moved up to higher, drier ground in the deeper recesses of the forest. We did see a green blur dashing off into the undergrowth, which we thought might have been her, but then gave up and turned back.

Above & below
Kakapo: not quite wrapped up in cotton wool, but almost.

Later that afternoon the lake next to our hut had shrunk to a pond and Jo persuaded Stephen to venture outside.

'It's a nice forest, though, isn't it?' I said to him, as we slipped and slid our way deeper into the interior.

'Yes, it is a nice forest. But why do we have to hike for three hours, when it was just as nice after three minutes? Let's be brutally honest, when you've seen one muddy puddle and one dripping wet tree you've seen them all.'

I laughed.

'Because we're looking for signs of kakapo,' I said.

'Yes, but we always seem to be hiking our arses off. And walking uphill. And sleeping in huts, or tents. It seems to be an unrelenting theme in *Last Chance to See*. Are you absolutely sure there aren't any endangered species that live in flat parts of the world near comfortable hotels?'

A lot of the hiking was, admittedly, up and down steep hills. The rangers and volunteers were super fit. Well, they would be, wouldn't they, after hik-ing with rucksacks stuffed full of equipment and kakapo food every day? We weren't quite so fit. In fact, struggling to keep up, we quickly realised that we weren't fit at all.

'One day I'll be in good shape,' muttered Stephen under his breath.

I huffed and puffed in knowing agreement.

We hiked to the home range of a kakapo called Merty, named after Don Merton, on the east side of the island. We wanted to take a look at his track-and-bowl system, which was next to the base of a tree and overlooking a long, sweeping wooded valley.

'I've just had a thought,' said Stephen when we got there.

'What's that?'

'When you say "kakapo booming in a bowl" it sounds like a euphemism for drug-taking.'

Jo gave me a funny look and smiled to herself. Kneeling on the ground, she tenderly removed a couple of leaves from inside Merty's bowl, like an affectionate wife picking a loose piece of cotton from her husband's suit.

Then she went to check a grey box that was fixed into the ground nearby.

'This is a "Snark",' she explained, seeing our quizzical looks. 'It's named in honour of Lewis Carroll's poem.'

Stephen's eyes lit up, as they inevitably did whenever anyone mentioned anything to do with literature. Immediately, he began to quote from Carroll's longest poem (though what do I know? – I think it's one of the longest, anyway). He was word-perfect, as always.

He would have continued right to the end, if I hadn't interrupted just as he got to 'By a finger entwined in his hair'.

'Why name a grey box after *The Hunting of the Snark*?' I asked Jo.

'Well, the poem is all about trying to find a mysterious, unlikely creature, isn't it? And that's exactly what we're doing here. The Snark is an electronic box of tricks designed to monitor Merty's comings and goings. It's a data-logger that records the time he spends at his track-and-bowl system each night and how much time he spends with different females.'

'How does it do that?' asked Stephen.

'Like all the kakapo on Codfish, he carries a radio transmitter on his back. It's a bit like a child's rucksack, with straps around the wings, except it is so small that it's virtually invisible under his feathers. The transmitter sends messages to the Snark and we decipher the recordings to see what he's been up to. It's important to know that he is okay.'

We checked the two tracks leading up to Merty's bowl. Then we filled his feeding hopper with pellets, pouring out the rainwater first, and stood back to check we hadn't missed anything.

There was little else we could do, short of catching him and wrapping him up in cotton wool.

We thought we'd just witnessed the ultimate in hands-on conservation. But little did we know.

The highlight of the trip came on the very last day. We were sitting in the bunkhouse when we heard a message hiss and crackle over the field radio.

We strained to hear and could just make it out: 'Lisa is sitting on eggs! Repeat. Lisa is sitting on eggs!'

Lisa was well known to all the rangers as the 'early warning bird'. She was always the first kakapo to mate and, sure enough, several weeks ahead of all her contemporaries, she had already mated with a male called Basil.

Rather romantically, their little rendezvous had taken place on Christmas night (nothing, but nothing, in the world of the kakapo is private).

She'd mated with Basil the year before, too. Lisa liked Basil. But then so did all the other female kakapo – he was a strong and impressive boomer, the Elvis of the kakapo world, and considered a pretty good catch.

It was exciting news, because these were the very first eggs of the season. Everyone in the bunkhouse whooped and cheered with delight.

We were given special permission to go and visit Lisa on the other side of the island. It meant another long, steep hike and I turned around to see Stephen's face. But he was already tying his bootlaces, eager to go.

We made it in record time and set up base camp about 50 metres (170 feet) from the nest.

First, we had to put up a tent. I say 'we' but I was helping to prepare the high-tech nest-monitoring equipment and Stephen was busy watching Jo doing the actual putting up. He did do a bit of directing, shouting snippets of helpful advice, as he supported his elbow with one hand and his chin on the other.

Stephen sat on a rock to recover, while Chris, Ness and I crept up to the nest to have a closer look. It was hidden inside a dark cavern under the tangled roots of a fallen tree.

We took it in turns to peer inside, which wasn't as easy as it sounds. One by one, we had to lie at a 45-degree angle and stick our heads inside the muddy main entrance with our feet sticking up into the sky. We emerged looking like coal miners at the face of a pit.

It was my turn and I struggled to get into position, using an infrared camera to see inside without causing any unnecessary disturbance. There was Lisa, just a metre (3 feet) or so away, blinking innocently back. Her eyes lit up in the way human eyes light up when they are being filmed with infrared in the dark.

'Are you absolutely sure there aren't any endangered species that live in flat parts of the world near comfortable hotels?' asked Stephen.

I was staring at a wild kakapo sitting on the very first eggs of the season. I couldn't believe it.

Like surveyors checking a property for potential house-buyers, Chris and Ness did a thorough inspection of Lisa's new home. There was lots of frowning, and pondering, and debating in hushed tones, but eventually they pronounced it fit for kakapo habitation.

'What if it hadn't been okay?' I whispered.

'Well, if there had been anything wrong,' answered Ness, 'we would have done some home improvements.'

'Like building a new roof,' added Chris, 'or more flood-proof walls.'

I watched as the two of them set up an infrared trip beam inside the nest cavity. They unravelled the cable, like a couple of bank robbers preparing to blow up a safe, all the way back to Stephen and the tent.

At last, we could talk normally.

The tent was for a couple of volunteers to camp out in the forest, where they could keep a watchful eye on Lisa and her valuable eggs each night. It looked a lot less cosy and waterproof than the nest.

During the course of a typical breeding season, every single kakapo nest is observed and protected round the clock. Whenever the birds come or go, they break the infrared beam and a loud doorbell rings inside the tent and wakes up the willing volunteers inside.

They have to get up in the dark and set to work on two main tasks before they can go back to bed.

First, they have to keep watch for intruders, such as seabirds or wandering male kakapo, to stop them stumbling about in the nest and accidentally damaging the eggs.

Second, they have to time the mother's absence whenever she leaves the nest.

If she is gone for too long they have to cover the eggs with a little electric blanket to keep them warm. This used to be made out of a whoopee cushion filled with wallpaper paste and heated by a battery-powered element, but nowadays it's a little more high-tech.

The volunteers have to sleep in the tent for about a month, until the eggs have hatched.

Timing her absence once the hatchlings have emerged is just as important. Kakapo eat food which has a very low nutritional value and so they need large amounts to survive: a foraging trip, on foot, can often take several hours. But if a mother stays away for too long, the volunteers have to report her to the rangers. This requires another long stint in the tent: the chicks don't fledge until they are about ten or eleven weeks old.

Above
Caught on the infrared camera – Lisa blinks innocently back from inside her nest hole.

Kakapo are excellent parents, but if food is scarce they make a habit of wandering off and leaving their eggs or chicks for far too long. Monitoring by volunteers enables early detection of this problem so that the eggs or chicks can be whisked away to the relative safety of an artificial incubator next to the bunkhouse.

What we were witnessing was the ultimate in eleventh-hour micro-conservation. The kakapo is so endangered, so close to the edge, that caring for its population as a whole, in the traditional sense, is no longer an option. The only real hope for the last few survivors is round-the-clock individual care and attention.

Whatever happens, the female kakapo are remarkably trusting and forgiving about all these intrusions. Perhaps they understand that everyone is there to help? Or perhaps it's simply this: they'll never learn to worry?

Soon after leaving Codfish, I had a call from Ness with the almost unbelievable news that another ranger, Chris, had just caught a male kakapo, called Ranji, that had been missing for an astonishing 22 years. That made a grand total of 91.

But there was more good news to come. The year 2009 proved to be a particularly busy and exciting one for everyone involved in kakapo conservation. It produced a bumper breeding season, with a record number of eggs and chicks.

The population, at the time of writing, now stands at 124.

Dear old Ralph, meanwhile, boomed heartily for the rest of the season.

5

POISONED
DAGGER

Our confusion over dates and time zones continued with a trip to Southeast Asia. Stephen flew from New York to London and on to Singapore, while I flew from San Francisco via Seoul. He had gained a day, I had lost a day, and somehow, as if we were travelling in weird parallel universes, we bumped into one another in a lift at the airport.

We'd both had haircuts and developed dark rings under our eyes in the week since we were last together, in New Zealand. Or was it Madagascar? Or perhaps it was Kenya? We'd clearly been on the road far too long.

'Sometimes I dream about staying at home, in my own time zone, and sleeping in my own bed,' said Stephen. 'Where are we going now? Oh God, don't tell me. It's Komodo, isn't it?'

It was. Komodo occupies a murky something-to-do-with-dragons place in most people's minds. It's a small island in the middle of the Indonesian archipelago, which stretches like a jewel necklace from the coast of Southeast Asia 4,800 kilometres (3,000 miles) into the Pacific Ocean. I hadn't particularly enjoyed my first visit there, with Douglas Adams, and must have mentioned this to Stephen. I remembered it as a hot, dusty and rather unwelcoming place.

'And we're looking for a great, scaly, man-eating monster?' he added almost to himself, clearly remembering my comments.

We were.

Opposite
Komodo – home to the largest and most dangerous lizard in the world (and to some of the most tolerant people).

Below
Making miniature great, scaly, man-eating monsters out of wood.

The animals on Komodo can be divided into three main categories: highly venomous, mildly venomous and large, scary and drooling. Okay, I'm exaggerating a bit – but the island does have a reputation for having more venomous snakes per square metre than anywhere else on the planet. It is also one of those places where you have to check for fatal surprises at every turn, whether it's inside your boots, behind a bush or underneath the toilet seat.

And it is home to the largest and most dangerous lizard in the world.

Maybe I was just tired but, to be honest, if I had been given the choice between another visit to Komodo or a week tied up in a sack on a compost heap in Nigeria, I'd probably have chosen the compost heap. At the best of times, Stephen would rather go somewhere that could be enjoyed through Ray-Bans from the fluffed up cushions of a comfortable sofa.

But you know what they say about keeping your expectations low? It guarantees a pleasant surprise. Besides, we were doing a bit of island-hopping first, through the Malay Archipelago, and we were both looking forward to that.

'Did you know I'm the same age as Malaysia, by the way?' asked Stephen.

'What? 63? You're looking surprisingly good for someone nearing retirement age, all things considered.'

'No,' said Stephen. 'I'm not talking about when British Malaya was dissolved

just after the war – I'm talking about when it gained independence in 1957.'

I had been reading about Malaysia on the plane, but the walking-talking encyclo-paedia, Stephen Fry, happened to know it all anyway. Maybe it had been a question on *QI* in one of the earlier episodes? He remembers every single fact and figure divulged since the first programme aired in September 2003. Test Your Knowledge competitions with him were always a foregone conclusion, so I gave up.

We were starting our travels in Borneo, for no better reason than that we both really wanted to go there (Borneo does count as Malaysia, by the way – the island is shared by three countries: Malaysia (which owns Sabah and Sarawak), Indone-sia (which owns Kalimantan) and Brunei (which owns, well, Brunei – one of the smallest countries in the world).

Three hours into a very bumpy flight to Kota Kinabalu, on the northwest coast of Sabah, we hit a heavy thunderstorm.

'I've flown through more terrifyingly bumpy thunderstorms in the past six months, travelling with you, than in the whole of the rest of my life put together,' complained Stephen, as if it were my fault.

'That's the trouble with rainforests,' I said. 'As we discovered in the Amazon, it rains a lot.'

We did try to land, but aborted at the last possible moment and accelerated back into the storm clouds. Once the plane had settled at a safe cruising altitude, the pilot announced that we were being diverted to a place called Pulau Labuan, about 70 kilometres (43 miles) away as the hornbill flies. We blamed Komodo im-mediately for all the inconvenience.

We landed on a little airstrip and the pilot and co-pilot emerged from the cockpit, sweating profusely but grinning like a couple of released hostages. They slapped one another on the back, hugged the stewardesses and shook hands with a few of the passengers in the two front rows. It all seemed a bit melodra-matic, but everyone else was apparently in on the celebration. It was beginning to feel as if we'd just escaped a terrible near-catastrophe, so I asked one of the stewardesses what had happened.

'We only just had enough fuel on board for the diversion,' she explained. 'We don't normally carry any more than we actually need. So the pilot was flying the plane on empty.'

I glanced at Stephen, whose eyes had noticeably widened.

'Good grief!' he whispered. 'Maybe we should offer to buy some spare fuel, just in case? Have you got your American Express card? We've still got to get back to Kota Kinabalu.'

We made it to KK, eventually, and spent the rest of the week exploring some of the most beautiful and wildlife-rich places you could possibly imagine.

We travelled across mirror-calm, crystal-clear, turquoise seas, visiting one tropical paradise after another. There were small islands with golden beaches and Bart Simpson haircuts, formed by all the sticky-up palm trees; and there were even smaller islands with just enough room for one person to sit on, leaning against a solitary palm tree, with the warm seawater lapping at their feet.

'If I see one more dazzlingly gorgeous, holiday-brochure tropical island I think I'm going to be sick,' joked Stephen.

We had a mud bath in a pool of hot, bubbling mud on the island of Pulau Tiga. Stripping down to our swimming trunks, we rolled around and played in the sludge like a couple of wallowing rhinos. The mud was so thick we could have lain on the surface and fallen asleep.

'I feel like one of those Pompeii figures,' said Stephen, 'caught in a posture of "here comes a volcano".'

We pushed and pulled one another up the slippery bank, while he sang 'Mud, mud, glorious mud' (I knew he would, eventually), and tiptoed our way through the forest towards the sea. We were literally covered in mud from head to toe and, much to the amusement of the crew filming us, instinctively avoided stepping in muddy puddles along the way.

Something caught our attention as we approached a little stream flowing towards the beach. We saw some fish jumping up and down at the water's edge. This may strike you as an odd thing for a fish to do, but these curious critters were mudskippers – and, in defiance of all biological logic, they spend most of their time on land.

They survive by storing mouthfuls of water in large gill chambers, which are a bit like the aqualungs used by scuba divers – except, of course, that they are filled with water instead of compressed air. As a safety backup (presumably in case they sneeze or laugh, and lose all the water in their gill chambers), they can also breathe through their skin.

Above & opposite
Mud, mud, glorious mud – and some creatures that evolved out of it.

We watched as the mudskippers showed us how they got their name, by skipping across the mud and limping on their fleshy fins, like a crowd of people with broken legs hobbling about on crutches.

Once in a while, a male would try to impress the girls by raising his brightly coloured dorsal fin and showing off his athletic prowess. He would leap into the air, using his tail like a coiled spring, land with a little plopping sound, and then look around with his frog-like bobble eyes to see if anyone was looking.

'Never again will I use the expression "like a fish out of water",' said Stephen, as another fish the size of his little finger went flying through the air.

Mudskippers are not really related to the first land-walking animals that emerged from the sea about 375 million years ago. But we know so little about that missing evolutionary link – the fish that turned into a four-legged tetrapod – that studying the amphibiousness of mudskippers may help to shed some light on what these wonderfully named 'fishapods' might have been like.

It felt as if we saw more wildlife during that first week in Borneo than most people see in a lifetime. One of the many highlights was an afternoon spent with several troops of proboscis monkeys, in a mangrove reserve. It's hard not to point out that these are rather ridiculous-looking monkeys, with pot bellies and red, pendulous noses (the Indonesians used to call them 'Dutch monkeys' as a dig against Dutch sailors and plantation owners). They even have ready-made cushions – thickened, hairless patches of skin on their backsides – for that extra-special comfort when sitting down.

The male is particularly impressive, with a jet-black scrotum, a bright red penis – and a permanent erection. I found it unbelievably difficult to take a picture of one that wouldn't result in legal proceedings from Mr and Mrs Outraged from Surrey.

Stephen couldn't help laughing at their honking and groaning vocalisations, 'They sound like old codgers in the Garrick Club,' he said. 'Guffaw, guffaw, ruff, ruff. I don't know why he's been given a peerage. What's he ever done? Oh, I see from my paper that you're dead. Eeee. Uh? Ruff, ruff.'

We fed water monitor lizards with scraps from the breakfast table ('I used to be a water monitor at school,' offered Stephen), we were chased by crab-eating macaques ('the poorer relatives of lobster-eating macaques') and we released a rescued pangolin – a mammal with reptilian scales ('it looks like the illegitimate child of a dachshund and an artichoke,' said Stephen).

In fact, there was more wildlife in our assortment of cabins and huts than in some entire nature reserves in Britain. I remember on one particular night I woke up sensing a slight movement on my chest. Instantly, my brain kicked into gear and all sorts of possible explanations flashed through my mind. Snake? A venomous yellow and black mangrove snake had been caught in someone else's cabin just the night before. It moved again, ever so slightly. Maybe it's just a harmless mouse? Or a giant moth? But then a moth wouldn't be heavy enough to wake me up. It's amazing how many thoughts your brain can process in a mere nanosecond, especially when it's a potentially life-threatening situation.

I fumbled for the light, trying to move as little as possible for fear of triggering a venomous bite, and switched it on. There, cleaning its whiskers, was a small black rat. We stared at one another for several seconds, before it sniffed, ambled down the entire length of my body to the bottom of the bed, and jumped into the darkness beyond.

During the course of our travels in Borneo, I noticed that Stephen was becoming a little eccentric (or, should I say, a little more eccentric). Maybe it was sheer tiredness, or a case of sensory overload, but he was saying 'hello' to all the animals we came across. 'Hello fish,' he would say. 'Hello frog', 'Hello orangutan', 'Hello Muscovy duck'.

I asked him why.

'Oh dear,' he said. 'Have I been doing that? You're right, I have. Sorry. I'll try to stop. I think my brain is struggling to compute everything we're seeing and doing. It's all a bit much.'

We decided to take the evening off. We lay in hammocks strung between palm trees at the back of a beach, watching the usual implausibly fiery red sunset (remind me why everyone keeps saying 'ooh, you're so lucky'), and the conversation turned to Alfred Russel Wallace.

We are both huge fans of Wallace, a 19th century British naturalist who gave Darwin a run for his money. Wallace worked in the Malay Archipelago, where he collected no fewer than 125,600 plant and animal specimens for his own private collection and for various museums, and in the process wrote one of the most influential journals of scientific exploration published during that time. It was called *The Malay Archipelago*.

Most importantly, he came up with an idea that closely resembled Darwin's theory of evolution. Darwin had been tinkering with his own theory for more than twenty years and was plunged into despair when he received a letter from Wallace outlining his thoughts. But it shocked Darwin into action and, in a bit of a panic, he published *On the Origin of Species* the following year.

It just goes to show what happens when people don't have stringent deadlines.

Douglas Adams was notorious for missing deadlines ('I love deadlines,' he used to say. 'I love the whooshing sound they make as they fly by'). He developed problems keeping to deadlines early on in his writing career, and it got worse the more he wrote.

By the time we were writing the original *Last Chance to See*, he had the science and art of missing deadlines down to perfection. He was living in a rented villa in Juan les Pins, in the South of France, at the time – and I joined him for the

After four solid months in Juan le Pins we emerged with a grand total of one page written – and eve that didn't make into the book.

dreaded task in hand.

We had a year's worth of memories, many hours of BBC recordings for the radio series, and thousands of photographs from which to draw. Douglas had also made copious notes in the field using his latest toy, a Z88 electronic notebook, but unfortunately he sat on it while we were in Chile and had lost absolutely everything.

But the biggest problem was the South of France itself. There were just too many things to distract us from working.

Every day, we would get up fairly late and start talking about how we must knuckle down and start the book. We'd decide to go for a stroll along the seafront and maybe have a coffee while we talked through ideas for the structure and style of the first chapter. Then coffee would merge into lunch and we'd order some wine, to help ideas flow a little more freely. By the second bottle, we would agree to enjoy one last leisurely meal before heading straight back to the villa some time late in the afternoon to start work. Back at the villa, having failed miserably to discuss the book at all, we agreed that the day was going to be hopeless for writing so we might as well enjoy it and then start properly the following day. We usually went out to eat in the evenings, sometimes driving all the way to Monte Carlo for one last good time before the hard work really began. Then we followed the same routine the following day…

After four solid months in Juan les Pins we emerged with a grand total of one page written – and even that didn't make it into the book. Afterwards, we returned to London where the publisher locked us in Douglas's house in Islington, until it was done. We had nearly finished writing by the time the book was published. There were just a couple of chapters still to go (our search for Amazonian manatees in Brazil and an expedition to look for Juan Fernandez fur seals in Chile – both of which made it into the radio series but not the book), and the last chapter was considerably shorter than the others. But the publisher (understandably) decided that enough was enough and, having made us finish the page we happened to be working on, took the manuscript away and let us out for the first time in weeks.

I'm not sure if any of Douglas's writing procedures or techniques rubbed off on me, but my absolute final deadline for this book was 30 April and the date today is 27 June. So if there isn't another chapter after this one, lashings of apologies all round.

Something I really must tell you about, before it's too late, is one of the greatest evenings of Stephen's life. I know that's true because he actually said 'That was one of the greatest evenings of my life.'

It was one of mine, too.

We were still off the north coast of Borneo, this time on Selingan Island, in Turtle Island National Park. And we had 24 hours to spend quality time with a heavily protected population of endangered green sea turtles.

There is a turtle hatchery on the island and we were shown around by Nicholas Pilcher – a fellow Brit as well as a world-renowned turtle expert. The hatchery consisted of hundreds of artificial turtle nests in neat rows across the sand next to the park headquarters. Each nest was labelled, with a date and the number of eggs inside, and protected with a circle of plastic mesh roughly the size of a bucket.

One of the many threats facing sea turtles around the world is egg-collecting (the eggs are taken from the nests and eaten), so transferring the eggs to properly guarded hatcheries is a good way of keeping them safe.

We actually collected some from a female who had dug a nest under the mangroves at the back of the beach. I had the enviable job of leaning right into the depression behind her and scooping up her clutch as the eggs came out. She laid 95 altogether. They were warm and roughly the size and shape of table-tennis balls, though much heavier and softer.

We carried them back to the park headquarters, where they were placed inside one of the artificial nests.

'It's another example of how conservationists have to do almost exactly the same as poachers,' observed Stephen. 'Here we are collecting eggs – just like poachers. The difference, of course, is that we're doing it to help save the species.'

We took a closer look at some of the nests already under protection. We paused at one of them and looked at the marker post: 81 eggs buried on 13 January 2009. It was 24 March 2009 – exactly seventy days later. Suddenly, a tiny hatchling appeared out of the sand. Then there was another, and another. Just as we realised what was happening, the entire nest erupted and they all scrabbled out like bubbling lava. I leant in towards the nest and it sounded like a pot of boiling water.

Nick was delighted.

'On the day of hatching,' he said, 'they make their way up towards the outside world and wait patiently in a queue just beneath the surface of the sand. As soon as the light starts to fade, as it is now, they begin to emerge.'

Nick went to get a basket and, very gently, we lifted the tiny, perfectly formed turtles out, one by one. Their shells were soft and leathery, and they felt incredibly delicate.

'It'll be a while before they harden,' Nick told us.

'Ooh!' said Stephen. 'Aah! My darling!'

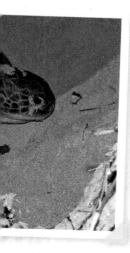

(The last time I'd heard him talk like that was when we released the adorable little Madame Berthe's mouse lemur in Madagascar.)

Sixty-three hatchlings made it out altogether. It was a heart-wrenching moment, because we knew that very few of them would survive. The life expectancy of turtle hatchlings is worse than for drug-taking members of street gangs in Los Angeles – as few as one in a hundred survive long enough to become mature breeding adults.

'Can you tell if these are male or female?' asked Stephen.

'Not just by looking at them,' answered Nick, smiling. 'But my guess is that they will be female. Have you noticed that the hatchery is half in the shade and half in the sun?'

Stephen looked up at the green fabric roof above our heads and nodded.

'Well, that's intentional – so that half the nests are slightly warmer, by a couple of degrees, than the other half. The warmer nests will produce mainly females and the colder ones mainly males. It enables us to manage the population more carefully.'

We carried the basket of scrabbling turtle hatchlings down to the beach.

'We'll release them here,' said Nick. 'We need to give them a run-up before they enter the sea. That gives them a chance to get their bearings, to set their internal magnetic compasses, so they are able to navigate when they get out to sea.'

'Where will they go?' I asked.

'Nobody knows for sure. The next few years of their lives have been dubbed "the lost years" because they are hardly ever seen. They probably get swept along at the mercy of the ocean currents. How they eventually get their bearings and swim back to the place they were born is a complete mystery.'

We watched in awe as the hatchlings made their perilous dash for the sea.

'Notice how they're all heading straight towards the setting sun,' said Nick. 'They always head for the brightest point in the sky. It's a big problem when they emerge from nests on tourist beaches, of course, because they head for the hotel lights instead.'

'Oh my God!' shouted Stephen suddenly. 'One's been grabbed.'

We rushed over to see a hatchling disappear down a hole in the sand. I rescued it just in time and let it go a safe distance away. I know you're not supposed to intervene in nature, but I'm afraid I couldn't resist. Our hatchlings needed all the help they could get. Plus they were irresistibly cute.

'That was a ghost crab,' said Nick. 'Lots of hatchlings get picked off on their way to the sea, not just by crabs but by gulls and rats and things.'

The hatchlings ran straight into the surf without skipping a beat, diving into the waves and swimming as if they'd been doing it their whole lives.

'Unbelievable,' I said to Stephen. 'I just can't believe this is the first time they've ever set eyes on the sea – and yet, there they go, as if it's the most natural thing in the world.'

'I suppose it *is* the most natural thing in the world,' he replied.

Without the benefit of swimming lessons, the baby turtles started swimming automatically. Their flippers did an intriguing mix of doggy-paddle and breaststroke, while their heads bobbed up and down so they could breathe. They looked just like clockwork toys.

'I wonder how many of them will make it?' asked Stephen.

'I'm afraid the odds are not very good,' answered Nick. 'They've survived the hazards of the beach…'

'With our help,' I interrupted.

'Yes, with our help,' smiled Nick. 'But now they have to run the gauntlet of the reef, where there are loads of hungry fish that would love to snack on them. They'll just keep swimming frantically for a day or two until they are far out in the open sea, where they might be able to hide in floating seaweed and be a little safer.'

The hatchlings will be looking over their shoulders for about a year, by which time they will be roughly the size of saucers and their shells will have hardened enough to make them less easy prey for predators.

Opposite
Turtle hatchlings erupt-
ing out of their nest like
bubbling lava.

Below
The sunny side of the
turtle hatchery will
produce mainly
females.

But even as adults they face a barrage of threats. One of the biggest dangers comes in the form of fishing nets – tens of thousands, if not hundreds of thousands, of sea turtles die in them every year.

We watched as the last of the hatchlings disappeared beneath the waves.

'Hopefully,' said Nick, 'one of them will be back, in maybe 20 or 25 years' time, to lay her eggs on the same beach, right here, where she was born.'

'Good luck,' called Stephen to the now-invisible babies. 'I've never seen anything quite so magical in my entire life.'

We flew from Kota Kinabalu to Tawau, in the southeastern corner of Sabah, and had the shock of our lives. We travelled over a never-ending expanse of man-made plantations. Vast swathes of what was once tropical rainforest had been cleared to make way for row upon row, mile upon mile of identical palm trees.

'I've seen the future of Malaysia – and it's bleak,' said Stephen, staring out of the window in dismay.

'How do you know?' I asked.

'I've read its palms.'

He was absolutely right. The rapid expanse of palm oil plantations in Southeast Asia could be the single most immediate threat to the greatest number of species on the planet.

Palm oil is one of those things we've all heard about, but probably couldn't discuss in any depth at a dinner party. Don't worry – most politicians couldn't, either. It's a bit like 'global warming', 'sub-prime mortgages' or 'saturated fat'. Just hearing those words sends an automatic signal to the brain that says 'bad', though we're not entirely sure of all the details.

This is one of the few times in the book when I am going to rant, because palm oil is a bigger disaster than you think, regardless of how big a disaster you think it is. It's about as environmentally friendly as dropping some plutonium into the reservoir at Staines. Vast areas of tropical rainforest are being cleared to make way for palm oil plantations – millions of hectares in Borneo alone in the last few years.

Palm oil is derived from the fruit and seeds of a particular species of tree called, rather unimaginatively, the oil palm. This oil is a key ingredient of many processed foods (though we don't know about it most of the time, because it is listed simply as 'vegetable oil'). It is in great – and growing – demand as a source of non-hydrogenated vegetable fats. It's used as a cooking oil, too, and in everything from soap to washing powder.

Food and cosmetics companies, smelling huge profits, are driving the demand for new supplies and turning a blind eye to illegal habitat destruction in the process. The incentives to produce palm oil are so great that national park and reserve boundaries are often changed to make way for new plantations.

It is also in great demand for biofuel. How ironic is that? Apart from anything else, clearing the forests releases huge amounts of carbon dioxide into the atmosphere, causing damage that far outweighs the benefits of switching to a so-called environmentally friendly fuel.

When the forests go, so do most of the native plants and animals. And, in a place like Borneo, that means a heck of a lot of different species. There is a well-known story of a botanist spending a few days tramping around about 10 hectares (28 acres) of jungle in Borneo and discovering no fewer than a thousand *new* species of flowering plant. I am no botanist, but even I know that is a lot (more species than are found in the whole of North America, as it happens).

Apart from the obvious ethical and emotional reasons for worrying about some multinational company coming along and bulldozing that 10 hectares of forest, and everything that lives in it, there are some practical reasons, too. Nearly a quarter of all prescribed medicines are derived from just forty plants, and the vast majority – at least 99 per cent – have never been tested for their potential

healing properties. Just imagine what medical nuggets those 10 hectares might be harbouring. And 10 hectares is just the tip of the iceberg.

Malaysia is far and away the largest exporter of palm oil in the world, and Indonesia comes a very close second. Their economies rely on it – and so do the livelihoods of millions of people. But there are solutions. For example, there is plenty of non-forested land that would be perfectly good enough to meet the growing demand for palm oil plantations. It's not being used, though, because the corporations responsible for palm oil find it cheaper and easier to bulldoze tropical rainforests – and, of course, the rainforests provide valuable timber that gives them an extra financial bonus.

We landed at Tawau, still in shock, and drove through yet more endless palm oil plantations as far as Semporna. We passed a convoy of tankers along the way.

'You know what?' said Stephen. 'I think I've just discovered the least environmentally friendly job on the planet.'

'What's that?'

'Driving a petrol-driven palm oil tanker.'

It's hard to know where to begin with the island of Sipadan, our next stop. I'd heard about it for years and was actually getting quite tired of friends raving about the place, claiming that it's home to the world's best dive site, richest coral reef, clearest water, blah, blah, blah. I don't mean to be rude but, honestly, I'd got it. Sipadan is 'bloody, bloody brilliant', as one friend exclaimed.

Well, I've been to Sipadan at last, and I'd like to add my own particular perception to the fray: it's bloody, bloody brilliant. I can't think of a better way of putting it than that.

Right on the border with the Philippines, in the Celebes Sea, Sipadan is a pile of living coral sitting on top of an extinct volcano. It rises steeply from the sea bed, which is 600 metres (2,000 feet) away down in the depths, and breaks the surface by no more than the height of a man. The island itself is quite small – about 12 hectares (30 acres) – and consists of a slash of gleaming white sand topped with verdant palm trees. Imagine a cartoonist's impression of the ultimate desert island – and that is exactly what it's like.

We were completely spellbound as we approached in our dive boat. It's the kind of place that makes you want to paint a picture, write poetry, sing songs and, I'm afraid, phone all your friends to bang on about it until they tell you to shut up. It's so spectacularly breathtaking that your brain struggles to process so much heavenly wonderfulness. And that's just the view from above the surface.

'You know the saying "the grass is always greener on the other side of the fence"?' said Stephen. 'Well, this *is* the other side of the fence. It doesn't get much better, does it?'

We had to sign in with the marine park authorities first, so docked at the rickety wooden jetty. A small Malaysian navy boat appeared alongside. There has been a heavy military presence on Sipadan since 2001, when 21 people were kidnapped at gunpoint by Filipino terrorists (most were held for about a year, then slowly ransomed off for millions of dollars).

The military is also there to deter illegal fishermen. We're not talking about a couple of men with nets or fishing rods – it's much, much worse than that. One of the great scourges of coastal seas in Southeast Asia is fishermen armed with lethal weapons. Many coral reefs in the region have been destroyed by dynamite fishing (using home-made bombs to stun or kill schools of fish) and cyanide fishing (squirting cyanide into reef crevices, to stun the fish hiding inside, and then breaking away the coral with a hammer to collect them by hand).

The fishermen completely destroy the coral in the process. They are trying to catch live fish for the luxury food trade (live groupers and Napoleon wrasse, in particular, are in high demand in Hong Kong, Taiwan, Singapore and other parts of Southeast Asia) and for the aquarium trade (which has an insatiable appetite for colourful fish to sell to animal-lovers who like to put them in tanks).

'The worst thing in the world is to be born tasty,' commented Stephen.

'What's the second worst thing in the world?' I asked.

'To be born Welsh, obviously.'

[Stephen has just asked me to point out that this was, of course, a stupid joke and that he loves the Welsh more than you could possibly imagine, and he once went to Cardiff. Next time he promises to make a joke about the Scots, the Irish, and then the English. And the Americans.]

Even the heavy military presence on Sipadan didn't dampen our enthusiasm and we wasted no time in getting ready for the first dive of the day or, in Stephen's case, the first snorkel of the day.

I say we 'wasted no time' but I've never known anyone take so long to get into a wetsuit as Stephen. I was completely ready in my suit, fins and mask, with my weight belt around my waist, a tank on my back, the regulator in my mouth, and was sitting on the side of the boat about to do a Navy SEAL backwards roll into the water, when I realised that Stephen had barely got one leg inside his wetsuit. And it was back to front.

I made a mental note for next time: persuade him to get ready the night before and sleep in his wetsuit. Then we might have a fighting chance of getting in the water before sunset.

You know the grass is always greener on the other side of the fence? Well this *is* the other side of the fence.

Opposite
'I'm going to learn to dive,' said Stephen. 'I'm definitely going to learn to dive. And I'm going to do it right here in Sipadan.'

'These things are bloody impossible,' he complained to the world at large, puffing and panting and sweating profusely. 'This had better be worth it.'

He stopped to take a short break and started texting.

'What on earth are you doing?' I asked.

'Texting,' he replied bluntly, knowing that I was getting impatient. He didn't look up.

'Who are you texting now?'

'Alan Davies. He's a keen diver and I just wanted to tell him that we're here. Shouldn't you be sucking in nitrous oxide or helium or something?'

The phone bleeped.

'What did he say?' I asked, failing not to be intrigued.

'He says "Lucky bugger – even more jealous knowing it's completely wasted on you".'

'Have you never considered learning to dive?' I asked.

'Not really. It's always struck me as a bit like skiing, with lots of competitiveness and one-upmanship. I can just imagine sitting on a dive boat with people looking aggressively at my equipment and thinking "I'm a better diver than you" or "I've dived deeper than you" or "I don't like the look of your dive watch". You must admit lots of divers really fancy themselves, don't they?'

'Well some do, obviously, but so do people who play football or go to knitting classes. It's human nature. That shouldn't put you off, though.'

Despite all the protestations, I helped him into his wetsuit – 'ow!... stop, stop!... that hurts!... don't pull so hard... ouch!'. He just had to find his snorkel, spit into his mask and squeeze his size-twelve feet into a pair of size-eleven fins, and we were ready to go.

We peered into the crystal-clear water at all the big fish milling around by the side of the boat.

'Be careful when you answer, Mr Bond,' he said, in his best Bond-villain voice.

I rolled over the side and started to descend. The water wasn't just warm – it was positively, sizzlingly, magnificently balmy. I reached the reef fairly quickly and started to move down the sheer wall that plunged into the ocean depths, where I was joined by the rest of the crew. There was quite a strong current and we were suddenly whisked along like astronauts being sucked into outer space from the safety of the International Space Station.

The reef wall was teeming with outrageously colourful fish, spectacular corals and bizarrely shaped sponges. There were spirals of barracuda and schools of big-eye trevally shoaling in the open water. A couple of large grey reef sharks passed close by overhead and we encountered more white-tipped reef sharks on this dive than I'd seen in the whole of the past year diving in lesser parts of the world.

One of the highlights was coming face to face with an enormous male Napoleon wrasse – now an endangered species because so many have been taken for the live fish trade. It must have been at least 1.5 metres (5 feet) long. Bright purplish-blue in colour, with thick, fleshy lips and a protruding forehead, it was unlike anything else on the reef. The best thing about Napoleon wrasse is that they can change sex. Actually, it's only the females that can change into males rather than the other way round. There are lots of good jokes in that, but I'll let it pass.

The turtles were another star attraction. They were everywhere. Most of them were massive green turtles, but there were a few smaller hawksbills too. We must have seen at least a dozen altogether.

By the time we returned to the top of the reef, the current was so strong I couldn't fin hard enough to make any progress. I had to divert into a small gully and catch my breath. As I pushed back out into the maelstrom, and started kicking like a madman, I noticed that all the fish – even the tiddlers – were overtaking me. With no apparent effort, they were swimming up-current. The little buggers. Of course, I consoled myself, it would be a different matter in our world: put them on land and they'd be flailing about all over the place.

I surfaced right next to Stephen, who'd apparently been waiting impatiently

Top
The starfish that looks like a chocolate chip cookie.

Above
What a healthy coral reef should look like, without the damage caused by dynamite and cyanide fishing.

Opposite
A white-tipped reef shark with its fins still intact.

at the surface, and he started rapid-fire talking even before I'd removed my mask and opened my eyes.

'Holy mackerel!' he started (for once his favourite expression seemed to be perfectly apt). 'The intensity of the colours is absolutely astounding. I don't think I've seen any flower on the surface of the planet that has the same kind of purity and blazing intensity as those colours down there. And the clownfish. Did you see the clownfish? What about the starfish that look like chocolate chip cookies? Amazing. And all those things I can't identify? They are amazing, too. Not to mention all the turtles and sharks. But I have to say I really like the small stuff – I could have stayed in just one place for an hour and not got bored.'

He barely drew breath and was still deliriously talkative as we clambered back into the boat.

'I'm going to learn to dive,' he said. 'I'm definitely going to learn to dive. And I'm going to do it right here in Sipadan. I'm going to get one hell of a dive watch, too, just to annoy all the other divers. I'm going to come back here for a holiday. This has to be the most extraordinary place on the planet. I'm definitely coming back.'

Then he paused for a moment.

'The only trouble is I haven't had more than three days off in a row since I was eight.'

We discussed the Zen art of relaxation and the importance of taking time off, which neither of us knew much about, while Stephen slipped out of his wetsuit in the way a high-security prisoner might slip out of a straitjacket.

'But I do have one important question,' he said after catching his breath for a few minutes.

'Yes?'

'If swimming is so good for you, why are whales fat?'

Normally, it's me trying to persuade the director to let us stay longer, but this time it was Stephen who used all his powers of persuasion to win us another day of diving and snorkelling at Sipadan. I'll never forget when he knocked on the door of my luxurious stilted chalet to tell me the good news. He was obviously feeling a little guilty, because he looked like a small boy allowed to stay up late on a school night, but he was terribly pleased with himself all the same.

We did take time out to visit an underwater field of seagrass, to see if we could find a herd of grazing seahorses. We didn't find an entire herd, but, in about 2 metres (6.5 feet) of water, we did spot two thorny seahorses about the

So what do we humans do to celebrate and honour such magnificent creatures? We eat them, of course.

size of a travel toothbrush. They had wrapped their tails around grass stems near the sea bed. Careful not to kick up the sand with our fins, or the visibility would have dropped to zero, we took it in turns to duck-dive down to take a closer look.

The two unlikely fish were masters of camouflage and very easy to lose as they glided in and out amongst the stems. They reminded me a little of the aye-aye, in Madagascar. Not that they look anything like an alien lemur of course, but they do look as if they have been made from bits of other animals: a horse's head, obviously, but also a monkey's prehensile tail, a chameleon's eyes moving about independently, and a kangaroo's pouch.

The most astonishing thing about seahorses is that the male – not the female – gets pregnant, and the pouch is where it all happens. The female deposits her eggs into it, and the male fertilises them with his sperm. The pouch then acts like the womb of a female mammal, complete with placental fluid that bathes the eggs and provides nutrients and oxygen to the developing embryos. It even removes waste products.

The eggs hatch inside the pouch and, as the baby seahorses develop, the male begins to look decidedly pregnant. The babies (called fry – no relation) look like miniature versions of their parents, but with proportionately larger heads. They are usually born at night, when the male goes into labour, pumping and thrusting for several hours to release his brood. As far as is known, it's the most extreme form of male parental care in any animal.

So what do we humans do to celebrate and honour such magnificent creatures? We eat them, of course. Not all of us, admittedly, but a lot of people in China, Hong Kong and Taiwan put seahorses in boiling water and then drink the resulting broth as a tonic, a kind of pick-me-up. Countless tonnes of seahorses are also used every year in Traditional Chinese Medicine, to treat everything from incontinence and impotence to asthma. Just imagine how many tiny seahorses it takes to weigh 'countless tonnes' – and that's not including the hundreds of thousands captured alive every year for ornamental display (almost every seahorse you are ever likely to see in an aquarium or tank has been caught in the wild).

I was shocked to discover that the scale of the industry is so huge many Asian fishermen earn the majority of their income from seahorses.

We went into a shop in Borneo to witness the trade for ourselves. Stephen is incredibly polite most of the time but even he was struggling to maintain a degree of good manners, as we strolled past walls and shelves packed with a frightening assortment of animal products. There were huge crates full of shark fins and sea cucumbers ('they look like ossified turds' according to Stephen), while bags hanging from the ceiling each contained hundreds, if not thousands, of dried seahorses.

Unfortunately, no matter what the rest of us may think about Traditional Chinese Medicine, the fact is that a quarter of the entire human population thinks it works. And few of them give a damn about the impact it has on the world's increasingly endangered wildlife. It's one of the greatest challenges facing conservationists today.

We were sitting in an open-air bar in Labuan Bajo, a ramshackle little port on the western coast of Flores, looking out across a huddle of rusty tin roofs towards Komodo. Stephen was reading the local paper, the *Straits Times*, and I was busy fixing a problem with my camera.

'Mark!'

'Yes.'

'No, really, Mark.'

'What is it?'

'Listen to this. It's in the paper. "Man killed by Komodo dragons" is the headline. "Two Komodo dragons mauled a fruit-picker to death in eastern Indonesia, police and witnesses said yesterday, the latest in a string of attacks on humans by the world's largest lizard species." What do you think of that?'

It was unfortunate timing – not least for the fruit-picker. Stephen was yet to be convinced about the arguments for going to see a Komodo dragon in the wild, and the latest attack didn't help.

But Komodo dragons don't really deserve their dreadful reputation for killing people. Being a man-eater isn't necessarily bad in itself. Lions and tigers are man-eaters and, though we don't actually like to be eaten by them, we don't resent the very idea. I think it's because Komodo dragons are reptiles and, given a choice, we prefer to be eaten by mammals. This partly explains why we have such an irrational fear of sharks which, of course, are fish.

Besides, Komodo dragons attack people surprisingly rarely – and kill them even more rarely. There was an awful incident on 4 June 2007, when an eight-year-old boy was killed on the island of Komodo, but that was the first fatal attack in more than thirty years. Admittedly, a number of villagers can boast impressive Komodo dragon scars, so there is no denying that they are buggers to have living on your doorstep. The locals must be pretty tolerant to put up with them. There are benefits from living in a national park – and there is money to be made by selling carved Komodo dragons to tourists – but it can't be particularly easy

Opposite
A Komodo dragon and a tiny teddy. One has been on every *Last Chance to See* shoot and will be auctioned off for charity; the other hasn't.

Being a man-eat isn't necessarily bad in itself but, given a choice, prefer to be eate by mammals.

or pleasant. We make such a fuss in safety-conscious Britain whenever anyone mentions the prospect of reintroducing wolves that we should be in eternal awe of anyone prepared to live next door to Komodo dragons.

Stephen considered the implications of all this, looked for a moment as if he might say something, then shook his head and went back to reading the paper.

I'm afraid talking about dangerous animals is rocking one of my (many) hobbyhorses. I tend to get very irritated by our obsession with them. Komodo dragons aren't all sweetness and light, of course, but they have a fearsome reputation mainly because people love to exaggerate.

Certain television naturalists have added fuel to the fire by manhandling, provoking and bullying so-called dangerous animals to try and make themselves stars, pushing the hapless creatures to the limits to make, cheap, kiss-me-quick telly.

Their apparent determination to prove that all animals are baddies and out to get us means that virtually every creature they brandish in front of the camera is in distress. Have you ever noticed how it is always the TV presenters doing the chasing? The animals are trying to get away.

I've rubbed shoulders with great white sharks, slept with a puff adder, tripped over an alligator and had goodness knows how many other close encounters with supposedly dangerous animals over many years in the field. But I can count on the fingers of one hand the number of times I've been badly bumped, bitten or stung.

Some people argue that this style of television is the only way to reach a human population with virtually zero interest in wildlife. But I believe it encourages entirely the wrong attitude towards wildlife – manipulative, domineering and interfering. I'm sure the people responsible are well meaning, but I question the kind of interest this misguided programming inspires. Surely, some of the people responsible – in front of the camera and behind – must have stopped, just for a moment, and thought, 'This is wrong'?

That said, Komodo dragons have had a rather fearsome reputation for much longer than they've been appearing on television.

For centuries, the Chinese came to Komodo looking for its underwater treasure trove of pearls. They returned with stories of great scaly man-eating monsters with fiery breath – stories that are believed to have been the origin of the Chinese dragon myth, or at least to have enhanced it. It is, after all, a large creature with scales, it is a man-eater, and though it doesn't actually breathe fire, it does have 'the worst breath of any creature known to man' (to quote Douglas Adams, who was talking from personal experience).

People at the time used to write 'Here be dragons' on their maps when they saw a land they didn't like the look of. Komodo was such a land. Rumour has it that it was marked 'Here be dragons' in bold capital letters, underlined and with several exclamation marks (I'm embellishing the rumour – but it was definitely a place travellers were warned about for being dangerous and inhospitable).

And then, at the beginning of the last century, a pioneering Dutch aviator was attempting to island-hop his way along the Indonesian archipelago to Australia when he had engine trouble and had to crash-land his plane on Komodo. He survived the crash but his plane didn't. When he went to search for water, he found a strange wide track on the beach, so he followed the track, and suddenly found himself confronted with a dragon. Against all the odds he survived, and was rescued. But when he returned home, and described the great scaly man-eating monsters he had lived with for three horrible months, nobody of course believed a word of it. He may have survived, but his reputation didn't.

Strange tales continued to filter out of the region. Traders and fishermen brought back stories of giant prehistoric lizards, but they were assumed to be the ravings of men who had been at sea for too long. No one seriously thought such things existed, except in people's wildest imaginations.

Finally, the Dutch sent a scientific expedition to settle the matter. In the spirit of scientific expeditions at the time, they shot a Komodo dragon and sent it back for evaluation. It was identified as a member of the monitor lizard family and nothing less than the largest lizard in the world.

Fortunately, Stephen likes a good story – and nowadays he likes a good adventure, too – so he was in surprisingly high spirits when we set sail from Labuan Bajo on the *Felicia*, a traditional teak and ironwood sailing boat.

'Whoever would have thought Mrs Fry's little boy would one day be able to say that he is sailing the South China Sea,' he said. 'And what a heavenly place it is. Look at those islands. They've got that classic Southeast Asian humpiness – they're unlike islands anywhere else in the world.'

He was so glad to be on the way to Komodo, in fact, that he kept calling out completely irrelevant and unconnected thoughts (he does that when he is happy).

'Look – terns,' he said, as we passed a small flock of great crested terns. 'Shall we throw rocks at them? Aren't we supposed to leave no tern unstoned?'

A few moments passed and he uttered another little gem: 'Your karma ran over my dogma.'

He started to write some notes and, in a voice straight out of *Star Trek*, pretended to read them aloud: 'It's getting increasingly difficult to write these diary entries. Mark died this morning, dragged into the bushes by a gang of vicious dragons. It won't be long until the rest of us succumb…'

And so it went on for the entire journey to Komodo. Or, at least, it would have done if we hadn't stopped off en route to visit the neighbouring island of Rinca, which has its own population of Komodo dragons.

'Never wear polyester when you're walking in Komodo dragon country,' said Stephen as we clambered ashore.

'Why not?'

'Because Komodo dragons can't digest polyester.'

We walked along a well-worn path to the ranger post at a place called Loh Baru, on the southwest side of Rinca. We wanted to see the office of the Chief Ranger, Pak Maain, whom we'd met the day before we left Labuan Bajo. We walked up the steps and peered inside. The main wall and part of the floor were covered in blood, like a scene from a Quentin Tarantino movie. A few months earlier, the 55-year-old ranger had entered his office, as he had done many times before, and just as he went to sit at his desk he saw a 1.5-metre (5-foot) dragon loitering underneath. It grabbed him by the foot and an almighty struggle ensued. Pak Maain tried to shake it off and then attempted to prize open the animal's mouth with his bare hands. Eventually, he broke free and managed to climb on top of the office cupboard. By this time his colleagues, who had heard his cries for help, had come to chase the dragon away with sticks. His hand, arm and leg were all terribly swollen when we saw him, but he was expected to make a full recovery.

We left the office and continued along the path. There, lounging around under one of the stilted wooden huts, were seven giant lizards, ranging in length from less than 1 metre to well over 2 metres (3 to 7 feet).

Opposite
Just look at those beady eyes.

Below
Chief Ranger Pak Maain and his injuries.

We walked up the steps and peered inside. The main wall and part of the floor were covered in blood like a scene from a Quentin Tarantino movie.

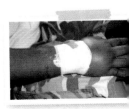

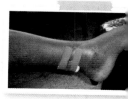

'Holy mackerel!' said Stephen (not so appropriate this time). 'I thought I was ugly, but this is ridiculous. They're really not the most attractive animals, are they?'

I'm afraid I had to agree with him. Komodo dragons are animals of minimal cuteness. Maybe they're an acquired taste, and we were still in the process of acquiring it.

I was going to say that only a Komodo dragon mother would love a Komodo dragon, but even that isn't true. A baby dragon is just food as far as Mum (or any other adult) is concerned. It moves about and has a bit of meat on it, so it's edible. If the adults ate all the youngsters, of course, the species would die out, so that wouldn't work very well. But the dragons survive because the babies have acquired an instinct to climb trees – and the much bigger adults can't. So the babies just sit up in trees, out of harm's way, until they're big enough to look after themselves.

The largest of the dragons under the rangers' hut was looking straight at me and I have to say it was far and away the most malevolent expression I'd seen in millions of years. It was more than 100 kilos (220 pounds) of malevolence wrapped up in loose, leathery skin, complete with unblinking, don't-mess-with-me eyes.

'Even its skin makes mine crawl,' said Stephen.

A giant lizard's skin is scaly, of course, and that's absolutely fine. But there is something a little unnerving about the way it hangs around in folds, crinkles and creases. The Komodo dragon is built like a concertina – the folds of skin give it plenty of room to expand when it eats. It can eat as much as 80 per cent of its own weight in one sitting (it swallows everything – including bones, horns and hooves), and the skin just stretches out like a great big bag.

Every single dragon was dribbling. Actually, I'm being far too polite – they were positively drooling. Saliva was pouring out of the sides of their mouths. And that saliva is very unpleasant indeed.

If you ever get bitten by a Komodo dragon, I'm afraid you are in very serious trouble. You see, when one lies in wait for a large animal such as a horse or a buffalo, it doesn't necessarily expect to kill it there and then. If it gets involved in a fight it might be injured, and there's no benefit in that, so sometimes it will just bite its prey and walk away.

Clearly, there is something in the dragon's bite that ensures the animal will weaken and die within a few days, whereupon the dragon can eat it at leisure (or another dragon can eat it at leisure, if it happens to find it first).

There was a well-known case of a Frenchman who was bitten by a dragon, while visiting Komodo. The wound festered and would just never heal, and he eventually died in Paris two years later. Unfortunately, there were no dragons in Paris to take advantage of it so the strategy broke down on that particular occasion, but normally it works very well.

The general consensus has always been that the secret lay in the dragon's fetid saliva. It contains a witch's brew of toxic bacteria – 57 different strains at the last count – which are so virulent the wounds never heal and the bitten animal usually dies of septicaemia.

I mentioned all this to Stephen.

'That's the creepiest way of earning a living I've ever heard,' he said. 'That's lower than a dung beetle. It's even lower than a banker or an estate agent.'

But recent research just published suggests that Komodo dragons may actually be venomous – making them by far the largest venomous creatures on the planet. For the first time, scientists have found glands in their mouths that produce venom as potent as that found in some of the world's most dangerous snakes. It works by causing a sudden and severe drop in blood pressure, sending the prey into shock, and then it prevents the blood from clotting, to ensure that the hapless animal bleeds to death.

This deadly combination of venom and sharp, serrated teeth works as well as a poisoned dagger.

Indonesia has between 17,508 and 18,306 islands altogether, depending on whom you believe. The exact number is a little vague because everyone who has ever tried to tot them all up has eventually lost count, or got bored. Komodo dragons live on only five of them – Komodo, obviously, and Rinca, but also the islets of Gili Motang and Gili Dasami, and a very tiny corner of Flores – all about 480 kilometres (300 miles) east of Bali.

There are believed to be fewer than 1,400 dragons in the wild (when Douglas Adams and I visited Komodo in 1988 the official figure was 5,000 – but everyone thinks that was probably a miscalculation). Even 1,400 sounds like quite a lot, but the problem is that fewer than fifty of them are breeding females. A forest fire, a disease outbreak or a sudden decline in prey species could wipe out the entire breeding population in one fell swoop.

We spent a couple of days with Deni Purwandana, Field Officer for the Komodo Survival Programme, and the man charged with understanding how the dragon population ticks. Information is crucial for conservation. Deni had worked with Komodo dragons since 2002 and knew more about them than almost anyone else alive. Perhaps that was why he always carried a stick.

He was quite a small man and the thought of him wandering around Komodo on his own made me think of a duck walking into a Chinese restaurant. But Deni lived and breathed Komodo dragons. The more I got to know him, the

Above
Proof that Komodo dragons are animals of minimal cuteness.

more he struck me as the kind of person who could make a crash-landing on Komodo and survive alone for three months with no problem at all.

Stephen got straight to the point.

'Do you actually like Komodo dragons?' he asked.

Deni laughed.

'I have to be honest,' he began. 'I didn't really like them at first. But I grew to like them after a couple of years and now I'm almost fond of them. I'm definitely proud to be working with them. They are uniquely Indonesian and part of our heritage.'

Komodo itself was an extremely pleasant surprise. It was nothing like the scorched, dry and dusty island in my distant memory. The hills undulated like the great heavy folds of a lizard's skin, but they were luxuriantly green. It happened to be the end of the rainy season and that made all the difference.

'The landscape looks surprisingly Welsh or Scottish,' remarked Stephen as we stepped onto the wooden jetty.

But you don't go to Wales or Scotland to catch a Komodo dragon. Deni had set a huge trap under a tree and there was a large male dragon inside.

It took four of us to sit on the giant lizard, with its feet trussed up like a rodeo calf and its slobbering mouth taped firmly shut. I was holding onto its tail – the same tail that could knock a fully grown buffalo off its feet. I gripped as tightly as I could, but still struggled with the mind-boggling surge of power every time it thrashed about. We had little choice but to be heavy-handed and I felt a little guilty. But I consoled myself with the thought that this research would at least benefit the dragons in the long run.

Deni took a few measurements (it was 2.63 metres/8.5 feet long), injected a bar code into its shoulder (which, at a later date, could be read like a bar code in a supermarket), and then attached a radio transmitter to its back (like a miniature rucksack).

'Right,' he said, when he had finished. 'We're ready. I'm going to count to three and I want everyone to let go straight away and make a run for it. Okay?'

We all mumbled a yes.

'Here we go. One... two... *three!*'

Stephen and I let go and ran so fast it didn't even take measurable time. But the dragon barely moved. Gradually it gained confidence, grasping the fact that it was free, and then celebrated by lunging at us with a spine-tingling hiss.

By this time, we were surrounded by at least a dozen other Komodo dragons and we'd run out of places to hide. They were everywhere, coming at us from all directions. Every time a twig snapped, we'd turn around and there would be another one.

There were several rangers with us and they used sticks to push them away

'Right,' Deni said, when he had finished. 'We're ready. I'm going to count to three and I want everyone to let g straight away an make a run for it Okay?'

whenever they ventured too close. There was no brutality involved – just a strong push was all it took. But they would always come back for more, and, eventually, we decided to retreat to the safety of the boat.

It was our last night on Komodo and we were anchored offshore, having a celebratory drink on deck. As the sun disappeared below the horizon, thousands upon thousands of large flying foxes, or fruit bats, streamed out of their roost in the mangroves.

Stephen was decidedly unmoved.

'They're like rats in leather jackets,' he grumbled. 'Just because they're mammals you're getting all excited. I'll tell you something – the starlings wheeling and turning near my house in Norfolk are far more impressive.'

'I hate to admit it,' I said, 'but you do have a point. If Komodo dragons were mammals, I think most people would probably like them a lot more, too.'

'Yes, we do tend to be very narrow-minded,' Stephen agreed. 'They're as ugly as sin, but, like all animals I suppose, they're very good at being themselves. You've got to respect their sort of Komodo dragonness, haven't you?'

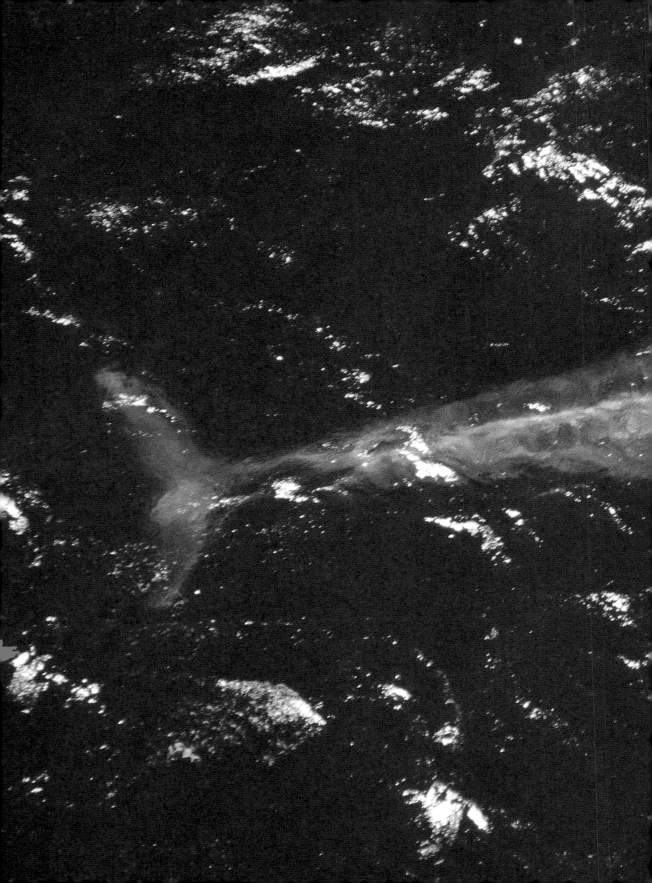

6

SINGING THE BLUES

Look at a map of North America and, down in the bottom left-hand corner, you will see a long stretch of land that looks rather like a giant chilli. This is Baja California – my favourite place in the whole world.

Stretching 1,300 kilometres (808 miles) south from the California border, this wild corner of Mexico is a whale-watching Mecca. You can see a greater variety of whales here in a couple of weeks than you can anywhere else on the planet.

I've been exploring Baja since the late 1980s, diving with sharks, snorkelling with turtles, surveying blue whales from the air, photographing lots of other whales and dolphins from boats, and much, much more. I couldn't cope without my annual pilgrimage. It is always utterly breathtaking.

Stephen and I decided to begin our little expedition to this 'Mexican Galápagos' with one of the greatest wildlife encounters on earth: a touchy-feely meeting with a friendly grey whale.

We were starting with greys because they are widely regarded as the friendliest of all the world's whales. The grey whale is so friendly, in fact, that I was quietly confident in getting Stephen as close to one as anyone could possibly get, without actually calling themselves Jonah and climbing inside its mouth.

We met at the southern end of California – in San Diego, to be precise, right on the border with the northern end of Baja. It was the first time we had seen one another for a little over a month and I must admit it was quite a shock.

Opposite
Baja California – Mark's favourite place in the whole world.

The Stephen Fry sitting at the hotel bar, sipping a vodka and soda, definitely wasn't the same Stephen Fry I'd started travelling with a year or so before. It wasn't even the same Stephen Fry I'd seen at the end of the last shoot.

There wasn't as much of him as there was before.

While we had been in Madagascar, Stephen decided – quite suddenly – to lose weight. I remember the moment quite clearly: it was just as we started to eat dinner one night in Antananarivo. He ceremoniously drank his last glass of wine, returned his bread roll to the bread basket, and that was that. The following morning he started a crack-of-dawn walking regime that continues to this day, and the kilograms started to fall off. In the four months between Madagascar and San Diego, he had lost an impressive 29 kg (64 pounds) altogether.

The trimmer and slimmer Stephen looked years younger and a heck of a lot healthier.

He was on cloud nine. Rarely had I seen him quite as euphoric as he was at the prospect of meeting a whale face to face. He was even wearing his 'lucky whale shorts', bought especially for the occasion, which were dotted with spouting humpback whales (at least, I think they were humpbacks – I didn't like to look too closely). It was the wrong species, but definitely the right idea.

Grey whales are inveterate travellers, commuting along the entire length of the western North American coastline, and back again, each year. The round-trip distance between their summer feeding grounds in the north and their winter breeding grounds in the south can be as much as 20,000 kilometres (12,400 miles), making their journey one of the longest migrations of any mammal.

In a grey whale's lifetime of about 80 years, that's the equivalent of swimming all the way to the moon and back – twice.

The vast majority of grey whales spend every summer in the icy Arctic waters of the Bering, Chukchi and western Beaufort seas, where they have three main objectives: eat, eat and eat.

Grey whales are messy eaters, feeding in the sediment on the sea bed. They use their mouths like vacuum cleaners, sucking up tiny animals called benthic amphipods, as well as considerable amounts of water, sand, mud and stones. No one knows why, but most of them feed by rolling onto the right side – they are right 'handed' – although a few roll to the left.

They have about five months to put on enough body weight to survive the rest of the year without another proper meal.

Early in October, the Arctic weather begins to worsen and the fat and blubbery whales prepare to leave. Their migration south is organised like a military manoeuvre: the pregnant females are first to go, followed by non-pregnant females, then mature males, immature females next and, finally, the immature males.

Below
Stephen's 'lucky whale shorts', bought especially for the occasion.

Opposite
One of the friendliest animals on the planet – a baby grey whale.

They file through Unimak Pass, a narrow gap between islands in the Aleutian chain, and head south along the coasts of British Columbia, Washington State, Oregon, California and beyond. With hardly a break, they average about 125 kilometres (78 miles) a day, and the entire journey takes them a couple of months.

They are heading for the Pacific side of Baja, which happens to be the winter home of practically the entire world population of grey whales. Safely sheltered from the pounding surf of the open ocean, thousands of them gather to socialise, mate and calve in a string of lagoons beside the desert.

The pregnant females are the first to arrive and they give birth to their gargantuan calves in the shallow backwaters of these lagoons, while many of the other whales are still on their way south.

The calves drink huge quantities of their mothers' fat-laden milk and gain weight rapidly. It's a relentless race against time. Within a few months they have to be fit and ready for their first journey north, to the Arctic feeding grounds, where the grey whale's annual cycle begins all over again.

But the most remarkable thing about grey whales is their willingness to forgive and forget.

They were hunted ruthlessly in the second half of the 19th century, and again in the early 20th century. Yankee whalers entered the Baja lagoons in small wood-

en rowing boats and harpooned grey whale calves, knowing that their mothers would come within range to protect them. And protect them they did – chasing the whaling boats, lifting them out of the water like big rubber ducks, ramming them with their heads and dashing them to pieces with their tails.

They would 'fight like devils', so the Yankee whalers dubbed them 'devilfish'. But despite their best efforts to fight back, they were hunted to the verge of extinction. Thank goodness, with official protection, they have made a remarkable comeback in the years since. The current population is about 21,000 – roughly the same as it was in the days before whaling.

Nowadays, the very same whales, once notorious for their ferocity in the face of danger, positively welcome whale-watching tourists into their breeding lagoons. Somehow, they seem to understand that we come in peace and, far from smashing our small open boats to smithereens, welcome us with open flippers.

We don't deserve it – but they have forgiven us for all those years of greed, recklessness and cruelty. They trust us, when we don't really deserve to be trusted.

We drove across the border from San Diego to Tijuana, increasingly notorious for its drug wars and assassinations, and continued south for an hour or so to the little town of Ensenada. From there we hitched a two-hour ride on a Cessna Caravan to San Ignacio Lagoon.

'It makes you wonder about evolution, doesn't it?' observed Stephen, looking out of the window at the desolate and rugged desert stretched out below. 'I mean, what animal would emerge from the sea onto dry land like this godforsaken place – and decide to stay? Obviously, not a particularly bright one.'

We landed on a sandy airstrip near the lagoon and, after a bumpy 45-minute drive in an ancient yellow school bus, eventually rocked up at a solar- and wind-powered eco-lodge nestled right on the shore.

'Oh my God to the power of ten!' exclaimed Stephen. 'What an absolutely magical place.'

'Oh my God to the power of a hundred!' he said a moment later. 'We're not going to be sleeping in those bloody huts, are we?'

We were. A row of small wooden cabins, roughly the size and shape of the beach huts found at many English seaside resorts, stretched out along the back of the beach. This was Cortez Camp – our home for the rest of the week. In fact, it was perfectly comfortable: my cabin had a shelf, a small window, a nail for a coat-hook, and a couple of single beds.

One of the disadvantages of being a zoologist is the constant lack of sleep. You always have to get up early in the morning and if you dare to mention the possibility of a lie-in to other zoologists they treat you with contempt for the rest of the day.

After a while, you just learn to sleep fast and keep quiet.

But one of the great advantages of whale-watching is that the whales are just as active after mid-morning coffee, or lunch, or even afternoon tea, as they are at the crack of dawn. So we started straight away.

The next few days were a blur of leaping, laughing, spouting, stroking, playing and patting. We had so many mind-bendingly close encounters with grey whales, we actually lost count.

On one occasion, we had a colossal calf literally leaning against the side of our small fibreglass boat. It lay there in ecstasy while we scratched it on the back and tickled it under the chin. It was as trusting and playful as a kitten.

Stephen ooh-ed and aah-ed over this 5-metre (16½-ft) long baby in much the same way as he had ooh-ed and aah-ed over the minuscule Madame Berthe's mouse lemur in Madagascar.

'Ooh!' he said when the baby opened its mouth.

'Aah!' he said when it looked him straight in the eye.

Suddenly, a huge cloud of bubbles erupted from the water underneath the boat. There was a slight swishing sound and a gigantic, bowed head appeared right alongside – giving me such a jump I almost swallowed my tongue. It was Mum, all 15 metres (49 feet) of her. She had been keeping a watchful eye on her calf, and no doubt on us, from the hidden depths.

I couldn't help thinking it was like watching the Mother Ship appear in *Close Encounters of the Third Kind*.

Another whale stayed with us for ages. Mottled grey, with a low dorsal fin instead of a hump and a series of 'knuckles' down the length of its tail, it was covered in barnacles. Grey whales are so heavily infested with barnacles – a large grey may carry several hundred kilograms of them – that, from a distance, they look suspiciously like rocks.

I managed to pull a whale louse from the middle of a barnacle cluster on its head. Named by early whalers, who had similar creatures crawling around in their own hair, whale lice are actually crustaceans rather than insects. My louse looked like a miniature crab (it was about a centimetre/half an inch long) that had been run over by a steamroller, and used its strong claws to cling on to the end of my finger. I had to prize it off before putting it back on the whale's head (I know it's only a louse but I felt responsible for its wellbeing).

Every time our new-found friend dropped out of sight, we stared into the murky water contemplating its next move. On several occasions, it surfaced so unexpectedly – and with such a loud explosion of breath – that we almost leapt out of the boat.

It was incredibly inquisitive and, most of the time, it was hard to tell who was supposed to be watching whom. It frequently spyhopped – towering above us as it lifted its head as high as 3 metres (10 feet) out of the water to take a closer look.

Then we had a group of no fewer than six adult whales lolling and rolling around next to the boat. We were surrounded. Every time they spouted we were showered and soaked in salty whale breath, and every time they rolled the swell almost tipped us over. For a heart-stopping moment, one lifted us up, ever so gently, and lowered us back into the water; another nudged us with the end of its snout and then energetically pushed us round in circles like a cat playing with a mouse.

At one point, filming stopped as the entire crew downed tools to pat, tickle and kiss the friendly whales around us. No one could resist.

Just a brief flirtation with a whale is often all it takes to turn normal, quiet, unflappable people into delirious, jabbering extroverts. On whale-watching trips almost everyone becomes the life and soul of the party. I have seen grown men and women dance around the deck, break into song, burst into tears, slap one

Above
Mark in his element.

Opposite
Whale barnacles and whale lice making themselves at home on a grey whale's head.

Opposite bottom
It was hard to tell who was supposed to be watching whom.

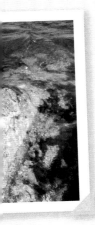

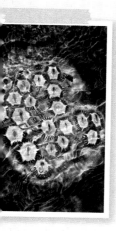

another on the back and do all the things that normal, quiet, unflappable people are not supposed to do.

I have done them myself and laughed as I watched Stephen and the crew falling under the spell. I knew that their lives would never be quite the same again.

There is something about whales that grabs you by the scruff of the neck and makes you think about them morning, noon and night. At the risk of sounding theatrical, emotional and (heaven forbid) unscientific, they make you feel good.

After a really close encounter, it is hard to remain emotionally stable for several weeks afterwards. Eventually, the jabbering and the delirium subside, but you are still left with a good feeling that never really wanes. There is an immense and lasting satisfaction in simply knowing that the whales are out there, wild and free.

By now, if you haven't already seen a whale, you may be wondering if six months on the road with Stephen has had some weird and deleterious effect on me. I wouldn't blame you. If I had read this thirty years ago, before my first close encounter with a whale, I would have been wondering exactly the same thing.

But it's not Stephen's fault. Ask someone else who has seen a whale and they will explain that I'm not quite as barmy and irrational as you might think. There are plenty of 'whale junkies' out there – people, like me, who have to see a whale at frequent intervals just to survive their normal daily lives.

ave seen grown
en and women
nce around
e deck, break
o song, burst
o tears, slap
e another on
e back and do
the things that
rmal, quiet,
flappable
ople are not
pposed to do.

So even if I am crazy, I am definitely not alone.

Stephen, for one, is a recent convert. He summed up our close encounters better than I've heard anyone sum it up before or since.

'Suck my pants and call me Noreen,' he enthused. 'What a phenomenal experience. Epic. Epic. Epic.'

It was our last evening in San Ignacio, so I poured myself a beer and sat alone on the beach, watching the natural world go by and the sun set over the water.

Squadrons of brown pelicans flew past in sullen procession, looking as if they had important business to attend to – like finding a suitable roost for the gathering night. They travelled in single file, beak to tail feather, their heavy wing beats and enormous beaks making them look like pterodactyls left over from prehistory.

After supper, I went to sleep in my hut with the curtain wide open, thinking about the events of the day and listening to the sounds of the night. Lying in the moonlight, I could hear coyotes calling from beyond the shower hut, a cacophony of barks from distant sea lions, an occasional whimbrel or American oystercatcher disturbed at their roost, waves lapping on the beach, and the

Opposite
And they all came
back complaining
that they hadn't seen
anything.

Below left
Grey whale breach-
ing – like a fleet of
juggernauts leaping
out of the water.

Below right
Brown pelicans looking
like pterodactyls left
over from prehistory.

thunderous blows of whales swimming about in the lagoon beyond.

I wouldn't have been at all surprised if Louis Armstrong had been sitting on my cabin steps, overwhelmed by the magnificence of it all and moved to sing *What a Wonderful World*.

It was truly idyllic. Good for the soul.

Meanwhile, Stephen hadn't been doing so well. The next morning he was behaving rather strangely.

I was walking past his hut, on the way to breakfast, when I heard him call out. He sounded really stressed.

'I can't find my glasses. Or my trousers. Someone has stolen my trousers.'

I went over to see what was happening. At first, I thought he was drunk. Tired and dishevelled, as if he had slept in his clothes, he was staggering about and bumping into things.

'Are you okay?' I asked, leaning through the open door.

'I've lost my trousers,' he replied.

'You're wearing your trousers.'

'No, no, not these trousers. Different trousers. Someone has stolen my trousers.'

'I don't think that's very likely. Are you sure you haven't just mislaid them?'

'Oh God, I don't know. What's happening?'

He sat on the side of the bed, his head in his hands, groaning and rocking slowly backwards and forwards.

By this time, Tim, the Director, had arrived. He was looking very concerned.

'Do you think he's had a stroke?' he asked in a loud stage whisper.

'I don't know,' I whispered back. 'He's certainly behaving oddly, but I haven't had much experience in diagnosing strokes.'

'He didn't seem himself last night, did he?' said Tim.

'That's true. He left supper incredibly early – some time between 7 and 7.30, I think – saying that he was tired and had a cold. He wanted to get an early night.'

'What are you talking about?' asked Stephen, sounding like a frightened child at the hospital.

'You don't seem very well,' I said, in what I hoped was a soothing voice. 'We're worried about you.'

We decided to call the BBC and a doctor for advice, and left Stephen sitting on the side of his bed while we went off in search of the satellite phone. Half an hour and several intense discussions later, we concluded that it probably wasn't a stroke but we ought to seek medical help just in case. We were due to leave Cortez Camp later that day anyway, so we'd just get going a little earlier than expected.

We went back to help Stephen pack his things, but the hut was empty. He had gone. We ran around in a complete panic, calling his name, until one of the staff said they had seen him wandering off into the desert.

Above
Muleteering about
to commence.

He was found fairly quickly, lying under a cactus, and brought back for safekeeping.

Fortunately, the weirdness didn't last long. He was noticeably better by lunchtime and almost back to normal by the time we checked in to a little hotel in San Ignacio town.

But it was several weeks before I found out exactly what had happened – and even then only after reading his Twitter entries for that fateful day:

'Tequila. That's all I have to say. Tequila. Damn you. Tequila. Odi et amo. Oh dear. Oh my.'

Apparently, he had drunk a couple of glasses of tequila and then taken two sleeping tablets, before turning in for the night. It had worked. At least, it had worked by sending him into a deep, 11-hour sleep. But as soon as he'd woken up the following morning, fitful sleep turned into hysterical delirium.

He hadn't had a stroke after all – he had just gone round the bend, albeit temporarily.

The good news is that his glasses turned up on the dining table in the main

hut of Cortez Camp, and his trousers miraculously reappeared – two days later – in a drawer by the bed in his hotel room.

We never discussed it again.

Tim casually dropped a bombshell one evening in San Ignacio town: the following day we had to be up early to go on a mule trek. Two hours up a mountain on the back of a mule, and then two hours back again. Four hours of hell on earth.

Throw me into a pit full of writhing vipers, hide a tarantula in my sleeping bag or tie a vampire bat to my hair. Anything, but anything, rather than put me on a four-legged animal with hooves.

Stephen wasn't the least bit happy, either.

'A thousand boiling arses,' was his immediate response.

I egged him on, like one of the keas we'd been watching in the car park in New Zealand, in the vain hope that Tim might buckle under pressure and abandon his plans for a death-defying donkey derby.

'I vowed never to sit on another four-legged animal again,' continued Stephen, getting into his stride, the human equivalent of a canter, 'and now you're going to make me break the promise to myself.'

'Oh come on – it'll be fun!' cajoled Tim, imagining the comedy TV moment (for everyone except us).

'Fun? Fun? It's all very well in a planning meeting in Cardiff, when you lot decide that it'd be nice to have Mark and me riding through the mountains on mules like a couple of learner cowboys – but the reality is dust, sunstroke, dehydration … and, ultimately, death.'

'But it's the only way to get to see some of the best pre-Columbian cave paintings in Baja.'

'I'll walk,' said Stephen, seeing through the wheeze.

'But you're not entering into the spirit of the occasion,' retorted Tim.

The pros and cons of riding on the back of a mule, watching other people ride on the back of a mule, walking alongside a mule or not going anywhere near a mule were discussed at length over drinks, then dinner, and finally coffee, until it was time for bed.

But Tim was having none of it. We were going and that was the end of the matter.

The next morning we drove the one-and-a-half-hour journey to our mule rendezvous point in sulky silence.

Heading east from San Ignacio, along ever-diminishing dirt tracks, we travelled through a sea of cacti, desert and rugged mountains. It was all very spaghetti western.

We arrived at a small ranch in a place called Santa Marta (although to all intents and purposes it was in the middle of nowhere) and were met by two grinning rancheros. They were wearing obligatory cowboy hats on their heads and thick leather chaps on their legs.

'Oh God,' said Stephen. 'It all looks a bit serious. Why the hell are they wearing those chaps? It's rather melodramatic, don't you think? Like it's going to be a proper expedition or something.'

We had one more last-ditch attempt at talking Tim out of the whole preposterous idea and begrudgingly climbed on to the backs of our respective mules.

Muleteering was about to commence.

We hadn't even left the car park (if that's the word for a dusty compound full of horses, donkeys and mules tied to various wooden fence posts) before we were getting into trouble.

'Oh hell! It's going backwards!'

'Mine's walking round in circles.'

'Help! No, seriously, help!'

'How do I stop it?'

Like a kidnap victim growing fond of his capto[r] I developed a special affinity for Bubba (I thin[k] that's what they said his name was) during our enforced time together.

Opposite
Stephen with a testicle snuggled in each armpit.

'Aaagh! It's jumping forwards with jerky movements.'

'Why is it going sideways?'

'Now it's bending down and eating. How do I stop it eating?'

Tim had to turn away to hide the tears of laughter rolling down his cheeks. The camera was quivering and quaking as the cameraman convulsed with laughter behind the eyepiece.

The rancheros gave us a helping hand and then gave the mules a stiff talking-to – or maybe it was the other way round – and we were off up the mountain track.

'This will make our inner thighs sit up and take notice,' groaned Stephen. 'And goodness knows...'

Just as he was about to continue a little tirade about the trials and tribulations of mule trekking, his mule suddenly lifted its head and made a strange and rather alarming sound. It started with a horse-like whinny, evolved into a donkey-like heehaw and ended with a pitiful whimper like a cowboy after a shoot-out gasping for breath. Stephen braced himself and sat bolt upright, waiting for something horrible to happen. But the mule just snorted and continued on its way.

I grew to become quite fond of my particular mule. In fact, to be honest, I felt

pangs of guilt for expecting it to be an obnoxious creature, with the asininity and stubbornness of a donkey and the stupidity and angst of a horse. But it seemed to have inherited the better characteristics of both parents: the sobriety, patience and sure-footedness of a donkey, and the strength, courage and self-assurance of a horse.

Rather like a kidnap victim growing fond of his captor, I developed a special affinity for Bubba (I think that's what they said his name was) during our enforced time together.

There was just one little hiccup in our developing relationship.

After an hour or so, it became blatantly obvious why the rancheros were wearing thick leather chaps. It definitely wasn't to look like Clint Eastwood. Our mules took inordinate delight in brushing us past every single viciously prickly cactus along the path. If there weren't any cacti along the path, they went off-piste to find some specifically to brush past. Even through long trousers the thorns ripped and snagged our legs. Had we worn shorts we'd have been red fleshy pulp from the waist down.

I called out to Stephen, who was a few metres behind me muttering under his breath.

'How are you doing?' I asked.

'Well, despite having raw and bloodied legs. And apart from having a testicle snuggled in each armpit, vowing never to descend again. And apart from my buttocks being more anguished and outraged than an Italian defender protesting innocence in the penalty box, I'm doing okay,' he called back.

Then he glanced up for the first time.

I looked around just in time to see his eyes pop out of his head. For a split second he looked like a bad actor in a Hollywood B-movie spotting a posse of arrow-firing Red Indians galloping over the brow of a hill.

'Holy mackerel!' he yelped, looking at the path ahead turning abruptly towards the highest mountain. 'We can't possibly be going up that slope. Surely not? It's far too steep.'

He watched as my mule followed the path and started up the slope.

'Oh my God, we are,' I heard him say to himself, almost in a whisper.

The mules bounced and jiggered, slipped and stumbled their way up the impossibly rough and steep mountain slope, until the path levelled and we breathed an audible sigh of relief.

You have to hand it to mules. For an infertile cross between a male donkey and a female horse, their mountain-climbing abilities are an absolute miracle. Thousands of years of evolutionary trial and error have given them perfect

four-hoof-drive precision far better than any four-wheel-drive vehicle designed by human engineers.

Not a moment too soon, our mules stopped walking and we were given permission to get off, or dismount I should say. We had arrived.

We turned and admired the view. The setting was spectacular – forbidding, arid, wild and vast. The rancheros told us that it rains in this particular corner of Baja only once or twice a year; sometimes it never rains at all. In that respect, at least, it bears absolutely no resemblance whatsoever to my home town of Bristol, where it seems to *stop* raining only once or twice a year.

The whole landscape spoke aloud of the dramatic elemental forces that move continents, form oceans and build mountains.

'It's all very well creating a backlit deer or an adorable baby whale,' observed Stephen. 'But why not make the earth safe and solid, instead of making it with tectonic plates that cause earthquakes and tsunamis?'

Behind us was a huge rocky overhang, which was literally covered in cave paintings. We recognised several different animals: lots of antelopes, a fish (or maybe it was a whale?), some rabbits, a couple of birds and a sea turtle. There were human figures, too, though they looked unlike any people we knew. Some were wearing what looked like top hats, others appeared to be in their pyjamas,

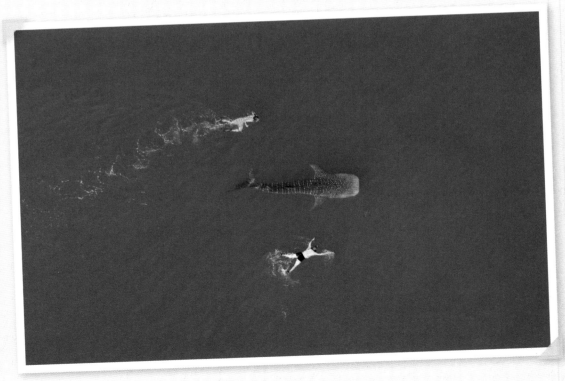

and several looked more humanoid than human. One, clearly a woman, had eye-catchingly long breasts that dangled down to her knees.

Some of the images were superimposed on top of one another, suggesting feverish bouts of artistic creativity.

The Mexicans call them 'rustic pictures'. I like that.

No one knows who painted them or how long ago they did it. Surprisingly little is known about rock art and even less is known about this particular collection. The most plausible theory is that they were produced by hunter-gatherers, between five hundred and a thousand years ago, and have something to do with shamanic rituals.

But it's all entirely speculation.

My favourite theory comes from a Cochimí Indian legend, which says that this remarkable mural was the work of giants who inhabited the mid-peninsula region a thousand years ago. It makes a lot of sense – they were the only people who could possibly have reached at least 10 metres (33 feet) above the ground without the advantage of a ladder or scaffolding.

Given the paintings' age and exposure to the rigours of the outside world, they were all surprisingly vivid and well preserved. Archaeologists reckon the exceptionally long-lasting paint was made from a mixture of urine and pulverised rock – a lesson to the builder who redecorated my bathroom with paint that barely lasted six months. The only problem is choice of colour – hunter-gatherer paint apparently comes in nothing but black or maroon (presumably depending on whether the urine was obtained from someone who either had, or had not, eaten beetroot the night before).

Reluctantly, we climbed back onto our mules and headed back towards the mule park. It was a bit of a shock to discover that going downhill was considerably worse than going uphill, and took even longer, but we made it just as the sun was setting – dusty and suffering a little from sunstroke and dehydration, but nonetheless alive.

'That was fun,' said Stephen, sarcastically. 'Aside from feeling tortured and tormented beyond all hope, as though I've been buggered by a train and stoned by a crowd of homo-hating fanatics, I feel great.'

'Get in the water! Jump! Get in the water!' shouted the skipper, as we came alongside the largest fish in the sea.

I dropped over the side of our small boat into the cool waters of La Paz Bay – a colossal bite out of the southeastern corner of Baja – and dunked my head

Opposite
Snorkellers with a *baby* whale shark – imagine how big its Mum must be.

Below
A whale shark: more like a fictional sea monster than a real-life fish.

below the surface. There, no more than a couple of metres in front of me, was a dorsal fin that would have made Steven Spielberg glow with pride. Covered with light-coloured spots and stripes, it was attached to one of the most gargantuan whale sharks I had ever seen: it was more like a fictional sea monster than a real-life fish.

Snorkelling with whale sharks is not quite as safe as watching breakfast television – simply because, in theory, any animal the length and weight of a bus is powerful enough to knock a person out of the water – but it comes pretty close. It's another one of the most exhilarating wildlife encounters on the planet.

I finned along with the shark, struggling to keep up as the giant feeding machine methodically worked its way through billowing clouds of plankton.

I could see its broad, flattened head far to the front and, briefly turning around, glimpsed its barn-door-sized tail swinging slowly backwards and forwards far to the back. Immediately below me was a huge pectoral fin, roughly the size of my kitchen table, covered with a motley collection of remoras calmly hitching a free ride.

Briefly, it made me think of a giant, spotty tadpole.

The shark swam with a smooth, graceful movement that belied its phenomenal size and, despite my attempt at Olympic-standard snorkelling, effortlessly left me behind.

Estrella stayed with it for a bit longer, but then she was considerably younger and fitter than me and made my pathetic attempt at speed-snorkelling seem somewhat less than impressive.

Esmeralda Estrella Navarro-Holm was a whale shark researcher. She had also recently been crowned Miss Baja California Sur. Marine biologist and model, she knew a heck of a lot about sharks and looked considerably better in a wetsuit than I did.

She swam over to where I was treading water and we waited to be picked up.

'Any luck?' shouted Stephen from the boat. 'That was a big one – I reckon it was at least 12 metres (40 feet) long.'

'No!' I called back. 'It was much too fast and the tape got tangled around my leg. We'll have to try again.'

We were in La Paz to measure the lengths of whale sharks with a long yellow tape measure. This involved four simple steps: 1) find a whale shark; 2) dive down and swim alongside it; 3) hold one end of the tape measure at the tip of its snout and the other at the most distant corner of its tail while it swam at the speed of a torpedo; and 4) remember to come up for air.

We had found several possible contenders in a shallow sandy bay opposite town, within half an hour of leaving dock, but were failing to complete the task in hand. The first step was relatively simple – but the remaining three were proving more difficult.

The larger whale sharks were, quite simply, too fast. They were surprisingly unperturbed by our peculiar antics, but a single, lackadaisical swing of their tails propelled them through the water faster than either of us could keep up. At least, it was faster than I could keep up. Estrella could stay with them for several minutes, but I was struggling. Swimming at top speed, while trying to hold the end of the tape in exactly the right position on the shark's moving tail, was a lot harder than it probably sounds. Several times, I had to drop back for fear of having a heart attack, or worse.

The smaller sharks (for 'smaller sharks' read 'five- or six-metre-long sharks') were a little slower and easier to keep up with. But if they dived more than a few metres beneath the surface, taking accurate measurements was pretty much out of the question.

It felt as if we were weird and whacky tailors measuring our 'clients' for new shark suits – except the clients wouldn't stay still.

Stephen decided to stay on the boat.

'I look such a twazzock in a wetsuit,' was his explanation.

So he became research assistant for the day. He was ready and waiting on deck, pen poised to write the latest shark dimensions on a scientific chart. But for the first hour or two he didn't have much to do. Leaping in and out of the water, following one whale shark after another, it was exhilarating, exhausting and fabulous fun, but we didn't actually measure a single shark.

We weren't short of possible contenders. La Paz Bay is among the best places in the world for close encounters with whale sharks.

But after years of intensive hunting, these extraordinary creatures have all but disappeared from many of their former haunts in other parts of the world. Unfortunately, it's hard to get most people, let alone governments, excited about shark conservation. There is no shortage of volunteers to care for orphaned orang-utans, campaign against the Canadian seal hunt, dive in front of Japan's explosive harpoons or climb Mount Kilimanjaro to raise money for endangered rhinos.

But who is fighting the fight for sharks?

Some are, thank goodness, but not many.

Our laissez-faire attitude towards shark conservation is perfectly understandable. Why should we protect an animal that wants to eat us? Protecting dangerous animals of any kind – whether venomous snakes, Komodo dragons or sharks – is always going to be difficult.

At least part of the blame must lie with the book *Jaws*, published in 1974, and with the high-profile movies that followed. They literally scared readers and audiences out of the water, and many shark conservationists believe they fuelled

Opposite
Bioluminescence – made when loads of microscopic marine organisms get together and convert chemical energy into light energy. Or something like that.

Below
Esmeralda Estrella Navarro-Holm – whale shark researcher and Miss Baja California Sur.

Below right
Yet another whale shark.

the anti-shark hysteria that has gripped the Western world ever since. Although to be fair to the author, Peter Benchley, many experts at the time were just as unenlightened. And he later became actively involved in shark conservation, publicly lamenting the impact of his book on our attitude towards sharks.

The truth is that sharks aren't really dangerous. Even if you spend a great deal of time in the sea, as I do, the likelihood of being attacked by one is ridiculously small. I've had hundreds of encounters with sharks over the years and not once have I been bitten. Quite simply, our collective fear has distorted the facts.

I know you don't believe me, so let me try to convince you.

How many shark attacks do you think there are around the world in a typical year? Bear in mind the tens of millions of paddlers, swimmers, snorkellers, divers, surfers and spear fishermen splashing about in the sea every single day. Maybe 1,000? Possibly even 10,000? No. Wrong. In the past ten years, the average number of people bumped, bitten, nipped or chewed by sharks worldwide each year was … 63. And just five of these, on average, have been fatal.

Given that nearly half of these attacks took place in Florida, it suddenly makes the rest of the world seem surprisingly safe, doesn't it? In fact, even Florida is surprisingly safe.

There is a simple reason why we think the situation is worse than it actually is: we get to hear about all the worst shark attacks, wherever in the world we happen to live. A headline reading 'Shark Attacks Man' sells newspapers – and so we assume it happens more often than it really does.

Statistics prove that we have nothing to fear. I know you can do anything with statistics, but let's look at them anyway. It's fun – and it puts the risk of shark attack into perspective:

Opposite
The front part of our
21-metre whale shark.

- there is a far greater chance of winning a national lottery than of being attacked by a shark;
- for every person attacked by a shark more than a thousand people drown;
- many times more people are killed by coconuts falling on their heads than are killed by sharks;
- and, best of all, according to figures published by the New York City Health Department, for every person around the world bitten by a shark, 25 people are actually bitten by New Yorkers.

So there we have it: sharks are not intent on hurting people at all. If they *were* out to get us, there would be many, many more attacks.

I'm not suggesting you jump into the sea during a feeding frenzy of tiger sharks, or waltz around with a gargantuan great white (although I have done that – and survived to tell the tale), but in the normal course of events your chances of being attacked during a relaxing holiday swim are just about nil.

Chinese medicin – trusted by near a quarter of the world's populatic – has a lot to answer for.

Having said that, I have an admission to make: I never wear yellow swimming trunks. There is some evidence to suggest that bright colours may attract sharks and, rightly or wrongly, 'yum-yum yellow' has a particularly bad reputation. But then I never run with scissors, either, so I am being over-cautious.

I also have a private pact with the sharks, which seems to have worked pretty well so far: I won't eat them if they don't eat me. I wish more people did the same thing, because sharks are in serious trouble and the fewer people who eat them the better.

Perhaps the most shocking statistic – and this really puts things into perspective – is that for every person killed by a shark we in turn kill many millions of sharks. In fact, the latest research suggests that 100–150 million sharks are killed by people every year.

Now that really is frightening.

The main reason is shark-fin soup. Once a rare delicacy consumed only by the Chinese aristocracy, since the mid-1980s shark-fin soup has become immensely popular with the growing middle classes in China, Hong Kong, Singapore, Tai-

wan and other Asian communities worldwide. Its traditional association with privilege and social rank makes it an essential dish at everything from weddings and birthdays to business events and Chinese New Year celebrations.

Since fishermen have been alerted to the commercial value of shark fins, what was once a small trade limited to parts of Asia and to certain species, finning has been transformed into a massive global industry involving more than 125 countries and virtually every known species of shark. Several are on the verge of extinction and many populations have completely disappeared.

Preparing shark-fin soup is a complex process, involving many different stages. But apparently the clear, glutinous broth is almost tasteless (I haven't tried it myself – remember my pact) and has little nutritional value. You have to add chicken or vegetable stock to give it any flavour.

Traditional Chinese Medicine nevertheless considers the soup to be an aphrodisiac and a tonic: strengthening the waist, providing a source of energy, nourishing the blood, invigorating the kidneys and lungs, and improving digestion.

Chinese medicine – trusted by nearly a quarter of the world's population – has a lot to answer for. It's responsible for the demise and collapse of wildlife populations, including tigers, rhinos and sharks, in all corners of the globe.

But shark-finning is more than a conservation issue – it is incredibly cruel, too. The fins are frequently removed from the sharks while they are still alive

Opposite
A fairly average sunset
in the Sea of Cortez.

and the animals are dumped overboard with terrible injuries, left to die slow, agonising deaths on the sea bed.

But there is a glimmer of hope.

In a bizarre twist of fate, recent research suggests that shark-fin soup could be dangerous to eat. It contains up to thirty times the maximum permitted levels of mercury and other marine pollutants, because the sea is heavily polluted and the pollutants get concentrated in the bodies of top predators. Shark-fin soup could actually render men sterile – a little ironic considering the number of people who consume the soup specifically for the qualities that are supposed to do the exact opposite.

So sharks are dangerous, after all, through absolutely no fault of their own.

Estrella and I decided to have one last go at measuring a shark. We spotted a particularly large one cruising just beneath the surface and slipped back into the water.

Suddenly, out of the planktonic gloom came a huge, gaping mouth. It looked more like the open cargo doors of an alien spaceship than the oral cavity of a fish, and I could have tumbled inside with room to spare.

Briefly, I made eye contact with its owner. The shark's prehistoric stare was mesmerising, but its eyes gave nothing away. It wasn't like looking into the knowing, enquiring eyes of the grey whales, and I could not tell if it was inquisitive or uninterested.

This gentle giant seemed to be swimming a little more slowly than the others and we were able to keep up just long enough to stretch the yellow tape along the entire length of its body. I took the measurement and swam back up to the surface, gasping for breath.

'21 metres!' (69 feet) I shouted to Stephen.

'Excellent. Brilliant. Well done!' our research assistant replied.

I peered under water again and saw Estrella rising to the surface some distance away.

'I got it!' she called. She had managed to take a DNA sample of the shark, by jabbing a special collecting instrument, like a large needle, into the skin at the base of its dorsal fin.

'How did the shark react?' I asked, thinking that I would have panicked and disappeared into the murk if someone had unexpectedly jabbed me with a sharp needle.

'It barely flinched,' came the happy reply. 'I'm not even sure that it noticed.'

Estrella was developing a technique to identify individual whale sharks by their DNA. She was looking for a kind of genetic name tag unique to each and every individual. This would help her to find out where they go between visits to La Paz Bay (whale sharks are among the least understood large animals on earth)

and would make it easier for other scientists to work out where they came from if – heaven forbid – their fins ever turn up in the shark-fin trade.

As we returned to La Paz, Stephen twittered something about the day to his half a million followers. The sun was shining, the sea was calm and we must have encountered at least a dozen different whale sharks during the course of the day.

The response was immediate and unanimous – we were a couple of lucky buggers.

'Yes,' he responded. 'It's been a heavenly day. We are absurdly lucky to be doing this. Preposterously. Outrageously. No excuse for it.'

We could easily have stayed in the delightful coastal town of La Paz for weeks, but we had a prior engagement: we'd chartered a boat to explore the extraordinary world of the Sea of Cortez.

The only major body of water entirely under the control of one government, the Sea of Cortez is a well-kept secret that tends to be overshadowed by the more famous grey whale breeding lagoons on the other side of Baja.

Visiting San Ignacio, without venturing into 'the Gulf', as the locals tend to

Opposite
The Horizon offered the
exciting prospect of
staying unpacked for
nearly a week.

Below
A humpback whale
showing off one of its
long flippers.

call it, is like buying a book and then reading only the first chapter.

We boarded the MV *Horizon*, a spacious 25-metre (82-foot) sportfishing vessel, late one evening and met captain Greg Grivetto and his affable crew. I had travelled with Greg several times before, cage-diving with great white sharks far out in the North Pacific.

Stephen and I were especially excited about the prospect of unpacking – and staying unpacked for nearly a week. One of the downsides of endless travel is living out of a suitcase, and, after months on the road, it was a rare treat to be in one place for a measurable length of time. The cabins were fairly small, but we had one each and spent a ridiculously long hour or more laying our books, boots, lenses, laptops, iPods and pants in neat rows and piles where we could see them all together for the first time in living memory. It was absolute bliss.

Stephen wandered upstairs and set up base camp on a table in the salon. Whistling and singing to himself, he carefully placed his laptop centre stage and laid out a motley collection of mobile phones and cables around the edge, like a child decorating a Christmas tree. I've rarely seen him happier.

We met on deck for a late-night beer and, with a well-worn map spread out on the baitfish tank, traced our proposed route. First, we were travelling south, crossing the Tropic of Cancer overnight, to spend a couple of days off the southern tip of Baja. Then we would head north and travel deep into the Gulf. The ultimate aim of our little expedition was to find the ultimate whale – a blue whale – but we had a few other things to do along the way.

Stephen was a little worried about seasickness, so he asked Mark, the boat's cook, for some tablets.

He looked at them suspiciously and signalled for me to join him in a quiet corner of the salon, out of earshot of the others.

'Do you think he's given me Viagra,' he whispered.

'Why on earth would he do that?'

'I don't know,' said Stephen. 'Look at them.'

He opened his hand surreptitiously, like a drug dealer on a street corner, and revealed two blue lozenges.

'I don't know what Viagra looks like!' I admitted, laughing.

'Nor do I!' said Stephen, as if I'd accused him of something. 'But I've seen pictures of it – and it looks exactly like this.'

He tutted, threw both tablets into his mouth and took a swig of beer.

'I'll await future developments with interest,' was his parting shot.

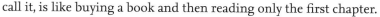

We'd taken a loudspeaker on the *Horizon* with us, and the next day, while floating about 10 kilometres (6 miles) offshore, we decided to set it up on the rear deck.

The speaker was connected to an underwater microphone, or hydrophone, which we carefully lowered into the sea at the back of the boat.

Stephen switched it on and, suddenly, the air was filled with a baffling medley of moans, groans, snores, squeaks and whistles. Some of the sounds were like the grating of an old metal hinge, others resembled the last gurglings of a drowning man, and there was one that could only be described as like the squawking of a chicken with a farmer standing on its toe.

In between, there was a beautiful operatic melody that reverberated around the boat and made the hairs on the back of our necks stand on end.

We were listening to the plaintive song of a male humpback whale. With elements of jazz, bebop, blues, heavy metal, classical and reggae all rolled into one, it's hard to describe the feelings that washed over us as we listened. It sparked a rollercoaster of emotions: soothing and melancholic, shocking and unsettling, mesmerising and awe-inspiring. There is nothing else quite like it.

When these unearthly sounds were first heard by an astonished world in the 1970s, thousands of people rushed out to buy recordings of them – making humpback whales the only animals able to boast a top-selling record in the pop charts.

But what we were listening to was not a recording. It was the real thing: a haunting and unforgettable live performance. We were eavesdropping on an unseen humpback whale earnestly singing from somewhere underneath the boat.

It was one of the few times during our travels together when Stephen was rendered completely speechless. He went to say something at one point – he even opened his mouth and a croaky little noise came out – but he closed it again and carried on listening.

So we stood there in silence, me leaning against the wooden railings and Stephen a few metres away on deck, his arms folded and his head tilted slightly to one side. He was smiling broadly.

I always find humpback whale songs a little overwhelming and humbling. I realise it's not very scientific to admit such a thing, and I'm sure my zoological colleagues will mock me for it, but a singing humpback seems to be so full of purpose and emotion.

Human words just don't do it justice.

I glanced around the deck. Every single person – director, cameraman, soundman, assistant producer and the entire boat crew – had stopped what they'd been doing. We were all perfectly still and quiet, listening together.

It was several minutes before Tim, the Director, snapped to attention, our brains had re-engaged and we were able to discuss for the camera exactly what we were listening to – in suitably hushed and respectful tones.

The humpback's song is the longest and most complex song in the animal kingdom. It can last for half an hour or more. All the whales in one area sing broadly the same song but, astonishingly, they are constantly refining and improving it. One whale adds a few new notes and all the others think 'Crikey! That sounds pretty good! I'm going to do that as well.' And so they incorporate each other's improvisations as they go along, as if they are writing and re-writing the music together.

This means that the song being sung one day is quite different from the one being sung several months later – to such a degree that the entire composition changes over a period of about five years.

It's hard not to read something into this remarkable process of reworking and fine-tuning. Does it suggest a degree of artistic sensitivity? Maybe. We don't know.

It would be great at this point to say that even the most elaborate bird songs are uniform and unchanging. But that wouldn't be true. Many songbirds change their songs as they grow older. During its first nesting season, for example, a young male indigo bunting sings a weird and wonderful song unique to itself. But gradually it begins to obey the unwritten rules of being an indigo bunting and comes to sound more and more like its neighbours.

Humpbacks living in different parts of the world sing very different compositions. They probably all croon about the same trials and tribulations in life, but it is as if the ones living around Hawai'i sing a sort of Polynesian jazz, while those living off the coast of Australia, for example, sing with a didgeridoo accompaniment, and the ones in the Caribbean sing a reggae version of the song. I'm exaggerating, of course, but you know what I mean. They are all singing the humpback whale song – it's just that they are singing variations of the same theme.

The differences are so distinctive that whale experts, like wine connoisseurs, can tell where – and even when – a humpback was recorded simply by listening to the intricacies of its unique and special dialect.

Again, the same thing happens with many songbirds. Indigo buntings living in one area sing their own version of the official indigo bunting song, while those living in another area sing a noticeably different version.

So maybe there isn't much artistic sensitivity, after all. But it's a nice thought.

It is only the male humpback whales that sing. They close their eyes and hang upside down in the water, heads pointing towards the sea bed and waving their enormous outstretched flippers up and down like conductors in front of an orchestra. Their aim is believed to be twofold: to serenade the females and to warn off unwanted competition from other males.

They croon day and night, sometimes repeating their songs over and over again, taking only brief, one-minute pauses for breath.

Our whale was still out of sight beneath the boat, but we could feel its presence through the haunting sounds still wafting around the deck.

We finished our piece for the camera and everyone lapsed back into reverential silence. We stood there for ages, quietly contemplating the secrets of the whale's world and wondering if we could extend our trip by an extra couple of days.

'Look out for a big black Cadillac with a major radiator problem' is how a naturalist friend introduces humpback whales on his whale-watching trips in Hawai'i.

They are, indeed, big – and predominantly black. Whether or not their bushy blows, or spouts, are like overheated radiators is a matter of opinion.

Actually, the humpback is best known for its outrageously long flippers, which can grow to nearly a third of the length of its body (5 metres/16 feet or more) and look more like wings than pectoral fins. Viewed from the air, a group of humpbacks looks surprisingly like a formation of jumbo jets.

If you wanted to design the perfect whale for whale-watching you couldn't do much better than a humpback. It's not too difficult to find, nice and easy

to identify, shamelessly inquisitive (if humpbacks had net curtains they would spend hours every day peeping through the gap in the middle) and capable of performing some of the most spectacular acrobatic displays on earth.

Herman Melville, who mentioned them in *Moby Dick*, knew what he was talking about when he described them as 'the most gamesome and lighthearted of all the whales, making more gay foam and white water generally than any of them.'

The next day was a baking-hot Saturday and we were still drifting off the southern tip of Baja, over an area called Gorda Bank. There were literally dozens of humpbacks in sight, including a tightly packed group swimming almost flipper-to-flipper in the whale equivalent of a chorus line.

We were incredibly lucky. Like flicking through pages in a book about whales, we witnessed almost every imaginable form of behaviour.

One whale was lying upside down on the surface, with its great flippers pointing towards the sky, like a sunbather reading a book on a sun bed; after a while, it slapped one flipper, and then the other, onto the water, rolled over and dived. Another turned upside down, literally reversed out of the water and repeatedly smacked its enormous tail onto the surface; it was making such a phenomenal splash that it was hard to see the whale itself through all the foam and spray.

As if for a grand finale, one particularly active humpback breached – leapt

Opposite
A bloodied male humpback whale after a bit of a scrap over a female.

Below
It is possible to tell one humpback whale from another by looking at the unique black and white markings on the underside of their tails.

out of the water – right in front of us. Flying through the air no more than 100 metres (328 feet) from the boat, the huge whale arched its back, turned slightly and then fell backwards. It seemed to happen in slow motion and, briefly, waving its flippers in the air, it looked like a giant, overfed parrot. It hit the water with a thundering splash, as if someone had dropped a submarine from a great height, and disappeared below the surface.

Why do whales breach? Well, the answer is the same as for many questions about whales: we don't know, but there are lots of interesting theories. It may be a form of signalling, because the noise of the splash can be heard for long distances above water, and even further underwater; it could be a way of dislodging parasites, such as whale lice or barnacles; or it might be a way of saying 'hello' or 'goodbye'.

Quite possibly, it could be something the whales do purely for fun. If I weighed nearly 40 tonnes (39 tons), and could leap out of the water like a fleet of juggernauts, I think I would probably do it just for fun.

Interestingly, many humpbacks seem to find breaching infectious: when one animal leaps others often join in, just like people giggling.

The whale breached again. Stephen whooped and cheered and slapped me on the back. He started to laugh – the kind of hysterical laugh people do when their brains are overwhelmed and can't quite compute the magnitude of what

is happening. I started laughing, too. Then the crew laughed. They put down the camera, the microphone and all the other paraphernalia that comes with filming, for the umpteenth time in a few days, and suddenly we were all slapping one another on the back and doing all the things that normal, quiet, unflappable people are not supposed to do.

We watched the whales and their antics for several hours and soon began to recognise certain individuals.

We are able to recognise one another by our faces. Take skippers and marine biologists, for example: some have red noses, others have long, straggly beards, a few are completely bald and several wear make-up. And that's just the men. Very quickly we can learn to tell them apart.

But humpbacks don't have faces – at least, not the kind that make individuals instantly recognisable. Instead, biologists use the unique black and white markings on the underside of their tails. These range from jet black to pure white and include an endless number of variations in between. No two humpbacks have identical markings and, with experience, it is possible to tell one animal from another simply by peering underneath as they lift their tails high into the air in preparation for a deep dive.

Biologists have been identifying animals as part of their research for many

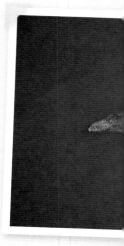

years. Jane Goodall used facial patterns to recognise chimpanzees in her classic study in Gombe Stream National Park, Tanzania. She found that each member of the group had a distinctive hairstyle, as well as a recognisable mouth and nose, and unique eyes and ears. Other studies have used striping patterns in zebras, the arrangement of whiskers in lions, and even the shapes, nicks and scars of elephants' ears to tell one individual from another.

In fact, many field biologists have become so proficient at recognising individuals that 'their' animals might as well be carrying passports.

Whale researchers often give the animals names, which are usually mnemonic. Cat's Paw, for example, has a jet-black tail interrupted only by a white paw print on the left-hand side; Fracture also has a black tail, but with a distinctive line down the middle; and Seal's tail – as you might imagine – has an image of a seal on the underside.

There are two basic rules in the humpback whale naming game. You are not allowed to use human names, like Bert or Beryl, because they are considered too anthropomorphic; and you're not allowed to use names that assume the sex of the animal, like Dr Spock or Lady Chatterley, because it is usually impossible to tell the difference (unless, of course, the whale turns up with a calf – in which case even I could tell that it is a female). Otherwise, anything goes.

Purists might argue that the use of names encourages biologists to become too attached to their study subjects. But imagine finding a group of whales off the southern tip of Baja and then trying to remember, with a complete absence of visual clues, whether you are looking at number 673 or 464. Worse still, try racking your brain to distinguish between WP14ZF and XY55PT. It simply wouldn't work – unless you have a retentive memory like Stephen Fry, of course.

Come to think of it, Stephen would make a terrific humpback whale researcher. He wouldn't need to resort to photographs or computer catalogues, like the rest of us. He could just remember the distinguishing marks, numbers and names of every whale he sees.

The purists, by the way, are missing the point: it's almost impossible *not* to become emotionally attached to humpback whales. So names are okay.

I remember going on a half-day whale-watching trip off the coast of New England. We were very close to two humpback whales when a couple of women in their late thirties, with matching outfits and jangly beads, were hopping and skipping around the deck. I had noticed them before and, while they seemed relatively normal at first, they had been acting increasingly strangely ever since our first close encounter with the whales. When they had finished their dance, they moved to opposite sides of the boat. One sat cross-legged on the deck and murmured a wild, half-sung, half-yodelled mantra, while the other leant over the

Above
Happy families? Not quite. Here is a female and her calf being harassed by a randy male.

Opposite
A humpback whale breaches so close to the boat Mark and Stephen almost swallow their tongues.

railings and whirled a short piece of hosepipe around in circles.

I was bursting to ask them two questions: 'What were they doing?' and 'What the heck were they doing?'. When I finally plucked up the courage to broach the subject, they talked about mystical experiences, golden energy fields, cerebral navigation, elevating vibrational levels and filling the vortex of life.

I still have no idea what they were talking about.

The same whales then surfaced a few metres in front of an elderly lady, who was sitting alone in a quiet corner of the deck. She watched intently as they put on an extraordinary show, this time one that seemed almost choreographed. One whale blew a tall column of water vapour high into the air, and the other blew a split second later; one dived beneath the surface, flukes pointing skyward, and the other dived a split second later.

The woman's face revealed nothing and she never said a word. But every time the whales took a joint curtain call, and disappeared from view, she clapped politely.

Later that morning, she confided that it had been the most wonderful and humbling hour of her life.

We took a last look at our whales. After several hours of unremittingly boisterous activity, the breeding group dispersed and, one by one, moved away.

Swimming alongside the boat, the last to leave arched its back, lifted its flukes and disappeared from sight. All that was left was an enormous 'flukeprint' – a large, perfectly formed circle of smooth water made by the swish of its tail close to the surface. Looking rather like an oily slick, and 3 or 4 metres (10–14 feet) across, it is the nearest a whale can get to a footprint.

We watched the flukeprint linger and fade, ever so slowly, until it was completely eroded and swallowed by the sea, and then we turned north into the Sea of Cortez.

'Here's that sick squid I owe you,' said Stephen, who was funny most of the time.

'Sorry, sorry,' he added. 'It would have been remiss of me not to say it. B-boom.'

We were with squid-wrangler and researcher Scott Cassell, floating off the coast of Santa Rosalia, to meet some of the strangest animals on the planet.

Scott was struggling into what looked like medieval armour – a protective steel-mesh suit, complete with hood and gloves, consisting of hundreds of thousands of electronically welded rings. Normally used by shark divers, it fits over a wetsuit and prevents a shark's teeth from penetrating the diver's skin.

'Seems a bit melodramatic,' Stephen whispered to me, as we watched him getting ready.

Opposite
Something out of an early episode of *Doctor Who* (the squid, not Scott Cassell).

Below
An unfriendly Humboldt squid.

'The squid are only about 50 or 60 centimetres (20–24 inches) long,' I agreed. 'It's like using a shark cage to dive with a manatee.'

We had caught six squid, with the help of a local fisherman and a very long fishing line, and they were swimming about in a pen at the back of the boat. Scott was preparing to join them and had strongly advised us not to get in with him.

'You don't have chainmail suits,' he pointed out, 'and you haven't been handling squid all your working life.'

'I don't want to get in the pen with them anyway,' retorted Stephen.

Humboldt squid, or jumbo squid as they are often called, grow up to 2 metres (6 feet 8 inches) long and can weigh as much as 45 kg (100 pounds). Unfortunately, all we had managed to catch were some relative tiddlers.

They are named after the cold current in which they are found, which flows along the west coast of South America and then out into the eastern North Pacific. And they are among the few animals we encountered during our travels together that are actually getting increasingly common.

We watched as the squid swam around the pen, rippling their diamond-shaped fins when they were merely pottering about or using jet propulsion to really shift (they suck water in through a siphon and then shoot it out again). Their skin colour changed constantly, from white to deep purplish red and back to white, like people blushing and recovering their composure in the blink of an eye.

'Mexican fishermen call them red devils,' said Scott, 'because they flash red and white when they are struggling on the end of a line.'

Incidentally, there is another kind of squid, called the Japanese firefly squid, which lights up like the Blackpool illuminations. Every year, from March to May, hundreds of thousands of these five-centimetre-long (2-inch) squid gather to spawn in a bay on the west coast of the Japanese island of Honshu. They are probably the most exuberantly bioluminescent creatures on the planet and they make the water flash, sparkle, shimmer and glow. The spectacle attracts visitors from around the world. Just thought you'd like to know.

'So why are you in a shark suit?' asked Stephen, going straight for the jugular.

'Because Humboldt squid are aggressive,' answered Scott. 'These are too small to do too much harm – although they could easily draw blood – but there are reports of larger ones attacking divers right here in the Sea of Cortez. They even attack one another, cannibalising injured or smaller squid in their own shoal. Just look at the weaponry on this thing.'

Scott grabbed a squid from the corner of the pen and held it up for us to see. It had eight arms, two tentacles and lots of suckers armed with sharp teeth. It looked like something out of an early episode of *Doctor Who*.

Opposite
Mark, Stephen, Scott and a red devil.

'It uses those teeth to grab fish,' explained Scott. 'Then it drags them towards that impressive, parrot-like beak to be ripped to shreds.'

The squid had huge eyes and stared back. I suppose it was understandable, given that it didn't have eyelids. It's hard not to stare without eyelids. Squid eyes are very similar to those of many higher animals, and they can see pretty well, so I wondered what it made of the man in the chainmail suit.

Scott put the squid back into the water and it squirted a cloud of dark ink.

'That's to confuse its predators,' he told us. 'The ink actually forms a cloud about the size and shape of the squid itself, to fix the predator's attention while it escapes.'

'Why do you get so excited by squid?' I asked, perhaps a little rudely.

'They're amazing animals,' replied Scott. 'There are lots of different kinds – something like 300 species altogether – and they range in size from a tiny Antarctic squid that could sit on the end of your finger to giant squid that reach phenomenal lengths of 17 metres (56 feet) or more. They're intelligent, too – among the most intelligent of all the world's invertebrates [animals without backbones]. They even have three hearts. I couldn't imagine studying anything else.'

One of the squid in the pen attached itself to his leg.

'They are formidable predators,' he continued. 'These guys hunt cooperatively –

Opposite
The largest animal
on the planet, diving
and blowing.

quite an extraordinary feat for an invertebrate – and they attack almost anything they don't recognise, as well as many things they do.'

Very little is known about Humboldt squid. They are difficult animals to study, living at great depth in the open ocean and rarely surviving more than a few days in captivity.

But it's vitally important to understand them, as Scott explained.

'We've fished out all their main predators – sharks, tuna, swordfish, marlin and suchlike. Now they're in seventh heaven. Their numbers are exploding and they are growing bigger and bigger. Hundreds of thousands, if not millions, are caught commercially every year, to provide calamari for the world's restaurants, yet nothing seems to be stopping them in their tracks.'

'Does it really matter? asked Stephen.

'Well, I think it's quite frightening,' said Scott. 'They are starting to dominate this corner of the Pacific and we have no idea what impact that is likely to have. We simply have to find out.'

One of the first things I learned in science at school was this: if it stinks, it's chemistry; if it doesn't work, it's physics; and if it's green or wriggles, it's biology.

Using the same basic principle, if it's almost as long as a Boeing 737 and lives in the sea, it's a blue whale.

It's impossible to prepare someone for their first encounter with a blue whale. It is stupendously, astonishingly, breathtakingly, bloody enormous. It is so large, in fact, that it stretches the imagination and boggles the mind.

We're talking about an animal with an average length – *average*, mind you – of more than 25 metres (82 feet). The longest ever recorded was landed by whalers in 1909 on South Georgia in the South Atlantic, and measured no less than 33.58 metres (110 feet) from the tip of its snout to the end of its tail.

The average weight is roughly 90–120 tonnes (88.6–118 tons). No blue whale has ever been weighed 'whole', of course. Sadly, all known weights were extrapolated during the whaling days, either by cutting them into smaller pieces or by adding up the total number of cookers filled with the meat, bones and blubber of individual whales at shore stations or on floating factory ships. But in this way the heaviest ever recorded was killed in the Southern Ocean, in 1947, and weighed a mind-boggling 190 tonnes (187 tons).

That's roughly the same as the entire population of the Scilly Isles (2,000 people).

Imagine a set of weighing scales. Big ones, naturally. Then put an average-sized blue whale on one side of the scales.

How much do you think you would have to put on the other side to balance the scales?

Well, you would have to put all of the following: half a dozen African elephants, a black rhino, five *Tyrannosaurus rex*, a couple of whale sharks, a hundred world-class Sumo wrestlers, the entire England football team and their respective wives and girlfriends, and my car. That lot together equals the weight of an average-sized blue whale.

Almost every aspect of the blue whale provides another superlative, another footnote for the record books.

A baby blue, for instance, measures at least 6 metres (20 feet) long when it is born. Biologists have made estimates about its first year of life: it drinks nearly 200 litres (44 gallons) of milk a day, adding 3.8 kg (8.4 lbs) of weight per hour or 90 kg (198 lbs) per day (that's the equivalent of putting on my total weight every single day). By the time the calf is weaned, when it's about eight months old, it is close to 15 metres (49 feet) long and weighs about 23 tonnes (22.6 tons).

Adult blue whales have the largest appetites on the planet – yet, in relation to body size, they eat the smallest prey. They feed on tiny, bright-red pelagic crabs and shrimp-like creatures called krill. The largest blues probably eat as many as five or six million of these tiny animals in a day. That's roughly 5 or 6 tonnes (4.9–5.9 tons) – equivalent to eating a fully grown African elephant. Fortunately, they have sufficiently voluminous mouths to cope with such a feast – big enough for a man to hold a dinner party for a dozen friends inside.

There's another related record, albeit an unofficial one, concerning food and feeding. It has no scientific basis whatsoever – it's based on nothing more than my own personal observations – but I'm absolutely convinced that blue whales have the smelliest droppings of any animal. And to add to the overall impact, they are nothing less than bright pink.

I've collected blue whale poo for research (just small samples – the largest animal inevitably does the largest poo), and the stench is utterly, mind-bendingly overwhelming. How some people do this kind of thing for a living I'll never know (I'll bet most people embark on a career in zoology imagining a lifetime spent observing tropical butterflies, or living with a family of elephants, or counting whales. Few would envisage years spent collecting and studying the smelliest poo on the planet).

Anyway, just to make myself perfectly clear: if you ever get the chance to do research work on blue whale diets, don't take it.

The low-frequency booms made by blue whales also break records. When vocalising across enormous stretches of ocean, their calls have been measured at

Opposite top
Imagine giving birth to a baby 6 metres (20 feet) long.

Opposite bottom
Blue whales have the smelliest droppings of any animal known to science.

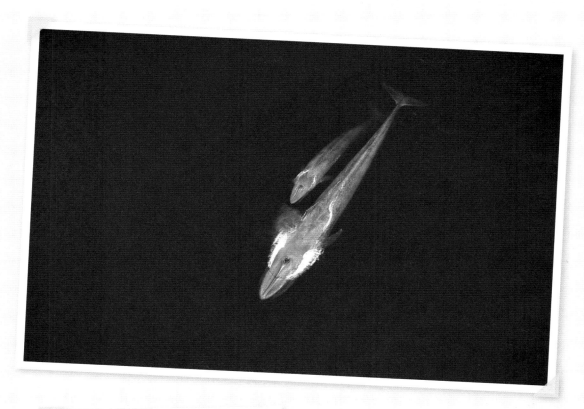

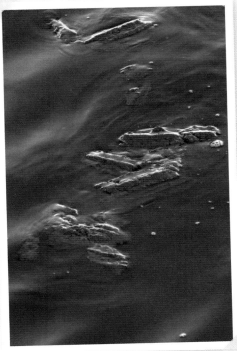

'Wow!' said Stephen. 'I think, for the first time ever, this may be the moment we can convincingly apply America's most popular word. Awesome.'

up to 188 decibels, making them the loudest sounds emitted by any living source. The sounds themselves are infrasonic (below the range of human hearing), but, using specialist equipment, they've been reliably detected from a distance of 3,000 kilometres (1,864 miles) away. It is unclear whether they are for long-distance communication or whether they form part of a long-range sonar navigation system, but biologists have established that blues calling off the coast of Newfoundland, in Canada, can be heard throughout the western North Atlantic and possibly as far as the Caribbean.

It almost goes without saying that seeing the largest and most impressive animal on earth is every naturalist's dream.

But it is a surprisingly difficult animal to find. You'd have thought something the size of a passenger jet would be impossible to miss, like looking for a sofa in the living room, but blue whales are frighteningly rare and these days there are few places in the world where they turn up with any regularity.

One of the grimmest blue whale facts is that more than 360,000 of them were killed by whalers during the 20th century alone. Can you imagine 360,000 blue whales? It beggars belief. It's one of the most dreadful and terrifying conservation failures in history.

The blue whale's size and speed saved it in the days of sail-boat whaling, but with the invention of explosive harpoons and fast catcher boats it quickly became the most sought-after species.

Blue whales were hunted so relentlessly that almost all populations were drastically reduced in size – some by 99 per cent.

The whaling was (and still is) unbelievably cruel, too. It is virtually impossible to kill whales humanely – especially ones as big as blues. They die slow, agonising deaths after explosive harpoons have blown huge, gaping holes in their bodies.

As one ex-whaler commented: 'If whales could scream, whaling would have stopped many years ago.'

The hunting of blues has been banned since the mid-1960s, but most populations have never recovered. Now there is serious concern about the future of these remarkable giants.

There is one population, however, that seems to be thriving. A splinter group of about 2,000 survived against all the odds and it divides its time between central and southern California, the Pacific coast of Baja, the Sea of Cortez and a place called the Costa Rican Dome (an upwelling of cold, nutrient-rich water off the coast of Central America).

I really wanted Stephen to see a blue whale. Plus I'd dug myself a little hole – having waxed lyrical about it for over a year, and whipped him into a frenzy of excitement, I had to make sure we found one.

So I persuaded a couple of old friends to lend us a hand.

Sandy Lanham is a pilot – one of the best I've ever flown with – who runs a non-profit organisation that conducts aerial surveys for underfunded conservationists and researchers in Mexico and the United States. She flies over everything from pronghorn antelopes and geese to sea turtles and whales.

We used to do aerial surveys of the blue whales in Baja together, many years ago.

Sandy very kindly flew her 1958 Cessna 182, called Emily, all the way from her home in Tucson, Arizona, to La Paz especially for a recce. Tim and I met her at the little airport (Tim by now had *very nearly* been forgiven for the mule debacle) and we spent a truly magnificent morning flying over the whale sharks in La Paz Bay and out into the Sea of Cortez to look for the elusive blues.

Within twenty minutes we had found one, right in the entrance to the bay. We could see the entire whale as it surfaced immediately below us – so large that it appeared to be moving in slow motion. With the window wide open, and the wind rushing through the cramped cockpit, Sandy expertly flew spine-tinglingly tight wheels and turns over the whale as we took pictures and film.

We continued north into the Sea of Cortez and found another, then another. In one little patch of water, off the northern tip of San Jose Island, we found a grand total of five different blues.

I felt an incredible surge of relief.

The next day I was back with Stephen and we were on the *Horizon* heading north, in the hope that our handful of whales would still be there.

Just in case, Sandy had offered to fly again and she appeared overhead the moment we spotted our first big blue. We chatted briefly on the radio, getting the precise location of some other blues she had seen a little way away, before she did a Red Arrows-wave goodbye and set off towards home.

It was a Monday morning. We hadn't even had breakfast and there were no fewer than seven gargantuan blue whales in sight at once. The sea was glassy calm, the sun was shining and the whales were spouting, their explosive columns of spray and vapour rising rhythmically towards the cloudless sky.

One particular whale came right alongside the boat and, looking through the blue filter of the ocean, its normally bluish-grey body turned unforgettably and startlingly turquoise. It surfaced to take a mighty breath – more of an explosion than an exhalation, followed by a noisy inhalation – and, for the first time, we could judge its length. We estimated 25 metres (82 feet), or roughly the length of the boat. It lifted its enormous flukes right in front of us and, as water poured off the trailing edge of its tail like an enormous waterfall, disappeared from sight.

'I wonder what the rest of the world is doing today?' I asked Stephen.

'Exactly what I was thinking,' he replied, smiling. 'I wouldn't swap places with anyone.'

We spent the entire day on deck, in the company of some of the grandest creatures on the planet, until the light faded and the sky filled with the kind of dazzlingly pink sunset that makes you marvel at the world and contemplate the meaning of life.

'Wow!' said Stephen. 'I think, for the first time ever, this may be the moment we can convincingly apply America's most popular word. Awesome.'

The next day we met up with another friend of mine, Diane Gendron, a French-Canadian blue whale biologist. She has the career that pretty much every marine biology student I've ever met would die for (except for the bit requiring detailed smelly poo analysis – proving that there is, after all, a downside to every job).

We met Diane at a place called Aqua Verde, just south of Loreto, where she was doing her studies from a bright yellow research boat. She was on the trail of a blue whale mother and calf, and, with research assistant Malie Lessard-Therrien hastily writing notes, was busy recording every intimate detail of their daily lives. If they took a breath or dived, turned left or turned right, Diane wanted to know about it.

She had spent more time with the 500 or so blue whales in the Sea of Cortez than anyone else in the world, but she was still as passionate and enthusiastic as ever. Every time the two whales reappeared she was noticeably more animated and excited than when they were hidden beneath the ocean waves.

Every time they dived – Mum lifting her flukes high into the air and baby trying to copy but failing to lift them high enough – we rushed over to collect some whale dandruff. Malie leaned over the side of the boat and scooped it up from the water surface with a child's fishing net. Then, like a surgeon performing a delicate operation, she picked the skin sample out of the net with a pair of tweezers and carefully transferred it to a test tube. DNA from the skin will help to unravel some of the many mysteries and get to the bottom of some of the unanswered questions about the world's largest animals.

We had spent six days and nights on the *Horizon* altogether, but it was nowhere near enough.

'Well, you promised it would be fun,' said Stephen on the very last day. 'But I can honestly say that was one of the best weeks of my life.'

China should have been the final stop on our world tour. We had hoped to go to the most populous country in the world to look for a blind, reincarnated princess otherwise known as the Yangtze river dolphin.

But in autumn 2007 we received the news we'd been expecting, but dreading, since we first started planning our travels together: the Yangtze river dolphin had officially been declared extinct.

Losing something as precious as a dolphin was quite a momentous event in the history of the world. There should have been a day of international mourning, some form of tribute to one of the most enigmatic and beguiling animals on earth.

But the passing of the Yangtze river dolphin went virtually unnoticed. It slipped away, quietly, while the rest of the world was apparently oblivious or entirely unconcerned.

Maybe I'm being unfair. Perhaps it's just that our senses are dulled as the inevitable and seemingly endless stories of doom and gloom about endangered wildlife become little more than background noise. Japanese whaling, the Canadian seal hunt, rhino poaching, rainforest destruction and so many other conservation issues have become as familiar a part of daily life as incompetent and dishonest politicians. We've heard it all before, so such revelations are less shocking than they once were.

But battle fatigue doesn't alter the fact that losing a dolphin is like losing the Crown Jewels or the Taj Mahal. In fact, I think it is even worse: we could rebuild the Crown Jewels or the Taj Mahal.

The Yangtze river dolphin, or baiji as it is often known, was unique to China. Once revered as the 'Goddess of the Yangtze', it was believed to be the reincarnation of a princess who had refused to marry a man she did not love and, for shaming the family, was drowned by her father.

A beautiful bluish-grey dolphin, it had a low, triangular dorsal fin, broad flippers and a long, narrow, slightly upturned beak.

It also had remarkably tiny eyes. There was little need to see in the turbid waters of its riverine home, where visibility can drop to just a few centimetres: if you were to snorkel in the Yangtze you would barely see the end of your nose. Its eyes were functional, but only just. So, like a bat finding its way in the dark, it relied on a sophisticated form of echolocation to build up a 'sound picture' of its surroundings, emitting sequences of tiny clicks and listening for the returning echoes.

Once upon a time, there were loads of dolphins living along a 1,700-kilometre (1,056-mile) stretch of the middle and lower reaches of the Yangtze River, from the magnificent Three Gorges all the way to the river mouth. The river used to be 'teeming' with them, according to Guo Pu, a scholar of the Jin dynasty who wrote about some of his local wildlife more than 2,000 years ago.

Douglas Adams and I went in search of them in 1988. We explored a small part of the Yangtze, which runs for 6,380 kilometres (3,964 miles) through the heart of China, but we failed to see a single baiji in the wild.

During our travels, though, we were overwhelmed by its phenomenally high profile in China. We drank Baiji beer and Baiji cola, stayed in the Baiji Hotel and used *Lipotes vexillifer* toilet paper (in case you're wondering, *Lipotes vexillifer* is the Yangtze river dolphin's scientific name). We even came across Baiji weighing scales and Baiji fertiliser.

Lending its name to so many things, it was very much a celebrity – the aquatic equivalent of the giant panda.

But it never really stood a chance.

First, it couldn't have lived in a more unwelcoming place. The Yangtze River basin is home to an astonishing one-tenth of the entire human population. With heavy boat traffic, agricultural runoff, industrial pollution, untreated sewage, riverbank development, dam construction and overfishing, the past fifty years have been a nonstop battle against the odds for its increasingly endangered wildlife – not just river dolphins but everything from alligators to paddlefish.

The final nail in the coffin was the Three Gorges Dam, the largest hydro-electric dam ever built, which has dramatically changed water levels, currents

The passing of the Yangtze river dolphin went virtually unnotice It slipped away, quietly, while the rest of the world was apparently oblivious or entire unconcerned.

and sandbanks. Smaller dams along other parts of the river fragmented dolphin populations, blocked their migration routes and made important feeding and breeding areas completely inaccessible.

You couldn't have come up with more threats if you had tried.

There was even a factory established for the sole purpose of making handbags and gloves out of Yangtze river dolphin skin.

Second – and this is even worse in many ways – the Yangtze river dolphin was as much a victim of incompetence, indecision and apathy as it was of environmental deterioration. It could have been saved, but insufficient funding, poor planning and incessant bickering among conservationists, scientists and the Chinese authorities meant it never really stood a chance.

Opposite
The Yangtze river dolphin, or baiji – now officially extinct.

A proper rescue plan for the Yangtze river dolphin was first mooted in the mid-1980s and consistently advocated until the day the last dolphin died.

The idea was simple: to capture some of the last survivors and move them to the relative safety of a 21-kilometre (12-mile) long, 2-kilometre (1.24-mile) wide oxbow lake called Tian'ezhou, in Hubei province. Right alongside the Yangtze River, the lake already had healthy fish stocks and a thriving population of finless porpoises (which were introduced from the river in the early 1990s). It was perfect. The dolphins would have loved the place and there is every chance they would have flourished and bred.

But it's one thing having a plan on paper, quite another putting it into action. Admittedly, a female was caught and relocated to Tian'ezhou in 1995, but she was found dead seven months later, entangled in the escape-prevention net at the outlet of the reserve.

One issue was money and, undoubtedly, it would have been an expensive strategy. It required boats to capture the dolphins, helicopters to transfer them, holding pens and veterinary staff to care for them before they could be released into the semi-natural reserve, a proper inventory – and management – of fish stocks, and round-the-clock protection.

But the dolphins should have been an international conservation priority. The fact that sufficient funding was never forthcoming is absolutely, utterly inexcusable.

Then there was the bickering. Can you believe it? Instead of taking urgent and decisive action, everyone argued about the pros and cons of moving the dolphins out of the main river for safekeeping. So many years were wasted that we lost the only real hope of saving the species from extinction.

From as many as 5,000 or 6,000 dolphins in the 1950s, the population shrank to around 400 by 1980, then 200 to 300 by 1985, and by the time Douglas and I arrived in 1988 it was down to fewer than 200.

Alarm bells don't ring much louder than that. Yet despite all the warnings, efforts to save the Yangtze river dolphin from extinction came far too little, too late.

Ten years later there were just thirteen left.

The last authenticated sightings in the wild were of a stranded pregnant female found in 2001 and a live animal photographed in 2002.

There was an intensive six-week search just before Christmas 2006. The survey, by professional and well-intentioned researchers from China, Japan, the US, Switzerland and the UK, used two vessels operating independently and covered the entire historical range of the species. They went up and down the Yangtze – not just once, but twice – looking through high-powered binoculars and listening for telltale squeaks and whistles with high-tech hydrophones.

But they were too late.

The conservation plan could have worked. Even in the shadow of China's economic boom and burgeoning population, the baiji could have been saved.

But it wasn't.

I realise it's easy to point an accusatory finger after the event and, of course, some conservation groups did make a positive contribution. But a surprising number were shouting about the plight of the world's most endangered large mammal, while doing little or nothing about it. Others withdrew their support because of the enormity of the challenge and the dwindling sense of optimism for the baiji's future.

It turns my stomach to read their official statements, expressing 'shock' and 'dismay' at the loss of the species. They should have been hanging their heads in shame. Despite all their workshops, conventions and meetings on the Yangtze river dolphin, many of them were too slow, too cautious and too downright inept to do anything constructive – so they must shoulder a large part of the blame.

Will we learn any lessons from the loss of the baiji? It's an important question, because there are other endangered species in the Yangtze River that could disappear soon, including everything from the Asian softshell turtle to the smooth-coated otter. In other parts of the world, we should be worrying about two of the baiji's closest relatives, the Indus and Ganges river dolphins, which face remarkably similar threats and are disappearing fast. And, of course, there is all the other, unrelated wildlife struggling for survival in all corners of the globe.

Sadly, I don't think we will learn any lessons. I'm not being unduly pessimistic – I'm just trying to be realistic. Without major changes in attitude and political thinking, I believe we will continue to make the same mistakes over and over again.

It makes me worry. If we can't save an appealing and charismatic dolphin – one that has lived on earth for more than twenty million years – what can we save?

Below
If we can't save
an appealing and
charismatic dolphin,
what can we save?

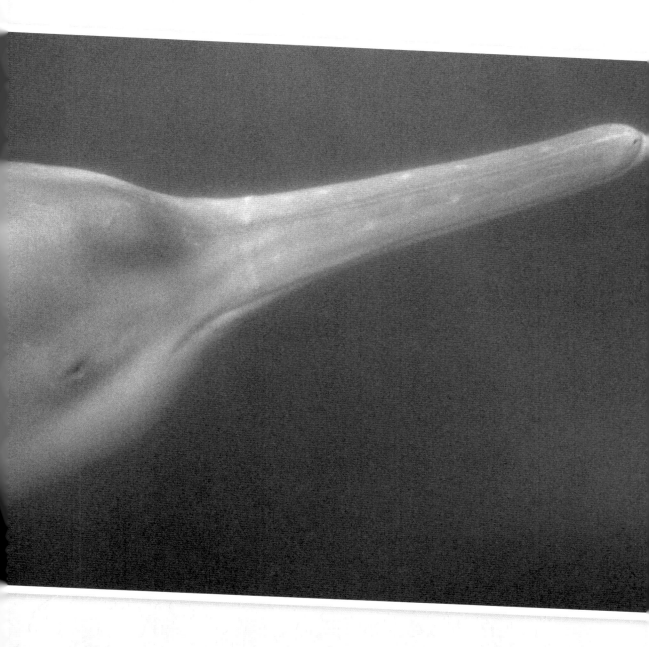

ONE MORE THING...

Our journey has left me with a mind-boggling mishmash of memories and impressions: exactly how much Stephen *hates* camping, for example, and the astonishing fact that he can learn a new language in just a few weeks.

I'll never forget meeting Madame Berthe's mouse lemur in Madagascar, tickling a thirty-tonne grey whale under the chin in Mexico, releasing a bucketful of turtle hatchlings in Borneo, or learning to love chimps in Uganda. Not to mention being ravished by a man-eating kakapo in New Zealand.

But there's one thing I can't get out of my mind. Twenty years have passed since my original travels with Douglas Adams – twenty years of rigorous and intensive conservation work, by countless people from all walks of life, costing untold millions of pounds. Yet for all these efforts, the natural world is not really a better place.

Yes, there have been some outstanding success stories and, of course, it's not all doom and gloom. But my overriding impression – and that of a great many of the people we met working in the field – is that we are slowly, but surely, losing the battle. Don't get me wrong – I haven't given up hope. The number of people who have devoted their lives to protecting the likes of gorillas, robins, turtles and lemurs is sufficient cause for optimism. Besides, we must be doing *something* right, if only because a large number of endangered species haven't (yet) become extinct.

Obviously, *Last Chance to See* can hardly be considered a global scientific review. It's a snapshot of a handful of countries and a few of their endangered animals, picked almost at random by sticking pins in a map. But the title did prove to be frighteningly prophetic. It really was our last chance to see one-quarter of the eight animals on our endangered species wish list. The mere fact that the Yangtze river dolphin and the northern white rhino have become extinct in the last twenty years is utterly shocking.

But it gets worse. If we were to continue the television series, searching for a different endangered animal each week, it would run for 162 years 10 months.

And that's just the endangered animals we know about. Then we'd have to start another series to talk about the ones we don't.

So far, we have named and described something like 1.29 million different animal species. We know so little about the vast majority of these that the conservation status of only a piddling 2.53 per cent (32,765) has been properly assessed. What we've found is that roughly a quarter of these (8,462) are threatened with extinction.

Bear with me, because this is where it gets really alarming. No one knows how many animal species exist on the planet in total, but 15 to 30 million wouldn't be a bad guess. So if a quarter of them are in trouble – a perfectly reasonable assumption given what we already know – we are left with somewhere between 3.75 and 7.5 million animals threatened with extinction. And I haven't even mentioned the fact that 70 per cent of all plant species assessed are endangered, too.

The situation seems bad enough when we hear about the kakapo hanging on by a thread, or thousands of whales being killed every year, or chimpanzee numbers in steep decline. But it goes off the scale when we realise that most endangered animals are likely to vanish before we have any idea they existed in the first place.

The point is that we cannot rely on an aye-aye to worry about the wellbeing of an Amazonian manatee, or a mountain gorilla to look out for a whale shark. Only we can do that. And through a combination of indifference, incompetence, ignorance and greed we are failing to do it properly.

There are many reasons. The biggest is the lack of political will. Most politicians either don't give a damn, or they pay lip service to the environment in return for votes, or they kid themselves (and us) into believing that conservation is painless. Their highly publicised 'easy solutions' lull us into a false sense of security – like recycling instead of tackling the real problem of over-packaging, or widening roads rather than improving public transport. Endangered species, in particular, are very low on their list of priorities.

Another reason is a lack of what I call 'predictive conservation'. We stand by and watch endangered species slide down the slippery slope towards oblivion and fail to act until their situation is so outrageously dire that they've almost reached the point of no return.

Take the catastrophic decline of the African lion – a species most of us simply take for granted. Sixty years ago there were half a million in Africa, twenty years ago there were fewer than 200,000, and today there are barely more than 20,000 across the continent. Yet this catastrophic decline seems to be passing the world by unnoticed. I know money is tight, and there are more than enough other animals even closer to extinction, but just how rapidly – and by how much – does a population have to decline before everyone is galvanised into action?

A good definition of a crisis is when you can't say 'Not to worry, it'll be all right in the end.' Well, it won't be all right in the end – unless we get off our backsides and do something about it.

Can you imagine a world without lions? Or Amazonian manatees, rhinos, aye-ayes, kakapo, Komodo dragons and blue whales, for that matter?

I can't.

Below
African lions: taken for granted, but in catastrophic decline.

IT'S A WRAP!
LAST CHANCE TO SEE
TRAVEL STATISTICS

Kilometres travelled:	**145,000**	By a motley collection of planes, helicopters, boats, cars, jeeps, buses and mules, as well as on foot (Stephen would argue, incorrectly, that most of it was on foot)
Carbon offset:	**World Land Trust**	Stephen and Mark donated to one of Mark's favourite charities
Meals eaten:	**379**	
Socks lost:	**17**	
Languages learnt:	**2**	Stephen learnt Portuguese and Malay; Mark learnt to leave all the translating to Stephen
Endangered species seen:	**5**	In the wild: kakapo, aye-aye, komodo dragon and mountain gorilla from the original book; in a research station: Amazonian manatee; plus everything from Madame Berthe's mouse lemur to blue whale along the way
Endangered species failed to see:	**2**	Northern white rhino and Yangtze river dolphin, because they are both extinct
New watches bought:	**23**	All by Stephen
Photographs taken:	**27,747**	27,104 by Mark and 643 by Stephen
Malaria tablets popped:	**224**	
Arms broken:	**1**	
Weight lost (lbs):	**52**	Stephen lost an impressive 64lbs, but unfortunately Mark gained 12lbs
Arguments:	**½**	A mild disagreement about giant jumping rats in Madagascar

LAST CHANCE TO HELP...

Here are some organisations really worth supporting

AMAZONIAN MANATEES

INPA (Instituto Nacional de Pesquisas da Amazônia)
Av. André Araújo,
2936,
Aleixo,
CEP 69060-001,
Manaus – AM, Brazil
Tel: + 55 (92) 3643 3377
Emails: bosque@inpa.gov.br;
lobato@inpa.gov.br
www.inpa.gov.br

NORTHERN WHITE AND BLACK RHINOS

Save the Rhino International
16 Winchester Walk,
London SE1 9AQ UK
Tel: +44 (0) 20 7357 7474
Fax: +44 (0) 20 7357 9666
Email: info@savetherhino.org
www.savetherhino.org

David Shepherd Wildlife Foundation
61 Smithbrook Kilns,
Cranleigh,
Surrey GU6 8JJ,
UK
Tel: + 44 (0) 1483 272323/267924
Fax: + 44 (0) 1483 272427
Email: dswf@davidshepherd.org
www.davidshepherd.org

CHIMPANZEES

The Jane Goodall Institute
Orchard House
51–67 Commercial Road,
Southampton SO15 1GG
UK
Tel: +44 (0) 23 8033 5660
Fax: +44 (0) 23 8033 5661
Email: info@janegoodall.org.uk
www.janegoodall.org.uk

MOUNTAIN GORILLAS

The Dian Fossey Gorilla Fund
800 Cherokee Ave.,
SE Atlanta, Georgia 30315-1440
USA
Tel: + 1 800 851 0203 + 1 404 624 5881
Fax: + 1 404 624 5999
Email: 2help@gorillafund.org
www.gorillafund.org

The Gorilla Organization
110 Gloucester Avenue
London NW1 8HX,
UK
Tel: +44 (0) 20 7916 4974
Email: info@gorillas.org
www.gorillas.org

AYE-AYE AND OTHER LEMURS

Durrell Wildlife Conservation Trust
Les Augrès Manor La Profonde Rue,
Trinity, Jersey,
Channel Islands JE3 5BP, UK
Tel: +44 (0) 1534 860000
Fax: +44 (0) 1534 860001
www.durrell.org

KAKAPO

The Kakapo Recovery Programme
c/- PO Box 631 Wellington 6140
New Zealand
Email: kakapovolunteers@doc.govt.nz
www.kakaporecovery.org.nz

KOMODO DRAGONS

Komodo Survival Program
Jl Pulau Moyo,
Komplek Karantina Blok 2 no 4,
Denpasar, Bali 80222,
Indonesia
Tel: +62 (361) 7420434
Fax: +62 (361) 710352
Email: komodosspi@centrin.net.id
komodosurvival.kbproject.org

BLUE WHALES

Environmental Flying Services
5900 South Camino de la Tierra
Tucson, Arizona 85746
USA
Tel: +1 520 578-5610
Email: sandy@eflying.org
www.eflying.org
(please specify donations are for blue whales)

Whale and Dolphin Conservation Society
Brookfield House
38 St Paul Street
Chippenham
Wiltshire SN15 1LJ
UK
Tel: +44 (0) 1249 449500
Fax: +44 (0) 1249 449501
Email: info@wdcs.org
www.wdcs.org

SHARKS

Shark Trust
4 Creykes Court
The Millfields
Plymouth
Devon PL1 3JB
UK
Tel: +44 (0) 1752 672008
Email: enquiries@sharktrust.org
www.sharktrust.org

RAINFORESTS

The World Land Trust
Blyth House
Bridge Street
Halesworth
Suffolk IP19 8AB
UK
Tel (UK only): 0845 054 4422
Tel (international callers):
+44 (0) 1986 874422
Fax: +44 (0) 1986 874425
Email: info@worldlandtrust.org
www.worldlandtrust.org

CORAL REEFS

Coral Cay Conservation
1st floor Block 1 Elizabeth House
39 York Rd
London SE1 7NQ
UK
Tel: + 44 (0) 20 7620 1411
Fax: + 44 (0) 20 7921 0469
Email: info@coralcay.org
www.coralcay.org

ACKNOWLEDGEMENTS

I would like to thank the following people for helping to make this project possible:

Lilly Arajova
Myles Archibald
Rachel Ashton
Jane Belson
Dan Bucknell
Betty Carwardine (Mum)
David Carwardine (Dad)
Simon Christopher
John Craven
Jo Crocker
JP Davidson
Adrian Davies
Lindsay Davies
Cathy Dean
Sue Doody
Emily Douglas
Simon Enderby
Suzi Eszterhas
Nick Garbutt
Tim Green
Greg Grivetto
Kes Hillman Smith
Roz Kidman Cox
Richard Klein
Michael Landau
Richard Lewis
Sally Lisk-Lewis
Janet McCann
Don Merton
Haley Miles
Caroline Montgomery
Doreen Montgomery
Sam Organ
Simon & Ange Peers
Ian Redmond
Jo Sarsby
Andre Singer
Ness Smith
Ben Southwell
Michaela Strachan
Miranda Sturgess
Emma Swain
Debra Taylor
Jane Thrift
James Thrift
Simon Watson
Joe Yaggi

And a very special thanks to Stephen Fry, for everything.

PRODUCTION TEAM

Head of Factual & Music
Adrian Davies

Executive Producers
Sam Organ
Andre Singer

Series Producer
Tim Green

Producers / Directors
Tim Green, Ben Southwell and JP Davidson

Assistant Producers
Sue Doody, Emily Douglas and Claire Messenger

Production Manager
Lindsay Davies

Production Assistants
Eleanor Hogan
Emma Samuel

Specialist Researcher
Jess Tombs

Camera
Will Edwards, Sam Gracey, Alan Duxbury, Robin Cox, Simon Ffrench and Simon Enderby

Sound
Tim A Green, Jake Drake-Brockman and Don Anderson

Editors
Alex Boyle
Paul Burgess

BBC Last Chance to See website
Jo Pearce, Anwen Aspden, Mat Fidell, Angharad Rhys, Sian Davies, Luke Baker, Steven Green, Simon Rooney, Andrew Dudfield, Kieran Bowler and Takako Tucker

INDEX

Entries in *italics* indicate photographs.

Adams, Douglas, 6–7, 7, 9, 13–15, *13*, *14*, *15*, 18, 26, 27, 54, 70, 73, 79, 83, 101, 120, 123, 124, 125, 135, 144–5, 188, 190, 196, 202, 207, 224, 232–3, 253, 306, 308, 312
Ajarova, Lilly, 93–4, 97, 99
Amazon, 16–67, 175
    aerial view of, *22*
    dam building in, 58
    dangers of, 20–2, 23
    destruction of, 54, 55, 58
    'emergent layer', 51
    Europeans first arrive in, 53
    fishing in, commercial, 58
    getting around in, 40
    height of trees in, 50–1
    indigenous people in, 53
    jungle canopy, 51–2
    missionaries in, 53
    rainfall in, 43, 44
    river, 23, 34, 34, 36, 37
    size of, 23, 50, 51
    swimming in, 34, 35, 36, 37
    unexplored areas of, 24, 28, 53
    variety of species within, 23–4
    wildlife in see under individual
      species name
Amazon Theatre (opera house), 29, *29*
anacondas, 34
Analamazaotra (Perinet), 150, 151, 152, 154
Andasibe-Mantadia National Park, 152
Antainambalana River, 124, 136
Antananarivo, 146, 155, 162, 260
Arauazinho Creek, 40, 44
Arauazinho village, *46*, 47, 50
aruanas, 30
aye-aye, 8, 13, *121*, *122*, *160*, *163*, 245
    appearance, 120–1
    fady and, 139–40
    female, 123
    lemur, 121–2
    mating, 123
    middle finger, 121, 122
    nocturnal, 124
    numbers of, 123
    'percussive foraging', 122
    role in ecological framework of
      the forest, 122–3
    search for, Douglas Adams and, 123–4, 133
    search for, Stephen Fry and, 156, 159, 161, 162

baboons, 83
Baie d'Antongil, 124
Baja California, 258–305
baobab trees, 142
barracuda, 242
BBC, 9, 27, 40, 64, 83, 268
    film crew, 27, 64–5, 134, 207, 216, 244, 268, 270, 287, 292, 303
Benchley, Peter, 279

Berenty, 134, 135, 137, 138
biofuels, 238
biographies, 320
bioluminescence, *279*
Black, Richard, 187, 188–9
blob fish, 24
boa:
    emerald tree, 162
    Madagascar tree, *126*, 127
bongo, 24
bonobo, 93
Borneo, 226, 227, 228, 232, 234, 237, 239, 240, 245
Bounty Islands, 24
Bwindi Impenetrable Forest, 99, 100–1, 102–4, 105

caboclo, 41
caiman, 34
    dwarf, 45
candiru fish, 35–6
Cape Peninsula National Park, 126
Cassell, Scott, 294, *294*, 296, *297*, 298
Cassiquiari, 40, 43, 45, 52
Central African Republic, 72
Chad, 72
chameleon:
    panther, *126*, 127
    pygmy, *128*, 129
Chatham Island, 168, 193, 194–6, *194*
    black robin, 168, 193, *196–7*, *196–7*, 198, 199–201, *200*, 205
    oystercatcher, 194, 195, *195*, 196
    shore plover, *199*
chimps, *92*, 93–9, *95*, *96*
China, 305
Chinese Medicine, Traditional, 245–6, 281
clownfish, 243
Cochimi Indians, 275
Com te Abreu, 62, 63, 65
Congo, 12, 102 see also Democratic Republic of Congo and Zaire
coral reefs, 239, 240, 243, *242–3*
Cordeiro, Ivano, 27, 44, 45–6, 48
Cortez Camp, 263–9
Costa Rican Dome, 302
Craig, Batia, 80

Da Silva, Vera, 55, 57, 59
Darwin, Charles, 133, 232
Daugherty, Professor Charles, 175, 176
Dawkins, Richard, 7, 8
De Brito, Marina Barahona, 27
Democratic Republic of Congo (DRC), 70, 72–3, 90, 93, 98, 101, 102, 104, 109, 162
    Garamba National Park, 70, 73–5, *73*, 80, 83, 84, 90, 91, 109, 114, 115
dendronautics, 51–2, 53
dik-dik, 24
dolphin, bottlenose, 198, *289*
dolphin, pink river (boto), 36, 37, *38*, 39, 162
dolphin, Yangtze river (baiji), 9, 306, *307*, *309*, *310–11*

appearance, 306
extinction of, 309–10
numbers of, 305, 306, 308, 309
Three Gorges Dam and, 306, 308
rescue plan for, 308, 309–10
Durrell, Gerald, 122
Dvur Králové Zoo, 115

electric eels, 34
elephant, *71*, 88–9, *91*
elephant birds, 133
ennis, 47, 48
eremomela, burnt-neck, 24
European Space Agency, 179

fishermen, illegal Southeast Asian, 240
Foing, Dr Bernard, 179
fossa, *146*, 147, *147*, 149
frog:
    poison-arrow, 53
    rot-hole tree, *127*
fruit bats, 255
    straw-coloured, 143
Fry, Stephen, *7*, 8, *19*, *20*, 33, 35, 37, *42*, 49, 58, *131*, 134, *178*, 228, *231*, *233*
    Amazon, reaction to, 50, 52
    appearance, 18, 260
    author, relationship with, 9–10, *11*, 18–20, 143–4, 155, 156, 194, 195, 216
    aye-aye and, 161
    baobab and, *116–17*
    breaks arm, 63–5, 66, 70, *70*
    brown lemur and, 138, *138*
    Chatham Island black robin and, 198, 199, 200, 201
    Chatham Island oystercatcher and, 195
    chimps and, 93, 94, 97, 99
    diving, 240–1, *241*, 242–3
    dolphins and, 289
    Douglas Adams and, 7–8, 9, 18
    extreme sports and, 186–7
    Fiordland and, 188, 190
    fossa and, 147
    frenetic lifestyle, 174
    giant jumping rat and, 143–4, *145*, 146
    gorillas and, 102, 103, *103*, 104, *105*, 105, 106, 108
    hedgehog tenrec, 130
    in quarantine, 170, *170*, 171, *171*
    intelligence, 18–19, 33, 227, 293
    jungle habituation process, 33–6, 35
    kakapo and, 166, 168, 169, 170, 202, 209, 210–11, *212*, 213, 216, 217
    kiwi and, 183, 184, *184*, 185, 186
    komodo dragon and, 224, 246, 248, 249–50, 252, 253, 254
    Last Chance to See, joins, 9–10
    on Madagascar, 162
    Madame Berthe's mouse lemur and 150
    Malaysia and, 226–7
    manatee and, 55, 58, 59, 61, 62, 63
    on noise of jungle, 100
    northern white rhino and, 75, 80, 81, 82,

84, 85, *86*, 87, 90, 92, *92–3*, 110, 113, *114*
on a mule, 269–72, *269*, 271
Peter Jackson and, 181, *181*, 182, 183
pink river dolphin and, 36–7, *37*
pygmy chameleon and, 129
rashes, 204–5
sea turtles and, 233–4, 235, 236, 237
sifakas and, 137
tequila induced delirium, 267–9
travelling, reaction to conditions during, 27, 41, 134, 136–7, 140, 143, 151, 152, 154, 155, 156, 205, 207, 215, 216, 218, 219, 249–50, 284, 285
travelling philosophy, 21
tuatara and, 172, 174, 176
weight loss, 260
weta and, 176, 178
whale sharks and, 276, 278, 283
whales and, 258, *262–3*, 263, 265, 286, 287, 288, 291, 293, 301, 302, 304, 305
Fry in America, 138

Galápagos Islands, 133
Garamba National Park, DRC, 70, 73–5, 73, 80, 83, 84, 90, 91, 109, 114, 115
Garamba River, 83
gazelle, Grant's, 83
gecko, leaf-tailed, 127, *127*
Gendron, Diane, 304–5
Gili Dasami, 253
Gili Motang, 253
giraffe, 74, 83
Gombe Stream National Park, 97, 293
Goodall, Jane, 97, 292–3
Gorda Bank, 290
gorillas, 93, 101–9, *107*, 162
  belch vocalisation, 105
  chest hair, 106
  Mubare group, 104
  rangers, 102, 104
  political troubles and, 102–3
  Rugendo group, executions of, 102
  Rushegura group, 104
  silverback, 102, 106
  search for, 103–5
  tourism, 108–9
  numbers left, 101
Greenman, Jo, 177, 178, 179
Grivetto, Greg, 285
gulls, red-billed, 198

Hairy van Pit-Bull, 44–6
hammock, sleeping in, 43
Henry Junior, Richard, 189–90, 196
Henry, Richard, 189
Hillman-Smith, Fraser, 83
Hillman-Smith, Kes, 74, 83, 84
hippos, dwarf, 133
Hluhluwe-IMfolozi Game Reserve, 76
Honshu island, Japan, 296
Horizon, 285, 305
Hutus, 102–3

indigo bunting, 287, 288
Indonesia, 12, 118, 224, 227, 229, 239, 246, 249, 253, 254
ivory, 88–9, *91*

Jackson, Peter, 181–3, 181
jambiyas, 87
Jaws (Benchley), 278–9

kakapo parrot, *164–5*, 166–9, *167*, 188, 201–20, 216–17, 315
  Codfish Island and, 206–20
  conservation, 189
  endangered, 168–9
  evolution of, 166, 168, 169
  life expectancy, 210
  mating, 202–3, 207, 218–19, 220
  parenting, 220
  Sirocco, 204, 210–11, *211*, 212, 213, 215
  name, 201–2, 219
  numbers of, 168, 189, 202–3, 206, 207
  search for, 166–9, 206–11
Kannerberg, Captain Wilson, 40, 50, 65
Karori Wildlife Sanctuary, 172, 174, 175, 179
Keall, Sue, 175, 176
Kenya, 79–90, 93, 109–10
Kenya Wildlife Service, 89, 110
Kenyatta International Conference Centre, 110
kissing bug, 24
kiwi, 183–6, *184*
Komodo, 224–55, *225*
  animals on, 226 see also under individual animal name
  landscape, 254, 254
Komodo Dragon, 12, *222–3*, *247*, *248*, *252–3*
  bite, 252–3
  dangerous nature of, 246, 248, 249, 252–3
  habitat, 253
  numbers of, 253
  reputation of, 249–50
  Survival Programme, 253

La Paz Bay, 275–6, *276*, 278, 284
Lanham, Sandy, 303, *303*, 304
lemurs, 12
  aye-aye see aye-aye
  baby ring-tailed, *119*
  black and white ruffed, 129, 156
  brown, 156
  indiri, *153*, 154–5
  giant, 132
  greater bamboo, 155–6
  grey bamboo, 156
  Madame Berthe's mouse, *148*, 149–50, 151, 235, 263
  number of species in Madagascar, 135
  pale fork-marked, 143
  red-fronted brown, *135*
  Verreaux's sifaka, 135, 136, 137–8, 156
  white-fronted brown, 127, 131
Leopold II of Belgium, King, 72–3
Lessard-Therrien, Malie, 304
Lewis, Richard, 144–5
lion, African, decline of, 313–14, *314*
lizard, monitor, 231
Lord's Resistance Army, 75
Luo tribe, 88
Lusaka Agreement Task Force, 84–5, 88–9

Maain, Pak, 250, *250*
Maasai, 88, 89
macaques, crab-eating, 231
Madagascar, 12, 13, 14, 118–62, 235, 260, 263, 296
  animals in see under individual animal name
  diversity of wildlife in, 131–3, 154
  driving in, 150–1, 152
  evolution of wildlife on, 131–3
  forest, disappearance of, 133–4
  Fort Dauphin, 134, 136
  human population, 133
  Kirindy Forest, 140, 143, 144, 147, 149

Morondava, 140
  superstition in/fady, 138–40, *139*, 162
malaria, 100, 204
Malay Archipelago, The, 232
Malaysia, 226–7, 237, 239, 240
Mamirauá Project, 61, 65
manatee, Amazonian, 56, 233
  appearance, 24, 26, 55, 56, 57, 58, 59, *59*
  breathing, 27
  character, 26–7
  dwarf, 44, 45, 46
  feeding, 46–8
  hair, 58
  movement of, 55
  numbers of, 58
  search for, 24, 44, 48–9, 54–7, 162
  swimming with, 57–8
  threats to, 58–9
  vegetarian, 27, 48
Manaus, 24, 27, 28, 29–30, *29*, 31, 34, 40, 50, 54, 61
  fish market (Mercado Municipal Adolpho Lisboa), 29–30, *31*
Mandrare River, 135
Marmontel, Miriam, 61, 62, 65, 66
Maroantsetra, 124, 150
Mauritius kestrel, 144–5
Merton, Don, 189, 190, 196, *197*, 198, 199, 200, 201, 205, 217
'Meeting of the Waters', 28, 29, *29*
mongooses, narrow-striped, 143
monkey:
  proboscis, 229, *230*, 231
  squirrel, *25*
moon, Noah's Ark on, 179–80
Mount Everest, 126–7
Mount Kenya, 79
Mount Kilimanjaro, 88
Mozambique Channel, 132
mudskippers, 228–9
mule trek, 269–75, *269*, *271*, *274*

Nairobi National Park, 109–10
Napoleon wrasse, 242
National Congress for the Defence of the People (Congo), 75, 102
National Institute for Amazon Research, 54–9
Navarro-Holm, Esmeralda Estrella, 276, 278, *278*, 283
New Zealand, 12, 166–220
  animals in see under individual animal name
  Chalky Island, 190
  Codfish Island, 170, 171, 172, 190, 203, 204, 205–20, *205*, *206*
  conservation in, 172
  Department of Conservation, 170, 171, 205, 209
  evolution of wildlife in, 171–2
  extinction of animals in, 171–2
  Fiordland, 187–9, *188*, 190, 201, 297
  Invercargill, 170, 203–4, 207
  Kakapo Castle, 188
  Little Barrier Island, 190
  Little Mangere, *197*, 198
  Mangere Island, 198
  Matiu-Somes Island, 176–8, 179, 204
  Maud Island, 189–90
  Queenstown, 186–8, *186–7*, 193
  Southland Quarantine Facility, 170–1, 203
  Stephen's Island, 172
  Stewart Island, 206, 207, 209
  Wakatipu, 187
  Wellington, 176, 181

Ngamba Island Chimpanzee Sanctuary, 93–9
Ngorongoro Crater, 126
Nkunda, Laurent, 102
Nosy Mangabé, 123–4, *125*, 127, 129, 131, 161

Ol Jogi Ranch, 110–14, *111, 112, 113, 114*
Ol Pejeta Conservancy, 79, 80–90, 110, 115, *115*
orang-utan, 93
organisations worth supporting, 316
Origin of Species (Darwin), 232
ostrich, 83
oystercatcher, Chatham Island, 194, 195, *195*, 196

palm oil, 237–8, *238*, 239
palm weevil, South American, 24
pangolin, 231, *231*
parrots, 12
    kakapo *see* kakapo
    kea, 190, *191*, 192–3
peanut-headed bug, 24
pelicans, brown, 266, *267*
People's Liberation Army (Sudan), 75
pigeon, North American passenger, 179, 207
Pilcher, Nicholas, 234
piranha, *21*, 30, *31*, 32, 34
pirarucu, 30
piti, 61–2, 63, *63*, 64, 65–6, *67*
plover, Chatham Island shore, *199*
poaching, 72, 73, 74, 75, 85, *86*, 87, 88–90, *91*, 102, 110, 113
potoo, great, *24*
Pu, Guo, 306
Purwandana, Deni, 253–4

rainforest destruction, 54, 55, 58, 237–9
Ramos, Carolina, 61, 62, 66
rat, giant jumping, *142–3*, 143–4, *145*, 146
Razafindramanana, Josia, 134, 137, 138
recognising individual animals, 292–3
rhino, black, 110–14, *112, 113*
rhino, northern white, 9, *68*, *73*, *77*
    colour of, 75–6
    discovered, 72
    mouth, 76
    population numbers, 72, 75, 76, 115
    search for, 73–5, 90, 109, 162
rhino, southern white, *77*, *78*, *81*, *82*, 84, 110
    conservation of, 76, 79, 84
    evolution of, 75
    Fry and author meet a, 80–2, *81*, *82*
    numbers of, 76
rhino horns, sale of, 85, *86*, 87–8
Rhios, 12
Rinca, 250, 253
Rio Aripuanã, 40, 49
Rio Negro, 27, 28, 37
Rio Solimões, 28
robin, Chatham Island black, 168, 193, *196–7*, 196–7, 198, 199–201, *200*, 205
Rocha, Miguel, 40, 41
Roosevelt, Theodore, 30
Rwanda, 101, 102–3, 109

San Diego Wild Animal Park, 115
San Ignacio Lagoon, 263, 266, 268, 270, 284–5
    cave paintings, *273*, 274–5
San Jose Island, 304
sea lions, 266
Sea of Cortez, *282*, 284–5, 294, 296, 302, 304, 305
seahorses, 244–5, *245*
Senegal, 97

shark:
    bull, 34
    conservation of, 278–80
    dangers of, 278–80
    great white, 280
    killing of, 280–4
    large grey reef, 242
    shark-fin soup, 280–1, 283
    shark-finning, 281, 283, 284
    tiger, 280
    whale, 275, 276, *277*, 278–9, *279*, *281*, 283–4
    white-tipped reef, 242, *243*
shrews, lesser white-toothed, 45
Sidaway, Matt, 177–8
Sipadan, 239–41, *241*, 243, 244
sirenians, 24, 26
Sirocco (kakapo), 204, 210–11, *211*, *212*, 213, 215
snakes:
    hog-nosed, 143
    mangrove, 231
    venomous, 21
snark, 217
spider, no-eyed big-eyed wolf, 24
squid, 294, *294*, 295, 296
    Humboldt, *295*, 296–8
    Japanese firefly, 296
squirrel monkey, *25*
St Peter, 47
Stanley, Henry Morton, 72
starfish, 243, *243*
Steller, Georg Wilhelm, 47
Steller's sea cow, 47

Stephen's Island Wren, 172
stingrays, 34
Sudan, 72, 75, 88

Tambaqui, olive-green, 30
Tanzania, 97, 126, 293
Tefé, 61
tenrec, hedgehog, 130
Three Gorges Dam, China, 306, 308
Trans-Amazonian Highway, 54
travel statistics, 320
trevally, big-eyed, 242
Trounson Kauri Park, 184–5, *184*, 204
tuatara, 172–4, *172*, *173*, 179
    Brother's Island, 174
    common, 174
    mating, 173
    metabolic rate, 174–5
    nest, 175, *175*, 176
    numbers of, 174
    third eye, 173–4
Turtle Island National Park, 234
turtles, green sea, 234–7, *234–5*, *236–7*, 242, 296
Tutsis, 102

Uganda, 72, 75, 90, 91, 93, 100, 101, 102, 103, 104, 109
Unimak Pass, 261
United Nations, 75, 88, 90, 109–10

Virunga Volcanoes, 101, 102

Wallace, Alfred Russel, 232
waxy-tailed planthopper, 24
weta, 182
    exoskeleton, 178
    giant or Cook Strait, 176–7, *177*, 178, 179, 180
    numbers of, 178, 179
    various species of, 177
whale, blue, 297, *298*
    average size of, 299
    average weight, 299–300
    booms, 300–1
    calves, *301*
    droppings, 300, 301
    feeding, 300
    finding, 301, 303–4
    numbers of, 301
    pigmy, 45
    whaling, effect upon, 299, 301
whale, grey, 258, *261*, 260, 266
    barnacles on, 264
    calves, 261, 262, 264
    feeding, 260
    friendliness, 258, 262
    hunting of, 261–2
    migrations, 260–1
    population, 262
    swimming with, 263, 264–6
whale, humpback, 285, *286*
    breaching, 289, 290–2, 293
    calves, *293*
    character, 290
    flippers, 288
    flukeprint, 294
    lobtailing, *285*
    mating, *291*, 293
    naming, 293
    search for, 290–1
    size and colour, 288
    song, 286–8
    tail breaching, *289*
    tail markings, 290, 292
wildlife watching, best time for 125–7
World Bank, 54

Yangtze River, 9, 306
Yangtze river dolphin (baiji), 9, 306, *307*, *309*, *310–11*
    appearance, 306
    extinction of, 309–10
    numbers of, 305, 306, 308, 309
    Three Gorges Dam and, 306, 308
    rescue plan for, 308, 309–10

Zaire, 70, 71, 101 *see also* Democratic Republic of Congo (DRC)